ASSESSING REVOLUTIONARY AND INSURGENT STRATEGIES

RESISTANCE MANUAL

Johns Hopkins University Applied Physics
Laboratory (JHU/APL) Contributing Authors:

Meg Keiley-Listermann

W. Sam Lauber

Christine Martin

UNITED STATES ARMY SPECIAL OPERATIONS COMMAND

Resistance Manual is a work of the United States Government in accordance with Title 17, United States Code, sections 101 and 105.

Cite me as:

Lauber, W. Sam, et al. *Resistance Manual*. Draft. Fort Bragg, NC: US Army Special Operations Command, 2019.

The authors would like to acknowledge the important contributions of Melissa Ellison, Grant Sutton, David Nobles, Bruce Milligan, and MIDN Justin Rojas.

Reproduction in whole or in part is permitted for any purpose of the United States government. The analysis and the opinions expressed within this document are solely those of the authors and do not necessarily reflect the positions of the US Army or the Johns Hopkins University Applied Physics Laboratory.

Comments correcting errors of fact and opinion, filling or indicating gaps of information, and suggesting other changes that may be appropriate should be addressed to:

United States Army Special Operations Command
G-3X, Sensitive Activities Division
2929 Desert Storm Drive
Fort Bragg, NC 28310

All ARIS products are available from USASOC at https://www.soc.mil/ARIS/ARIS/html.

CONFLICT
RESEARCH
GROUP

ASSESSING REVOLUTIONARY AND INSURGENT STRATEGIES

The Assessing Revolutionary and Insurgent Strategies (ARIS) series consists of a set of case studies and research volumes conducted for the US Army Special Operations Command by the National Security Analysis Department of the Johns Hopkins University Applied Physics Laboratory. The purpose of the ARIS series is to produce a collection of academically rigorous yet operationally relevant research materials to develop and illustrate a common understanding of insurgency and revolution. This research, intended to form a bedrock body of knowledge for members of the Special Forces, will allow users to distill vast amounts of material from a wide array of campaigns and extract relevant lessons, thereby enabling the development of future doctrine, professional education, and training.

The ARIS series follows in the tradition of research conducted by the Special Operations Research Office (SORO) of American University in the 1950s and 1960s, by adding new research to that body of work and in several instances releasing updated editions of original SORO studies.

RECENT VOLUMES IN THE ARIS SERIES

TABLE OF CONTENTS

INTRODUCTION AND BACKGROUND

Overview

This manual is for the US Army Special Operations Forces (ARSOF) soldier. Whether attending his/her first course at the John F. Kennedy Special Warfare Center and School (SWCS) or already deployed, the ARSOF soldier must be a student-practitioner of his/her craft: providing support to or countering a resistance movement.

This manual is a product of the Assessing Revolutionary and Insurgent Strategies (ARIS) project. The ARIS project consists of research on the phenomenon of resistance conducted by the Johns Hopkins University Applied Physics Laboratory (JHU/APL) for the US Army Special Operations Command (USASOC) G3X Special Programs Division. The ARIS program produces operationally relevant and actionable information for ARSOF soldiers encountering resistance movements. ARIS studies are academically rigorous and operationally relevant research materials that address challenges that ARSOF soldiers can encounter when conducting their mission sets. ARIS' multi-disciplinary research seeks to inform the ARSOF operator's mission preparation through applied learning of historical case studies, topically focused studies, and selected specialized topics across the global security landscape. The ARIS project further seeks to expand the study of resistance by synthesizing academic research, informing doctrinal development and professional education and training, and translating academic findings into operational impact.

In addition to drawing on case studies and topical studies in the body of ARIS products, this manual further draws on the body of academic work from the scientific study of resistance to provide a fundamental understanding of a resistance movement. It leverages the 2018 ARIS study *Conceptual Typology of Resistance* to identify variables relevant to the actors, causes, environment, organization, and actions that a resistance movement develops, operates, and uses to achieve its objectives.

Goals of the Manual

The *ARIS Resistance Manual* is designed to support teaching about resistance in the training and education of the ARSOF soldier. Accordingly, the goals for this manual are set in the context of instructional design theory. Specifically, each section in the manual provides application-based discussion questions for the reader to further explore the lessons embedded in that section.[1] In turn, the manual identifies the content alignment to ARSOF doctrine and concepts by marking the specific sections of the content that directly correspond to the ARIS publications.

The specific goals for the *ARIS Resistance Manual* are:

1. **Identify** the aspects of resistance that an ARSOF soldier must understand to be an effective practitioner of his/her profession.

2. **Categorize** the features of the conceptual typology (actors, causes, environment, organization, and actions) and **map** the factors to existing ARIS literature and emerging academic work in resistance studies to provide the ARSOF soldier with foundational understanding of the phenomenon of resistance.

3. **Integrate** ARIS historical case studies and topical deep dives into the ARSOF soldier's operational preparation and planning.

4. **Incorporate** emerging academic literature into ARIS historical case studies and the features of the conceptual typology to enable the ARSOF soldier to **differentiate** between various features of resistance movements.

These goals endeavor to assist the ARSOF operator to independently:

1. **Use criteria for evaluation** in SWCS classroom studies, independent study, and practical application.

2. **Design/plan** unconventional warfare operations in the SWCS classroom, independent study, and practice.

The Narrative

To provide academic content in a more relatable format, this reference book uses an overarching narrative to facilitate contextualizing and applying the material. This narrative tells the tale of a local leader in a fictional country on the brink of political change. The reader should adopt the perspective of an ARSOF operator tasked with planning operations to support this leader as he builds a resistance.

Arturo Bolanieves and the Sarca Resistance in Estatu

Estatu *is a country that recently experienced an election that favored an administration focused on the majority population. It spearheaded two controversial pieces of legislation: (1) an economic stimulus bill widely viewed as benefitting the wealthy, in part because it funded infrastructure improvements in the expensive downtown districts of the country's two megacities but not for rural areas and (2) a language law that makes minority languages invalid for government business and all contracts. Estatu has two megacities because rural populations have been migrating from those two urban centers in search of more economic opportunity. These populations struggle to find it and have built extensive shanty towns on the outskirts of those cities, and technology companies installed a temporary Internet infrastructure in these shanty towns as a humanitarian effort. The rural provinces of Estatu contain large deposits of rare metals where foreign companies have set up extraction industries. The towns there, however, lack sufficient infrastructure and local residents lose jobs to foreign workers tied to the extraction companies. Geographically, Estatu is predominately flat plains, except for a few forested areas and a large river running north and south cutting the country in half.*

Arturo Bolanieves, *a regional politician in the country of Estatu has risen to prominence by advocating resistance against the central government. He is a charismatic figure who comes from a humble background and rose to the upper middle class as a business owner. The movement he leads is known as Sarca. It began as a not for profit assisting minority populations with translation needs after the central government made the majority language the only legally acceptable one for contracts and government services. When Bolanieves was impeached for questionable reasons, he became the CEO of Sarca and broadened its mandate to advocate for better economic and infrastructure conditions for*

minority and poor populations. He rose to national prominence in part by using popular social media to highlight the struggles that the poor in his province face.

Sarca began as a not for profit to help minority language speakers adapt to the new language law. However, as Bolanieves expanded its scope, it also expanded its operations. It became a broad-based movement not only for changing the language law but for bringing social and economic change to improve the lives of the poor, whether in rural or urban areas. Sarca needed to increase its funding. Sarca continued its original fundraising approach of charitable donations and community events but added fundraising from the diaspora and foreign donors. As its operations continue to grow, it struggles to find more sources of funding. Some within the group advocated taking over local natural resources to sell on the open and black markets. Others advocate partnering with the companies engaged in resource extraction. Within Sarca, Bolanieves struggles to balance its radical and moderate elements. The radical elements undertake violent activities in the shadows to pressure the central government, while moderate members pursue nonviolent approaches.

Ajust, an advocacy group by and for the middle class in the megacities, developed almost in parallel to the rise of Sarca. The group advocates for economic reform that will bring more investment into its communities, impose higher taxes on the wealthy, and reduce its own tax burden. Leaders in Ajust view Sarca as a radical movement, and the two groups occasionally criticize each other in the media.

The Decision to Engage in Unconventional Warfare

The US president approved the employment of unconventional warfare (UW) in Estatu because the president views the goals of Sarca to be in alignment with the United States. The president tasked USASOC to take the lead in UW planning and execution. US ARSOF must plan a UW campaign for Estatu. This campaign will not be in support of a conventional forces campaign. This UW campaign must accomplish the president's goal of a change of administration in Estatu without resorting to conventional forces.

An Operational Detachment Alpha (ODA) was instructed to support Bolanieves and Sarca to replace the current administration threatening oppression of minority groups.

Therefore, the ARSOF soldier needs to understand the definition of, tactics employed for, and measures taken in support of a resistance. This reference book will enable that understanding. It will revisit Bolanieves' story intermittently throughout the text to provide opportunities to practice thinking about how to support a resistance leader. The first step is to understand where the resistance, Sarca, is in its evolution, and then the ODA can determine what the resistance needs.

ATP 3-05.1
2-6

States of Resistance[2]

From guerilla warfare practitioners, such as Mao Tse-tung, to the doctrine writers behind the Army Technical Publication (ATP) on Unconventional Warfare,[3] to academics studying resistance as a social phenomenon, many frameworks describe the evolution of resistance movements. In this vein, the ARIS program produced a study that considered various phasing constructs from different arenas and disciplines and developed its own based on the similarities across those constructs.[4]

TC 18-01
2-6

The construct proposed in the ARIS study contains four main states of resistance: preliminary, incipient, crisis, and institutionalization. The fifth and final state is the resolution state that can be reached from any of the four other states via a variety of resolution paths. The following paragraphs describe those states and provide an example for each.

The ODA tasked with supporting Bolanieves can use these states to map out the current state of Sarca's resistance as well as its future goals. Then the ODA can use its training and education to help achieve future states.

Preliminary

Increase in general unrest among disparate actors without coordination. Unclear or multiple conceptions of grievances, responsibility for them, and how to solve them.

The first state of resistance is the preliminary state, also referred to as "latent" in Army doctrine[5] or "emergent" in modern social movement theory.[6] **The preliminary state's most defining feature is the growth of unorganized and unattributed unrest**. It occurs when the population begins to perceive that its legitimate aspirations are repressed or hindered, albeit without knowing exactly how, why, or necessarily by whom. This is the **infancy of a resistance**, well before a conscious effort to build an organized movement.[7] Whether characterized as **incubation**,[8] or "**milling**" and "**circular interaction**," undirected restlessness slowly becomes directed.[9] Mao Tse-tung, ATP 3-05, and French military scholar David Galula did not propose phases similar to this preliminary phase in their writings; those constructs assume the preexistence of an aggrieved population and offer the organization of an already motivated population as the first phase.[10]

RESISTANCE IN FOCUS: Solidarity[11]

The years 1956 to 1976 marked the preliminary state of the Solidarity movement in Poland. In this state, the movement was not represented through the single organization of Solidarity but through emerging disparate groups and activity. Aggrieved social groups, primarily students, workers, and intellectuals remained disparate and acted independently. For example, during workers' strikes in 1956 and 1970, students did not participate, while the workers did not participate in the student protests in 1968. Meanwhile, intellectuals distanced themselves from protests in favor of focusing on concessions and reform within the government. Despite separate, uncoordinated actions, demands for free organization, speech, and association were largely in concert across the resistance's groups. During this period, economic downturns and subsequent government cuts brought about an increase in general unrest and insecurity. Despite a surge in unrest, the goals and strategies of the resistance remained uncertain.

This state was also characterized by a renewed focus on and vocalization of historical, political, and religious grievances among Polish citizens. A history of Russian oppression tracing back to the eighteenth-century blended with dissatisfaction against the standing Soviet-backed regime to foster a Polish identity for the resistance against a common enemy. The influence of the church in the resistance also contributed to the narrative of a common struggle against oppression by providing the resistance with symbols and rituals that resonated with the people. This renewed focus on history and identity provided a

salient narrative to a population willing to come together in struggle against a common enemy, enabling Solidarity to amass a popular following that reached fourteen million members.

Incipient

Leaders and organizations emerge as conceptions of grievance, responsibility, and solution narrow and crystallize. Outlook becomes formalized and strategic instead of short term/haphazard, as does the pattern of action the resistance engages in. As the organizational level increases and views crystallize, factions develop.

Transition to the next state of resistance occurs when disparate factors coalesce into a clearer and identifiable narrative. The incipient state also features loose and/or formal organizations mobilizing. One can think of this state as having participants with a clear sense of what is wrong and who is responsible, and they are beginning to take limited actions, including organization.[12] This phase is called coalescence in much of social movement theory,[13] but it has also been referred to in the literature as the **incipient phase**.[14] The defining feature of the incipient state is **the development of intentional organization and a common narrative. Leaders come forward and shape the movement.**[15] **Grievances become explicit, widespread, and open.**[16] **Coordination between once separated actors becomes organized and strategic in its outlook**.[17] Some specific indicators identified in the literature include the formation of an intellectual cadre,[18] as well as early signs of factions within the movement.[19] Incipient state activities are evident in Mao's organization and political unification phases, as well as the Special Operations Research Office's (SORO) organization and covert activity phases.[20] The word incipient implies progressing to the next state, or achieving the next action, but recall that, as in all incipient things, reaching the next state or achieving the next action is not guaranteed. Some resistance movements might not make it past the incipient state.

RESISTANCE IN FOCUS: Orange Revolution[21]

The Orange Revolution in Ukraine experienced the incipient state from 1999 through 2004. Opposition to President Leonid Kuchma's standing government coalesced throughout 1999 and 2000, most notably after three events in 2000: Kuchma's rumored authorization of the murder of an investigative journalist, his removal of Deputy Prime Minister Yuliya Tymoshenko, and the subsequent removal of his popular prime minister, Viktor Yushchenko. These events, on top of claims of electoral fraud from the 1999 election, brought previously disparate groups together and provided a clear sense of what was wrong and who was to blame. Discernable collective action and mobilization against the regime ensued, exemplified by the "Ukraine without Kuchma" campaign and anti-government protests in Kiev through 2000 and 2001.

This period also saw the development of resistance leaders and an intellectual cadre. Interestingly, this leadership evolved largely from Kuchma's removed inner circle, most notably Tymoshenko and Yushchenko. Strategies developed with a focus on resistance and revolution through electoral channels and peaceful protest. One example was the formation of the "Our Ukraine" Party by Yushchenko in 2002 and the party's get-out-the-vote campaign leading up to the 2004 elections. Believing that the overwhelming public support for new leadership (Kuchma, facing term limits, handpicks Yanukovich to run as his successor) would bring about change simply by getting people to the ballot box, the resistance focused solely on getting citizens to vote rather than advocating for its own nominee, Yushchenko, against Kuchma's handpicked successor, Yanukovich. The first round of elections in October 2004 did not produce a winner, and a runoff election was planned for November 21. Rampant electoral fraud in the runoff election incited massive protests, marking the revolution's transition into the crisis state.

Crisis

Escalated and overt confrontation with opponents (violent or nonviolent) that demonstrates clear division of resistance and those opponents. Real threat to opponent's interests, authority, and/or existence such that they must respond.

The crisis state distinguishes resistance movements from social movements more generally. The essential characteristic defining a resistance in the crisis state is **a decisive moment of escalated confrontation with opponents, however long or short**. This moment can be violent or nonviolent. By allowing for both, this construct blends social movement theory with political science and military thought. Moving from an incipient to crisis state occurs **when the movement grows powerful enough to pose a serious threat to its opponent**. A threat becomes serious when the opponent of the resistance, **the state, escalates its approach because previous methods of countering the resistance failed**. A resistance can be incentivized to escalate its actions, violent or nonviolent, when an incipient resistance gains power and influence. **That escalation can bring about a confrontation with and real risk to the government**. The idea of movements escalating to a state of outbreak or crisis is prominently acknowledged in the early literature on revolutions,[22] but this notion became less common after the field shifted away from revolutions and toward the study of social movements more generally.[23]

The crisis state features actions that mark the clear separation of the resistance from the state.[24] **Scholars identified signals of this state to include a decisive loss of legitimacy by the government, financial collapse, breakdown in authority, strong symbolic actions, and perception of dual sovereignty or provisional authority, among others.**[25] This state is often characterized as the peak in revolutions, where a shift occurs from academic to militaristic values, structured collective action, and the strategic exercise of new power.[26] Maoist and related constructs straddle the crisis state between transitional stages— particularly the second and third phases of Mao's three phases, buildup and employment, as labeled in ATP 3-05 on unconventional warfare, and SORO's transition from expansion to militarization.[27]

RESISTANCE IN FOCUS: Provisional Irish Republican Army[28]

From January to July of 1972, the Provisional Irish Republican Army (IRA), known locally as the Provos or the RA, was in the crisis state. The maintenance of barricaded "no-go" and "free" zones in Derry/Londonderry and Belfast during this period contributed to perceptions of provisional authority and separation of resistance from opponents. Heightened contention and escalation of resistance action occurred after British troops killed thirteen civilian demonstrators at the civil rights march that became known as

"Bloody Sunday." Public and international backlash against the British government increased its vulnerability to resistance demands.

Additionally, an escalation in resistance action occurred in retaliation, most notably a violent bombing campaign. As the resistance threat intensified, the British government initiated secret talks between the IRA and British Secretary of State. The secret talks were unsuccessful, and in July 1972, IRA bombs exploded across Belfast in what is known as "Bloody Friday," resulting in nine civilian deaths. Despite backlash from the "Bloody Friday" bombings, the IRA persisted through the crisis state and transitioned into the institutional state.

Institutionalization

> Resistance has survived crisis confrontation(s) with opponents and needs to consolidate gains. Viewed more equally to its opposition and possesses long-term staying power. Resistance organization establishes its role in society.

Referred to as bureaucratization in modern social movement theory,[29] the institutional state of resistance exists if the group or movement either persists through, or gains strength from, the crisis state. Surviving the crisis state deepens its organizational and strategic prowess as an established opposition player, and it broadens its appeal and long-term staying power. In other words, **the essential characteristic of a resistance in the institutional state is an established role in society.**

Scholarship characterizes this post-crisis state by the need for the resistance to consolidate its gains and authority and to secure its role in stability.[30] As Professor Hopper claims in his social movement theory work, "the out group must finally be able to legalize or organize their power" as a permanent organization "that is acceptable to the current mores."[31] Maoist and derivative phasing constructs regard the institutional state of specifically violent resistance movements in the variously named consolidation, transition, or regaining lost territories phases.[32] The institutional state is the most mature phase of resistance before resolution (either successful or otherwise), but **it can persist almost indefinitely if resolution is not achieved.**

RESISTANCE IN FOCUS: Hizbollah[33]

Hizbollah in Lebanon is an example of resistance in the institutional state that presently remains in this state. In July 1993, Hizbollah transitioned into the institutional state after cease-fires ended the Seven Day War against Israel. By this time, there existed a perception of Hizbollah as a provisional authority and legitimate representative of the Shi'a population in Lebanon. Additionally, Hizbollah operated as a political and paramilitary organization, participating in Lebanese elections as well as armed confrontation against Israel. For these reasons, Hizbollah transitioned into the institutional state as an equal opposition player with broadened appeal.

Hizbollah's organizational and strategic prowess deepened in this period as attacks against Israel/Israeli targets became more sophisticated, characterized by cyber attacks, rocket launches, terrorist activity, and war from 2006 to 2008. The group structuralized its role through control of media outlets, including a satellite channel and several radio stations and newspapers, and signaled its consolidation of authority and gains in domestic support with significant electoral victories in 2009. Hizbollah demonstrated its continued staying power through its recent involvement in the Syrian Civil War, fighting with Assad against Sunni rebels, and in domestic political conflicts in 2011, 2013, and 2014. The institutional status of Hizbollah was further signaled by international recognition of the political arm of Hizbollah within Lebanese politics, with only the armed wing considered a terrorist organization.

In the following diagram (Figure 1)[34] depicting the states of resistance, one can see "off-ramps" along the bottoms of the states. These represent paths to resolution. Scholars and analysts identified a variety of forms of resolution, and one can see that several of them repeat. That is because a resistance movement can take that path to resolution from multiple states. Just as the diagram aims to show the fluidity of the states, the resolution states should not be interpreted as strict or rigid. Resistance groups may experience multiple resolution states at once or over a period of time. Likewise, resolution does not only mean the absolute termination of the movement. The resolution state is simply another state, meaning a resistance group can move into and out of it as the circumstances evolve.

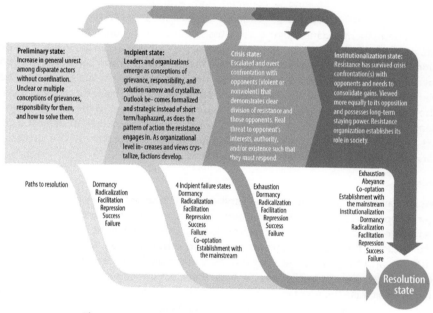

Figure 1. Proposed states for phasing construct analysis.

Resolution States

Radicalization

Radicalization can be reached from all of the states. Radicalization is "a shift in ideological commitments toward the extremes and/or the adoption of more disruptive and violent forms of contention."[35] Radicalization can be thought of as a "mechanism for

demobilization" often simultaneous with the resolution of a rival wing of the movement via institutionalization; one wing radicalizes while the other institutionalizes itself in society.[36] As the institutionalized wing moderates its positions and tactics, the other wing radicalizes further toward nonnegotiable positions and tactics that are more escalatory, confrontational, and violent.

> **RESISTANCE IN FOCUS: The Chechen Revolution**[37]
>
> A wing of this movement experienced a radical Islamist shift, distancing the movement from its initial nationalist-separatist demands. Increased Russian opposition caused regionalization, dispersion of resources, and exacerbation of internal cleavages. This resolution state also resulted from Vladimir Putin's hardline rhetoric of the resistance as terrorists, highlighting the gap between the resistance and the Chechen people.

Institutionalization

Institutionalization as a resolution can be reached from the institutionalization state. Institutionalization is the opposite of radicalization: the resistance adopts more conventional views and less disruptive actions. The process of institutionalization is characterized by a group seeking "accommodations with elites and electoral advantage" by moderating its tactics and goals.[38] During this resolution process, the group transforms itself into a permanent organization "acceptable to the current mores."[39] The group loses its resistant nature and becomes absorbed by the status quo. Unlike in the state of institutionalization previously mentioned, where the resistance group continues to oppose the government but as an established part of society, here the resistance group resolves into being the status quo and no longer resists. As noted earlier, this institutionalization can often occur simultaneously with radicalization by another wing of the group. While both lead to a decline in the movement, institutionalization may be seen as at least a partial success of the movement. However, depending on the perceived extent of this success, the resistance movement may lose its initial motivations.

Repression

Repression can be reached from all of the states. Repression occurs when the government or other authority uses force to stop movement organizations from functioning or prevent people from joining.[40] The tactics of repression include indictment, infiltration, physical attacks, harassment, threats to job and school access, the spread of false information, and "anything else that makes it more difficult for the movement to put its views before relevant audiences."[41] While those actions can lead to resolution on their own, it can also cause the resistance to splinter.[42] Repression is the resolution state when the government effectively halts the resistance, but if the government's actions create a more radical offshoot, the resolution state may be radicalization.

Facilitation

Facilitation can be reached from all of the states. Facilitation occurs when the government or its agents bring about the decline of a resistance by satisfying at least some of the claims of contenders. This acquiescence can be accomplished at the same time as using limited and selective means of repression.[43] This form of resolution functions by dividing the resistance. When the government facilitates some but not all of the resistance group's claims, such efforts can attract moderates to legitimate action or satisfy elites with the government response. Meanwhile, satisfying only some of the group's demands, with public acceptance by the moderates, can frustrate and inspire radicals who want more change. In turn, such a split can weaken the resistance, especially if it coincides with a decline in popular support because the larger population is satisfied with the government's responses and does not support the radicals. It should be noted that it is possible to end in multiple states of resistance.

RESISTANCE IN FOCUS: Provisional Irish Republican Army[44]

The Provisional IRA transitioned into the resolution state on April 10, 1998 through facilitation. The facilitation resolution state was marked by a decline in resistance through satisfaction of some resistance claims or demands by the government. In the case of the IRA, the decline of resistance occurred when the Good Friday Agreement (GFA) or Belfast Agreement in 1998 satisfied some demands of the IRA. The agreement enacted policing reforms, released political prisoners, set up provisions for a popular vote on Northern Ireland's status, and established power-sharing institutions in line with IRA demands. After the agreement, Sinn Fein, the political arm of the IRA, became one of largest parties in Northern Ireland and remains active to this day. The agreement also led to the disarmament of the IRA, and in 2005, international observers announced the complete demobilization of the IRA. Popular support for the agreement was displayed when 71 percent of voters in Northern Ireland and 94 percent in Ireland voted in favor of the resolution in 1999. Despite these achievements, the primary movement goal of an independent and unified Ireland was not met, and the resistance entered the resolution state. Although the IRA transitioned into the resolution state, one should not confuse the resolution state with the resolution of the real (or perceived) grievance and/or the holistically resolved conflict.

Success

Success can be reached from all of the states. Success is not as simple as it sounds. A resistance can set goals, achieve them, and then fade away, no longer being a resistance but part of governance. However, it is more common for movements to be forced into compromises that include concessions by the government that also transform them into mere interest groups.[45] The shape of success, and the concessions required, also reveal internal fractures within the resistance movement that lead to impotence and decline. For instance, some members of the resistance movement may see success when certain goals are achieved, but others may see success only when the movement continues to grow. However, growth may also include the addition of members who are less committed to the original resistance than earlier members, leading to factions that weaken the movement overall. In considering the complexity of a movement's success, one should consider how a resistance can be forced to change its values or demands and lose some of its identity or attraction to gain concessions from the government as part of a compromise. Therefore, in succeeding, the resistance ends up in some ways no longer claiming to represent an aggrieved or radical population. Scholars demonstrate that some within the resistance will view this concession as success, while others will not, leading to internal division that can neuter the resistance all on its own.

RESISTANCE IN FOCUS: The Orange Revolution[46]

The Orange Revolution in Ukraine is an example of a resistance movement that transitioned to the resolution state through success. Resolution through success indicates some degree of fulfillment of resistance goals, as well as the decline of the resistance in response to those successes. The Orange Revolution transitioned from the crisis state to the resolution state through success on December 26, 2004, when a third election took place and Yushchenko, the resistance's candidate, won by a clear margin. After a prolonged legal battle waged by Yanukovich, the Supreme Court upheld Yushchenko's electoral victory, and Yushchenko was sworn in as Ukraine's president on January 23, 2005, signaling the successful resolution of the resistance. The resistance further deteriorated after the decisive election due to the absence of a unifying enemy (Kuchma/Yanukovich), and ultimately Yanukovich was elected as president in 2010, defeating former resistance leader Tymoshenko. The re-emergence of the resistance continues to be debated in light of the 2014 uprisings in Kiev, the ousting of Yanukovich, and the ongoing conflict in Eastern regions of the country.

Failure

Failure can be reached from all of the states. An internal divide in a resistance movement can threaten the movement as a whole. Failure refers to the internal collapse of a resistance, rather than being undone by outside forces. This resolution state is particular to issues within the specific resistance organization, rather than attributable to overpowering external conditions (though the two can be related). Accordingly, factors that lead to the failure of a resistance in this sense are highly specific to the individual resistance, and commonalities are difficult to identify.

One scholar on the subject states that organizational failure takes two shapes: factionalism and encapsulation: "[F]actionalism arises from the inability of the organization's members to agree over the best direction to take," leading to an internal conflict that proves fatal to the organization.[47] "[E]ncapsulation occurs when the movement organization develops an ideology or structure that interferes with efforts to recruit members or raise demands," eventually causing a critical decline in mobilization and capabilities.[48]

Other scholars on this subject present four additional failure states specific to incipient movements. First, groups can fail by neglecting to establish "a preexisting network of communication linking those groups of citizens most likely to support the movement," effectively isolating themselves from growth or mobilization potential.[49] Second, the "failure of an emergent leader to incorporate...[other] leaders into his organization" can undermine a resistance group before it matures.[50] Third, a young movement may lack "a program to which a major section of the [participants] could give wholehearted support," stifling recruitment and internal commitment.[51] It essentially lacks a narrative and goals or values that appeal to enough people. The alternative is that the resistance's narrative and goals do not inspire people to commit to the movement. Finally, highly publicized failures can create a fatally "weakened . . . public image" and result in the resistance movement's rapid failure because it is discredited in a slow decline when confidence in the group fails to recover from the embarrassing failure.[52]

Co-Optation

Co-Optation can be reached from the incipient and institutionalization states. Co-optation occurs "when individual movement leaders are offered rewards [or positions] that advance them as individuals while ignoring the collective goals of the movement."[53] This reward approach serves to align the resistance leadership with the interests of the government or residing power.[54] Groups that are "highly dependent on centralized authority or on charismatic leadership" are especially vulnerable to co-optation.[55] Beyond co-opting leadership, this process also includes appropriating the language, symbols, and tactics of the resistance, assimilation of resistance participants, transformation of resistance goals, and regulation of enacted changes by state or vested interests.[56]

Establishment with the Mainstream

Establishment with the Mainstream can be reached from the incipient and institutionalization states. This state of resolution occurs when the resistance becomes "an accepted part of the system—typically after realizing some of their goals—so that although they continue to flourish, they no longer challenge the status quo."[57] The resistance essentially transforms from an opposition voice into another voice in the chorus of the mainstream. Although establishment with the mainstream is similar to institutionalization, when a movement enters this state, it is accepted as a voice within the dominant power structure while avoiding co-optation. This means the resistance is not just a radical wing of the many parties involved in governance but instead is involved in governance and decision-making. For instance, if the resistance becomes a marginal, radical party that only holds a few seats in government, it likely reached the resolution of institutionalization or co-optation, whereas if it becomes an active voice in a ruling coalition, the resistance becomes established with the mainstream.

Exhaustion

Exhaustion can be reached from the crisis and institutionalization states. After a resistance movement matures, particularly in the face of an extended crisis state, the movement may experience gradual decline through "psychological exhaustion which undermines the emotional foundations of the revolution."[58] This slow deflation of zeal for resistance accompanies the eventual success of the status quo and a return to normalcy.[59] Some scholars also cite the personal costs of resistance as contributing to this form of resolution: "although street protests, demonstrations, and violence are exhilarating at first...[resistance movements] involve risk, personal costs, and, eventually, weariness and disillusionment."[60] This dynamic can also contribute to movement radicalization or institutionalization.

Abeyance

Abeyance can be reached from the institutionalization state. Abeyance (sometimes referred to as dormancy[61]) is technically not a resolution because it does not mark the end of the resistance. Instead, it occurs when the resistance group or movement consciously practices little or no mobilization and reverts to an incipient state of "inward... focus on identity or values."[62] Essentially, the resistance chooses to remain in the incipient state and does not progress. During this time, it avoids decisive confrontations and reduces recruitment efforts. Scholars argue that abeyance allows movements to "sustain themselves...through internal structures" and orient themselves internally to maintain their values, identity,

and political vision.[63] Another scholar similarly theorizes that a movement's abeyance provides a measure of continuity for groups. It allows them to successfully build a base of support despite confronting a political and social environment unreceptive to its message or struggle.[64] A resistance movement, despite falling back into an incipient state through abeyance, can reemerge and remobilize after reinforcing its group identity and developing a larger support base. Therefore, abeyance can be thought of as deliberately prolonging the time spent in the incipient state, as opposed to continuing to drive toward a confrontation with the opposition or a resolution.

To use the aforementioned states of resistance construct, or any other phasing construct, in analyzing this manual's narrative for Estatu, the ODA will need information to inform its decisions about where Bolanieves and Sarca are in their evolution and the help they will need. An integral part of that information is the actors in the resistance and its society; the characters in their story and their roles. Another important piece of information is the motivations of Sarca. Why do its members participate in resistance? The ODA will need to be aware of the physical, social, and economic environment in which Sarca and Bolanieves operate. What is the stage on which Sarca's story plays out? To be effective advisors, the ODA needs to understand Sarca's organization. How are the characters' roles connected? Finally, the ODA will need to learn and advise which actions Sarca and its characters have available to them and which they should take. Each of these will be considered in turn through the rest of the manual.

ACTORS

Thus far, this reference book has covered the states of resistance movements. It will now examine the different elements of a resistance, specifically the actors that could become a part of it, the causes and motivations that could start and drive it, the environment in which it operates, the organizational approach it could take, and the actions that a resistance could undertake against the standing government. Each resistance movement is specific to its time, place, and circumstances, but no resistance movement is entirely unique from its historical predecessors; there are commonalities in resistance. Accordingly, while all the constructs, theories, observations, lessons, and ideas covered in this manual that were derived from the history of resistance movements may not apply to a specific resistance, it is imperative to learn from past resistance movements to understand current and future ones. The discussions about the elements of resistance that follow do not instruct the reader on what to do; rather, the following discussions use the narrative in the blue text to assist the reader in conceptualizing and thinking through a resistance generally. It introduces and walks through the general concepts and ideas that emerge from the history of resistance. The first area where these general concepts will be covered is the element of actors involved in resistance.

As a resistance leader, Bolanieves will need to answer several questions about the actors that are and potentially could be part of the movement. Actors can be individuals or groups, such as nongovernmental organizations, private businesses, foreign governments, or a diaspora.

Who does he need to recruit? How will he recruit them? What functions does he need fulfilled? What kind of people does he want and need in which roles? What will his leadership style be? What actors are needed to exercise control and govern the movement?

When it comes to planning, ARSOF operators should know Bolanieves from the news and intelligence sources.[65] However, what about the actors surrounding him? How do supporting elements fit into Bolanieves' leadership style? Maybe they lack the charisma to lead groups but possess exceptional managerial skills that can be used in organizing underground operations. As Bolanieves builds a shadow government, who will he put in charge of its different functions? Governance requires effective leadership in finance, law enforcement, and logistics to name a few. Who can Sarca entrust to make choices dividing resources between military operations and providing governance? If Sarca is ultimately successful and supplants the government it will need talent and experience in all aspects of a society and government to facilitate a smooth transition to governing. Resistance movements need more than just charismatic leaders and brave fighters. How can the ODA facilitate Bolanieves getting the right people into the right roles? How will ARSOF operators learn about his supporters and his critics? What other actors should the ODA need to consider? Resistance and UW are human centric[66] and therefore require knowing the humans involved, how to persuade them to participate, and how to lead them.

Leadership[67]

Leaders mobilize institutional, political, financial, psychological, and other resources to motivate, engage, and satisfy members of a resistance.[68] They also work to develop the group's ideology, legitimacy, and strategy and to build the organization according to the physical, human, and security environments. In this section, the reader will examine a series of different components of leadership that will be important for deployment: transactional and transformational leadership; charismatic leadership, targeting leaders, leaders chosen from inside the resistance, and leaders chosen from outside the resistance.

JP 3-05.1
I-14, B-4

TC 18-01.1
E-1

Resistance leaders can find themselves operating inside or outside the country. For example, a well-known resistance leader may be targeted by the government and forced to flee. Or the resistance may be capable of protecting the leader so s/he does not have to leave the country. Leading from outside the country can challenge the leader's legitimacy by bringing into question his/her loyalty (if s/he cares about the country, why did s/he leave?) or by distancing the leader not only in space but also in understanding the resistance group and the larger population. However, being outside the country can provide an advantage. For instance, if the leader flees to a democratic country, then s/he could have more access to information, better communications, and a greater ability to develop outside support for the resistance, moral, political, and material.[69]

ATP 3-05.1
1-5, 2-4, 2-20, E-4

TC 18-01
1-5, 2-3

Bolanieves has been the de facto leader of this resistance, but he will need to cement his position. Legitimacy is important for leadership, so Bolanieves will need to find a way to establish that legitimacy and credibility to a variety of audiences. Sarca may have a wide variety of society members, and all of them cannot be managed or led in the same fashion.

Bolanieves will have to decide whether he should be a transformative or transactional leader and in relation to which members. He will also need to develop a charisma that appeals to a sufficiently broad population and not alienate segments important to the resistance's efforts. For instance, alienating the overt, more moderate Sarca members (the public component) could dissuade them from supporting the covert, less moderate Sarca members (the guerilla, underground, and auxiliary components).

Transactional and Transformational Leadership[70]

Studies about leadership highlight two types: transactional and transformational.[71] In transactional leadership, the focus is on monitoring employees and rewarding and punishing them based on performance. It can be an effective style, but it can become counterproductive if overused. Transformational leadership inspires and communicates common purpose. This style has shown to more directly impact productivity than the transactional style. It also better increases trust and group identity.[72]

Based on that research, an ODA might advise Bolanieves to adopt a transformational leadership style. However, this decision may depend on the cultural aspects of Estatu society. Are people in Estatu like Americans on whom that research was done? How are they different?

Studying the corporate world, researchers also identified three categories of leadership behaviors: task, relationship, and change:[73]

Task Behaviors	Relationship Behaviors	Change Behaviors
Plan short-term activities	Provide support and encouragement	Monitor the external environment
Clarify task objectives	Provide recognition for achievement and contributions	Propose an innovative strategy or vision
Monitor operations and performance	Develop member skill and confidence	Encourage innovative thinking
	Consult with members when making decisions	Take risks to promote necessary changes
	Empower members to take initiative in problem solving	

As organizations expand, this range of leadership functions must be accomplished by teams, not individuals, because of the amount and complexity of the work to be done. Also, different leadership styles have different advantages and disadvantages. Effective leaders surround themselves with a team that both accentuates their strengths and complements them where they are weakest.

Accordingly, the ODA may want to identify Bolanieves' weaknesses and help him find the right team members to complement him as a leader. It is important for Bolanieves to understand how the right team members will re-enforce the skills, resources, and organizational capacity that he envisions. The ODA might consider assessing whether he is able to and has enough support to accomplish all the tasks previously listed and others that may not have been captured in the corporate literature, such as the more practical parts of resistance leadership, such as logistics and intelligence.

Charismatic Leadership[74]

Charisma is the "quality of an individual personality by virtue of which he is set apart from ordinary men and treated as endowed with supernatural, superhuman, or at least specifically exceptional powers or qualities."[75] Charisma helps to begin movements by motivating populations and to keep resistance groups together through challenges. Charismatic leaders are seen as visionaries, and they demonstrate some combination of emotionality, activity, sensitivity to the sociopolitical landscape, intense interest in and empathy toward followers, superior rhetorical and persuasive skills, and exemplary behavior in sacrificing personal ambitions to the movement's.[76] Abimael Guzman[77] from the Sendero Luminoso (Shining Path), Velupillai Prabhakaran from the Liberation Tigers of Tamil Eelam (LTTE), Osama bin Laden of al Qaeda, and Mohandas Karamchand Gandhi are all considered charismatic leaders.

Charismatic leadership can be difficult to maintain as movements grow larger. Charismatic leaders must accomplish these four functions: (1) maintain the public persona of the leader; (2) moderate the effects of the psychological identification of followers with the leader; (3) negotiate the routinization of charisma; and (4) achieve frequent new successes.[78]

Group members need to see and hear from charismatic leaders on a regular basis. This can be done with large, staged, public displays, or with smaller appearances. These leaders might favor smaller appearances because their personalities have a more effective impact on smaller groups. A challenge facing the use of charismatic leadership is ensuring the safety and security of that leader. As a result, they might also avoid public displays because it places the leader at risk as a target. As a public figure, Bolanieves could make appearances regularly, and social media technology facilitates making appearances to a broad audience in a way that can feel intimate.

At the same time, charismatic leaders need to balance public appearances with maintaining auras of mystery or supernatural power. That isolation has its own drawbacks, like making decisions without sufficient information and therefore failure from internal fractures over the direction of the resistance.[79]

The ODA will need to consider how to balance these benefits and dangers. Integral to this is also keeping Bolanieves alive and at the head of Sarca. This can become a challenge because governments have historically targeted resistance leaders, both politically and violently.

RESISTANCE IN FOCUS: A Cautionary Tale of Charismatic Leadership

A limitation of charismatic leadership can be demonstrated by the LTTE's Prabhakaran, who had a force of personality that inspired followers but also meant he had little capability for political compromise. His unwillingness to compromise likely perpetuated the kinetic component of the conflict and decreased the bargaining room for the Sri Lankan government. This stubbornness in turn limited the Tamil minority's options for achieving

---

political objectives without more bloodshed, and it ultimately resulted in the destruction of Prabhakaran's movement.[80]

Leaders Chosen from Inside the Resistance[81]

Where do leaders come from? The answer often depends on the resistance group's origins. Bolanieves rose up after falling out of political office and moving on to lead a nonprofit advocacy group.

Undergrounds often form from existing networks, such as political parties, labor organizations, civic clubs, or military units. For example, the Euskadi Ta Askatasuna (Basque Homeland and Freedom, or ETA) resistance organization in Spain built around the Basque institution of the "cuadrilla," a group of friends roughly the same age who spent most of their time together drinking, sharing meals, and mountain climbing, with group ties often stronger than family ties.[82] A leader in these kinds of groups may emerge organically. *Bolanieves emerged organically from the pre-existing structures of his political party and the not-for-profit corporation.*

Leaders Chosen from Outside the Resistance[83]

Occasionally, the external government supporting a resistance selects and emplaces a leader in the resistance. In Yugoslavia during World War II, for example, the allied forces withdrew support from Dragoljub Mihailovic and recognized Marshal Josip Broz Tito because they felt he employed aggressive action against the Germans and would thereby be of greater assistance to the military mission. External sponsors can, however, decide to cease support of the resistance, for instance, because their objectives no longer align. This was the case in El Salvador with the Frente Farabundo Martí para la Liberación Nacional (Farabundo Marti National Liberation Front, or FMLN). The critical flow of arms, money, and training from the Soviet Union was curtailed in the late 1980s, which fatally weakened the resistance.[84]

Some movements may also demonstrate divided leadership, where political and military leaders function independently. Such an approach might be an option for Bolanieves to preserve his legitimacy by separating him from the violent elements of Sarca. One can easily see the challenges of such a leadership structure. Namely, ensuring the two leaders do not develop different visions for the resistance and take their respective elements away from the other. If Sarca split into multiple resistance movements, it might not withstand efforts by the Estatu government to subdue it.

If the ODA helps Bolanieves identify his leadership weaknesses, one option to fill that weakness is to recruit from outside Sarca. Members often join a resistance for a variety of reasons, but leaders more frequently join a movement for ideological reasons.[85] Accordingly, recruiting leaders can be very selective, and they frequently hold existing close associates or friends of current resistance leaders.

When a resistance grows, it needs middle-level leaders: provincial leaders, influential agents within a university or government agency, and military leaders. New capabilities, resources, and members can be gained by recruiting key figures who already wield great influence in a society, such as a provincial leader, clan elder, or local religious scholar. They can bring legitimacy to the resistance and bring the resources of their respective constituencies to help the resistance.

Those same influential community members can also serve as recruiting tools, whether based in convenience—a former KGB agent called such people "useful idiots"[86]—or in true conviction. Lebanese Hizbollah, for example, always benefited from Shiite clerics who lend religious authority and respectability to the insurgent movement. In this case, the insurgent leaders share the religious faith of the clerics, even if the two groups often differ on matters of strategy and tactics.

Targeting Leaders[87]

Regardless of the type of leadership or the leader's origins, resistance leaders are often the target of counter-resistance efforts, counterinsurgency, foreign internal defense, or counterterrorism. Younger and smaller organizations are more vulnerable to attacks that remove leaders than larger and more-developed organizations.[88]

Additionally, religious organizations more frequently survive the murder of leaders, while nonreligious ideological organizations more often decline and terminate after their leaders were killed.[89] Counter-resistance efforts can also discredit leaders and undermine their legitimacy. Leaders outside the country uniquely face the danger of counter-resistance efforts to manipulate or disrupt their communication with elements in the country to create friction in the resistance.

The Form and Function of Shadow Governance[90]

To manage the movement as a leader, Bolanieves will need to institute some form of governing system. If he and Sarca are permitted to remain in the country, they can create a shadow government. However, if they are exiled from Estatu, they will need to set up a government in exile. Bolanieves will need to establish his shadow government or a government in exile with the infrastructure set up to command and control the multiple components of Sarca. It is important also to note that one function of the shadow government (or government in exile) is to interface with other resistance movements and potentially with actors outside the state. Bolanieves might contact the diaspora for support and/or liaise with foreign governments sympathetic to his cause.

JP 3-05.1
I-15, IV-2

TC 18-01.1
APPENDIX L

Resistance leaders that remain in the country can form a shadow government (instead of a government in exile) and control a portion of the territory. A shadow government provides services to the civilian population in the territory it controls and carries out other typical governmental functions, such as bringing justice and collecting taxes.[91] In some cases, shadow governments gained greater legitimacy and popularity by successfully creating benefits for the people they govern, such as schools, hospitals, roads, clean water, and safety.[92]

ATP 3-05.1
2-21, 3-9

TC 18-01
2-12

During World War II, there were many governments in exile because Nazi Germany or the Soviet Union occupied their countries. Resistance groups today are more likely to establish an internal shadow government because they are challenging and seeking to change or replace the existing government. Resistance groups mimic the functions of the state to bolster a shadow government's legitimacy in the eyes of both its domestic and international audiences.[93]

Government Versus Governance[94]

State governments are backed by formal authority and police powers to enforce formal laws. Having a government, however, does not automatically mean it provides good governance. For instance, in weak states, there are state governments with formal institutions that lack the resources or ability to provide governance.[95] Shadow governments fulfill the role of state governments but without formal authority or institutions to enforce laws. In other words, taxation, education, and security are still provided without recognizable formal institutions, such as an Internal Revenue Service, a Department of Education, or formal police forces. Successful shadow governments provide good governance where state governments do not.

Shadow governance is part of the constant interaction between a resistance and the population.[96] Research identified attributes of shadow governance in competition with the government: extension of force, national identity and legitimacy, revenue generation, and provision of social services.[97]

In Uganda, the National Resistance Army, or NRA, adopted governance strategies supporting the civilian population until military pressure stopped them.98 The NRA offered a series of services, including health care and security, to the civilian population in its liberated areas. As its hold on those areas deteriorated during the war, the NRA evacuated civilians to safe pockets in the Luwero Triangle, still encouraging civilians to maintain the democratic village councils it established in its safe areas. Eventually, as its position became more precarious, the NRA was forced to terminate all ties with the civilian population to free the group from allocating resources to civilian defense. The NRA demanded that civilians leave the war zone. The NRA only resumed governance activities when its military position vis-à-vis the incumbent government considerably improved.99

When a resistance successfully uses force against the government, it can keep the government from exercising authority over that territory. For example, the National Union for the Total Independence of Angola's (UNITA) challenged the Angolan authorities:

> Lodged like a bone in the throat, [UNITA] offered a permanent challenge to Luanda's [ruling MPLA[100] party] authority, to its ability to implant policies that might ordinarily have improved the lives of Angola's people. It denied the very title that MPLA had won for itself as the Government of the People's Republic of Angola. Savimbi's campaign . . . meant that the MPLA did not, could not, govern the country.[101]

Similarly, when the Fuerzas Armadas Revolucionarias de Colombia (Revolutionary Armed Forces of Colombia, or FARC) took control of five municipalities granted to it by the Colombian government, the state admitted its inability to effectively govern those areas. The FARC stepped in with effective shadow governance and brought a significant drop in serious crimes, such as murders, robberies, and rape.[102] The FARC's experience illustrates the importance of providing security, perceived strength, and generosity to the people for legitimacy.[103]

Legitimacy[104]

Legitimacy, or the consent of a population that a political organization has the right to expect and enforce its obedience, is at the core of the governance relationship with the population. In Western liberalism, legitimacy is based on the social contract between the state and the people. Other sources of legitimacy include ancestral or religious authority. Colonial powers often created states without considering the diversity in identity. The Eritrean People's Liberation Front, or EPLF, used this fact to its advantage by appealing to the Ethiopian threat to put Eritrean identity above religious and ethnic divisions. Today, Eritreans have a strong sense of nationality.[105]

The ODA and Bolanieves should understand how legitimacy is gained in the eyes of Estatu's populations. Assuming Estatu society operates the same way as US society could be a trap for the ODA's efforts and doom Bolanieves' chances. It would be important for Bolanieves' legitimacy to be gained from the sources of authority that Estatu society views as valid and important.

Funding[106]

Even with ironclad legitimacy, a resistance movement's shadow government needs to generate revenue. Shadow governments and resistance groups raise funds in a variety of ways, including taxation, voluntary contributions, control over valuable natural resources, or criminal activity. Sympathetic populations may prefer to pay taxes charged by the resistance, such as during the Kosovo insurrection when the Kosovo diaspora in Germany paid informal payroll tax. In particular, if the resistance is seen as less predatory and more secure than the government, even non-sympathetic populations may prefer to pay taxes to the resistance.[107] Alternatively, UNITA faced challenges after its primary source of income, foreign assistance, evaporated after the end of the Cold War. The group's revenue-generating strategies transformed to rely heavily on territorial control of diamond-rich areas and leveraging other commercial activities in the group's territory—these strategies sometimes generated as much as $5 million a month.[108]

Providing Social Services

It is important for shadow governments to provide social services to the civil population, such as charitable acts, public services like education and health, and infrastructure development, such as telecommunications networks and roads.[109]

JP 3-05.1
III-20, III-28

Hizbollah has been especially effective in this regard. The group used half of Hizbollah's 2007 budget for social services, which were delivered to mostly Shia constituents.[110] The social services component of the group comprises six subgroups supporting various needs of the community, from reconstruction to provisions for the families of martyrs, women's welfare, and education. Hizbollah's social service efforts, such as the reconstruction of homes and structures damaged by the 2006 war with Israel, far outstrip those of the Lebanese state.[111]

ATP 3-05.1
3-9, E-11

RESISTANCE IN FOCUS: Good Governance by the LTTE

One of the most effective shadow governance activities systems was that established by the LTTE in Sri Lanka.112 Both the political and military wings of the LTTE were under the authority of a single commander. The political wing's ministries included finance, justice,

protection, economic development, health, and education. LTTE representatives oversaw the implementation of the group's governance directives in each of its territorial districts. The shadow government's relationship with the incumbent Sri Lankan state was particularly unique. Both the incumbent government and the LTTE vied for legitimacy among domestic populations and international audiences through the provision of services. As a result, the competing governments formed a symbiotic relationship whereby they worked jointly to provide health and education to local populations. In LTTE territories, governance activities were conducted under the auspices of a dual authority—an LTTE representative and a Sri Lankan representative. The LTTE benefitted from the relationship because it was able to meet the demands of the residents without taxing LTTE resources, and the Sri Lankan government benefitted because it was able to maintain a hold, however tenuous, on the population living under LTTE control.113

Like most insurgencies, the LTTE first established an effective policing and justice system that sought to "normalize" life for civilians in its regions. Its police force eventually grew to over three thousand officers and became a legitimate and respected institution among residents. An expansive judiciary not only mediated disputes among residents but also acted as a source of revenue for the civil administration through land courts that instituted annual property taxes. The taxes generated steady income for the LTTE, particularly from the wealthy diaspora concerned about property they still owned in rebel areas. Moreover, the LTTE set up a respectable legal system, which included elements of Sri Lankan penal code and Tamil cultural norms, after more informal and ad hoc measures generated complaints. The system provided the populace with swift justice, and the LTTE was very vigilant to keep corruption to a minimum.114

In terms of providing social services, the LTTE was more involved and effective in education than health services. The group faced numerous constraints in establishing health care infrastructure, including an embargo on medical goods and the flight of highly trained professionals upon whom health care depends. International aid organizations offered basic health care, mainly through mobile centers that often lacked physicians. Residents with serious health conditions typically sought care in government-controlled areas.115 The LTTE met more success in providing education. Tamil families traditionally place a great deal of importance on the education of their children as a path to social mobility. The Tamil Eelam Education Council was tasked with carrying out education tasks in concert with the government provincial representative. The result was an impressive continuation of the educational system despite interruptions due to the conflict. Before the cease-fire in 2002, 1,994 primary and secondary schools with an enrollment of 648,000 operated in the province.116

International aid and nongovernmental organizations (NGOs), which flowed into LTTE territory after the 2002 cease-fire and the 2004 tsunami, altered LTTE's governance system. The LTTE's civil administration expanded its efforts to facilitate aid money, setting standards for work and where and how to establish projects. Moreover, the tsunami and the influx of aid encouraged greater cooperation between the government and the insurgent administration as they developed joint mechanisms to distribute aid and reconstruction efforts. The government and international NGOs viewed the events as an opportunity to coax the LTTE into the mainstream. The goodwill between the combatants dwindled as the government stalled over a final settlement and the intransigence of the LTTE leadership, which would not accept anything short of full independence.117 The government soundly defeated the LTTE in 2009 through military measures.

Poor Governance by the Congolese Rally for Democracy

A lack of shadow governance activities can reflect a strategic decision to forgo governance of local populations or a failed attempt at governance.118 The Lord's Resistance Army, or LRA, in Uganda, for instance, opted not to control territory in favor of greater mobility and, as a result, makes no effort to govern local populations.

In contrast, the Congolese Rally for Democracy (RCD), operating in Congo, is a case of failed governance efforts.119

The group faced numerous internal and external challenges that prevented the execution of its governance strategy. Internally, the leadership was divided between those supporting governance strategies to gain popular support while another division wished to devote scarce resources to strengthening its military capacity. Additionally, well before the war began, the Congo state retreated from territory that came under RCD control,120 abandoning administration to a diverse set of non-state actors—NGOs, the Catholic Church, and civil society groups. The RCD proved unable to persuade these disparate groups to follow along with its governance project. Civil society leaders "[portrayed] the RCD as a tool of Tutsi domination," and Church authorities also evidenced resistance to RCD rule, expressing similar ethnic sympathies.121

Although the RCD attempted to integrate itself into the systems providing justice, health, and education to residents, it failed to do so. Non-state actors such as the Catholic-based Caritas and other humanitarian organizations offered more comprehensive and effectual dispute-resolution services to residents. Many residents viewed the security and justice structures operated by the RCD as tools for revenue extraction because justice typically went to those who could pay the higher bribe. Likewise, churches and international aid organizations provided most of the available health services in the Kivus. Although it took control of the health ministry, the RCD outsourced health services to the disparate groups already providing it to residents upon capture of the Kivus. The RCD's role was limited to monitoring and oversight of NGOs operating in the region and directing the type of health campaigns on which NGOs embarked and the areas in which they operated, typically limiting NGOs to areas known to be sympathetic to the RCD while precluding their operation in areas known to house the RCD's armed competitors.122

Lastly, the RCD failed to cultivate legitimacy among the civilian population and develop a strong local base. This failure can be attributed in part to the group's inability to present itself as a unifying, multi-ethnic revolution and its methods of revenue generation. The RCD's dependence on its external patron, Rwanda, and resulting close ties with Tutsi elements led to the perception that the RCD was a monoethnic organization and the puppet of its Rwandan patrons. The perception of this excessive Rwandan influence spurred opposition, including armed opposition, to the RCD's attempts to fully govern the Kivus. Similarly, the RCD's reliance on external patronage and extraction of natural resources precluded any pressing need for the group to cultivate popular support. With easy access to

weaponry through Rwanda and Uganda, the RCD's strategy was a quick military victory and regional control through coercive means.123

As Sarca grows to include more people and more territory, so too will its shadow government. It could use that shadow government to win over the population by providing good governance, including social services. These efforts, however, require raising revenue and fostering sufficient legitimacy so that people provide money voluntarily instead of by threat or extortion. One can see how Bolanieves might find himself in a cycle seeking legitimacy to gain revenue to provide services to gain legitimacy. How might the ODA help Bolanieves through that cycle? It is important for Bolanieves and Sarca to determine how they should assert legitimacy if there is a competing resistance movement.

Other Resistance Groups[124]

Recall that Sarca is not the only resistance group in Estatu. Ajust has been growing and developing at the same time. However, its aims are different, so it may or may not be an ally on different issues and at different times. Resistance groups can compete or cooperate, and they can do so on a case-by-case basis or as a principle applied to the group's decisions and actions. Bolanieves will have to figure out how best to interface with Ajust and its membership, as well as its recruiting pool. The ODA might consider how to assist Bolanieves in this task. The ODA might also consider assessing Ajust in the same way it assessed Sarca for its compatibility with US interests.

Intrastate conflict since the end of the Cold War has commonly involved more than one rebel group. For example, in 2002 and 2003, 30 percent of conflicts involved more than one challenger to the state,[125] and in 2009, 20 percent of conflicts involved more than one challenger.[126] Frequently, these multiple challengers to the state seek to "dominate, ally with, or destroy weaker rivals" in order to "establish national control by one's own forces."[127] Every group wants to win, whether by working together or eliminating the competition. The LTTE engaged in a bitter rivalry with other Tamil insurgent groups in the mid-1980s,[128] and the Provisional IRA's domination in the Northern Ireland conflict required the armed defeat of its rival rebel group, the Official IRA, in the early 1970s.[129]

The following presents two case studies in governance. The LTTE was widely recognized for its success in meeting the needs of the local population while boosting the influence and standing of the insurgent group among civilians. The Congolese Rally for Democracy, however, failed to exercise good governance.

The ODA will need to consider how similar and different Bolanieves, Sarca, and Estatu are to the actors in these cases. Bolanieves faces questions about population needs, perceptions that Estatu is not providing those needs, and Sarca filling those gaps. He also faces questions about the resources at his disposal to accomplish governance. What kinds of people does he need to help him lead? Are there persons available who already know how to provide social services, raise funds, and implement security?

Gaining Popular Support[130]

This narrative considered the definition and functions of a shadow government, but in line with effectiveness, a shadow government needs the support and trust of the population.

Otherwise, it finds itself in the same position as the government it challenges. If Bolanieves and Sarca establish an effective shadow government, they still face the related challenge of gaining and maintaining popular support. This means Bolanieves will have to invest in continuously building that effectiveness, assessing and mitigating risks to the population from the government and from Sarca's own elements and rogue groups, and not asking too much of the local populations. In short, it is a relationship that requires continuous work to maintain a healthy symbiosis from which both sides benefit.

Choosing Between Military Operations and Governance[131]

Groups have limited resources and often choose between military operations or governance activities. That calculus includes the impact on the population that the resistance is trying to gain support. When the government increases military pressure on the resistance, the movement can face difficult choices between protecting and serving civilians and the survival of the resistance.[132] When its survival was uncertain because of increased military pressure, the NRA abandoned its territory and halted all shadow governance activities until its position improved.

Bolanieves will have to weigh these issues, allocate resources, and mitigate risks as best he can. His goal should be gaining popular support and lowering the risk of losing that support, as it can be critical to the success of a resistance. After all, the fight for territory in resistance is second to the contest for the population. Could Bolanieves leverage the distributed network of NGO offices across the country to facilitate a shadow government? Where will he seek additional resources as governance activities increase? Should he limit the promises by the shadow government, so as not to risk losing popular support by over promising and under delivering? How does he distribute resources?

Setting and Meeting Local Expectations[133]

Providing governance can set expectations by the population that the resistance group will have to continuously meet or risk losing popular support.[134] The IRA's political wing, Sinn Féin, put a crude justice system into place in the urban enclaves under its control where regular police forces were unable to operate. At one point, because of the resources required to maintain the rudimentary justice system, the IRA chose to stop. Shortly afterward, public pressure led the Provisionals to reverse that decision.[135]

However, providing poor governance can also harm a resistance. Even after the Provisionals' reinstated its crude justice system, the punishments it ordered were gruesome and led victims and their families and friends to act as informants.[136] Even as the IRA transitioned away from violence to more political efforts in the 1980s, the legacy of that crude justice system and its cruel punishments made it difficult to attract the support of moderate populations.

Conversely, the NRA's operations in Uganda show that cultivating popular support through governance offers operational advantages. Yoweri Musveni, leader of the NRA in Uganda, formed local governments, or resistance councils, in areas under NRA control that included representation of noncombatants.[137] This ensured that locally elected members governed their communities. NRA leaders also set and enforced rules for how the group interacted with the civilian population. Stealing was not allowed, and by giving the role

of food collection to the village committees, the NRA leadership instituted policies that encouraged more voluntary participation and support.[138] In exchange, the NRA provided civilians security by developing early warning systems, alerting villagers to approaching enemy soldiers. The NRA also provided health care services to prevent and treat infectious diseases and other ailments in the liberated zones.[139]

Components of a Resistance[140]

JP 3-05.1
I-7

Sarca must develop the components of a resistance: the armed component, the underground, the public component, and the auxiliary. The armed component is the visible element organized to perform overt armed operations using guerila, asymmetric, or conventional tactics. The underground will be Bolanieves' clandestine arm to operate in denied areas or conduct activities unsuitable for the overt components. The public component of Sarca will be its overt political element. If Sarca is successful, it can become the new government or part of it as a political party, and the public component would fulfill that function. Often the public component works with the underground to make their propaganda and communications work together. Finally, Bolanieves will need to pull on the auxiliary. Persons in Bolanieves' auxiliary operate clandestinely and do not openly indicate their sympathy or involvement with Sarca. The auxiliary is different from the underground because its members participate occasionally while maintaining a full, "normal," inconspicuous life outside of the resistance. The functions they perform can vary, from providing food and shelter, to providing arms and ammunition, to joining the underground on a covert mission.

TC 18-01.1
A-4

ATP 3-05.1
2-16

TC 18-01
2-8

There are four main components to a resistance:

- **Underground**—A clandestine organization established to operate in areas denied to the armed or public components, or to conduct operations not suitable for the armed or public components. Its activities can include intelligence, counterintelligence, subversive media campaigns, logistics, clandestine medical support, financing, and material production (e.g., false identification).

- **Armed component/guerillas**—The visible element of a resistance organized to perform overt armed military and paramilitary operations using guerrilla, asymmetric, or conventional tactics. Guerillas are distinct from mercenaries and criminal gangs. They are not simply paid fighters; they fight for the cause of the resistance, not for profit. They are not freewheeling criminals; they are organized similar to military concepts. It is worth noting that historical and modern cases include elements of resistance movements that fight for other or additional reasons than just the cause of the resistance. The traditional conception of the guerila as an ideologically pure soldier of the resistance is being challenged by deeper understanding of the complexities of resistance movements.

- **Auxiliary**—The support element of the resistance with clandestine organization and operations, and members do not openly indicate their sympathy or involvement with the resistance. Members of the auxiliary are more likely to be occasional participants of the insurgency with other full-time occupations. The activities of the auxiliary can overlap with the underground. The difference between the two is that the auxiliary can be thought of as part-time members of the underground, while the underground is a full-time effort. Some of its activities include supporting logistics, providing early warning to other elements of the resistance, acting as communications couriers, and managing safe houses.

- **Public component**—The overt political component of a resistance. Some resistance movements pursue military and political strategies. The public component negotiates with the state government (or occupying power), depending on whether and how much the state permits the existence of a public component. If the state is extremely authoritarian, it may be impossible to have a public component.

Figure 2[141] illustrates the division of activities between these components.

At the termination of conflict, or occasionally during the conflict, the movement can transition to the sole legitimate government or form part of an existing government. Thus, the four components engage in an evolving relationship that changes in response to internal and external drivers. The public component's overtness distinguishes it from the clandestine underground. However, the public component and the underground can frequently overlap in some of their functions. Figure 3 provides an illustration of their relationship.[142]

That the "public component" represents the overt political element of a resistance, such as a political party or an NGO, means a resistance can and frequently does simultaneously engage in nonviolent and violent opposition. *Sarca and Bolanieves began as an NGO. They can continue to use that platform as its public component to deliver its political message and participate in the open debate. Specifically with the public component, Bolanieves and Sarca will want to keep an eye on the end goal because it is this component that transitions into governance. Armed components and guerilla forces may be incorporated into the armed forces or be disbanded, and the auxiliary can return to its normal life. However, as the overt political arm of Sarca, the public component will become the government if this resistance is successful.*

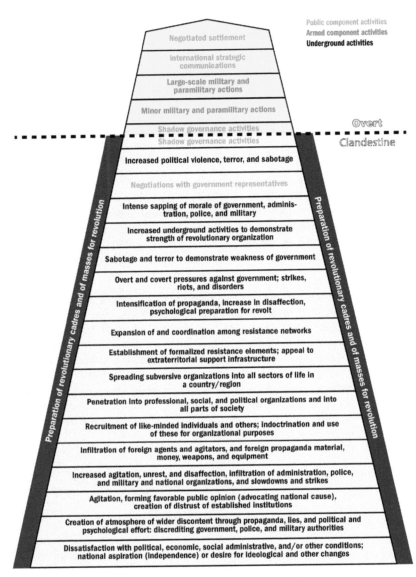

Figure 2. Covert and overt functions of an underground.

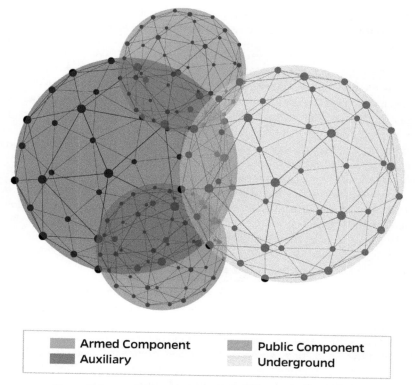

| Armed Component | Public Component |
| Auxiliary | Underground |

Figure 3. Components, phases, and functions of an insurgency.

Relationships between Components[143]

A study about the connection between terrorist groups and political parties shows that a very common relationship was for the political party to create the terrorist group, or some form of violent element. Sometimes this happens because factions break away from the political party or, other times, because the party supported an external violent element. The opposite, where a violent group creates a political component, like the IRA creating the Sinn Fein, is less common. However, the study also showed that political parties that turn to violence become unstable, while violent groups that turn to politics exhibited more stability, provided the transition to politics was successful.[144]

One reason violent groups establish political elements is to communicate with outside parties because their operations are clandestine. The clandestine group needs an avenue to communicate its objectives and messages to a variety of audiences.[145]

Take Hizbollah as an example. In Lebanon, Hizbollah is able to use public to include legislative representatives in government to announce its views.[146] In Israel, though, Hizbollah must operate clandestinely. Political wings, or public components, are

JP 3-05.1
II-6, II-10, IV-2, B-4

ATP 3-05.1
2-24, 5-11

critical for negotiating with the government because it provides the government with a negotiating partner not directly connected to the armed component.

> Unlike many armed opposition groups, Hizbollah laid the infrastructure for political activities, including establishing schools, mosques, hospitals, and voluntary welfare associations. From early in its career, "the aim of Hizbollah and Iran had been to strike roots in the Shiite society in Lebanon."[147] Hizbollah did not, however, contest a parliamentary election until 1992, several years after the death of Ayatollah Khomeini in 1989. Khomeini's death allowed Hizbollah leadership a bit of breathing room to follow a more independent path—one that included establishing a political party and participation in the Lebanese political process, a move now supported by Iran despite Hizbollah's abandonment of revolutionary goals. Hizbollah viewed participation as an opportunity to block any normalization of relations with Israel after the Gulf War, and it also provided the organization with an avenue of survival should it ever be induced to disarm. Additionally, the benefits of political participation, including "access to political resources such as governmental posts, contracts, authorizations, permits, and public exposure" proved attractive as well. The election of Hassan Nasrallah to the post of Secretary General of the organization solidified its dual military and political trajectory.[148]

A resistance can also abandon violent approaches and pursue only political methods. Factors that impact on that decision include ideological flexibility, strong centralized leadership, and internal cohesion among the support base. Some groups experience violence that ruins this transition, such as the Omagh bombing in 1998 by the Real IRA in protest of the IRA's Good Friday Agreement. However, groups that successfully transition often feature strong, committed leadership that moves the resistance toward a peaceful settlement.[149] Like Hizbollah, the IRA and Sinn Féin operated on dual tracks, with Sinn Féin taking a peripheral role. The balance did not switch, and Sinn Fein did not take on a larger role until there was a generational change in the group's leadership.

Gerry Adams took the reins of Sinn Féin in 1983, and by 1986, the Provisionals approved the pursuit of seats in the Republic of Ireland's parliament. After a series of operations that yielded civilians deaths, and dwindling popular support, Sinn Féin and the Provisionals sought a political solution to the conflict. Secret talks between Gerry Adams and the moderate leader of the Social Democratic and Labour Party, John Hume facilitated the solution.[150] In 2005, the IRA formally announced the end of its decades-long armed struggle and the decommissioning of its weapons.[151]

Researchers suggest that violent resistance groups are changing their tactics to include more politics for two main reasons.[152] First, becoming involved in the political process can remediate the original legitimate grievances, such as exclusion from political power. Second, involvement in a political process gives the violent component an incentive to reach a deal for peace. Support for this approach of including insurgencies in political processes to resolve grievances has been encouraged by the international community,[153] and it led to former resistance groups becoming new government parties, such as the African National Congress (ANC) in South Africa, opposition parties, like in Central America, or occupying seats in government according to power sharing agreements, like in Angola.[154]

Challenges of Transition[155]

Resistance groups face numerous challenges in transformation from an illegal, armed opposition group to a bona fide actor in the political process, and researchers stated that transitioning to conventional politics "requires adopting a new political culture, formulating a new programme, installing party organisational structures, recruiting party cadres, and building their capacity to govern."[156] A leader of the ANC in South Africa notes that despite the organization's victory in the 1994 elections after the peace process, it would have benefitted from paying more attention to building a team "ready to govern and build up its capacity to deliver."[157] Leaders within the Communist Party of Nepal–Maoist, or CPN-M, in Nepal anticipated obstacles to the transition:

> After 10 years of the People's War, we had entered into the phase of the peaceful development of the revolution. The form of our struggle had changed. Before, our activities were concentrated in rural areas and our main fighting forces were the PLA [People's Liberation Army]. But now, we had to do more in urban areas, with mass mobilisations and open activities as the primary focus of our work. We therefore had to train the party and PLA cadres in this new approach. For that purpose, Comrade Prachanda and I visited five regions throughout May and June 2006 to give political classes, mainly about how to develop the peaceful revolution.[158]

The CPN-M initiated many organizational changes to adapt the group to peaceful politics. PLA political commissars transferred from the military wing to the new party. Former members of the central committee became district-in-charges responsible for dialoguing with other political parties. The CPN-M also shifted its organizational structures to match those of the state administration and dissolved regional bureaus previously used to facilitate communication between the central committee and cadres in favor of state committees that were better reflections of the ethnic and geographic diversity of Nepal. Chairman Prachanda also dissolved all existing shadow government structures, the People's governments, and the parallel judicial system, the People's courts.[159]

Resistance groups also face dilemmas of transitional justice. This requires a balance between society's need for justice for crimes committed during the conflict and reconciliation of the parties with society. One approach is amnesty, total forgiveness, and legal release of responsibility for actions during the conflict. Another approach that can be separate or complementary is a truth and reconciliation commission, a body formed with the purpose of hearing the facts and striking the balance between justice and reconciliation. In South Africa, the interim constitution included provisions granting amnesty for offenses associated with political objectives during the conflict, as well as establishing a Truth and Reconciliation Commission. Similar mechanisms calling for amnesty established in other post-conflict settlements, such as in Aceh and Colombia.[160]

Fighters and Guerilla Forces

Recruiting into the Sarca resistance can target several population segments, but each must be approached uniquely by appealing to the motivations and passions among them. For some, that may be more transactional and pragmatic, such as resources or better

living conditions. For others, that may be more emotionally based, such as a sense of purpose expressed through an ideology. Potential members will be suited for a particular component. Bolanieves and his leadership circle will need to develop a method for attracting members and then evaluating and screening them for their particular value to Sarca or the underground or auxiliary components.

Recruiting Soldiers[161]

JP 3-05.1
IV-2

The armed component in a resistance needs security forces, local militias, guerilla armies, and/or conventional military forces. Recruiting these fighters becomes an important function of resistance. Sarca began as an NGO, so its original members may not be natural fits for the armed component of guerilla forces. Bolanieves will have to adapt recruitment strategies from those used for other components. Where will he look in Estatu's population,

ATP 3-05.1
2-21, 2-27,
E-9

and how can he convince people to risk so much for the cause?

In the case of the Viet Cong, it was relatively easy to find potential recruits who were hostile to Japanese, French, and later, American invaders. In the wake of World War II, Vietnamese nationalists cultivated a strong sense of resistance toward foreign powers seeking to occupy

TC 18-01
2-19

and exploit their homeland. Local militia and guerilla leaders based in villages were the main source of recruiting for the Viet Cong. Later, after 1964, as the Viet Cong began to adjust its aims toward the defeat of American forces, they provided manpower for more conventional forces to fight wherever needed. Recruitment therefore became more difficult, and communist leaders resorted to forced conscription and methods of deception and coercion to keep drafted soldiers in their assigned military units.[162]

Terrorists, and particularly suicide operatives, often have a strong sense of victimization, and propaganda methods to recruit them exaggerate the degree of victimization. Members of a resistance who later engage in acts of terror or suicide operations often first engaged in more benign activities. This is a case where fighters are recruited from within the organization, as opposed to outside it. That initial participation could have been casual or devoted, including protest marches, financial support, participation in the militia, or housing other operatives before being approached and recruited for more violent activity.

Psychologists studying the phenomenon of terrorist recruitment describe a recruit being pulled in opposite directions. The incentives not to engage in terrorism include family ties (in cases in which the family is not friendly to the insurgency), jobs, and associations with nonviolent organizations. The incentives pulling toward violent involvement include monetary incentives (for the member and/or his family), the perceived impending success of the insurgency, and even intangibles such as the respect of elder leaders and group acceptance.[163]

The LTTE portrayed suicide operations in a semi-religious light and cultivated a wide acceptance of such acts as necessary for the hastening of the day when they would achieve autonomy.164 Other organizations, such as the New People's Army (NPA) in the Philippines, leveraged peer pressure in youth organizations as a means of gaining new recruits, while young foot soldiers in Sierra Leone and Nigeria were often drawn to (or kept in) the Revolutionary United Front (RUF) and the Movement for the Emancipation of the

Niger Delta (MEND), respectively, because of the availability of drugs and money (blood diamonds, bunkered oil, etc.).165

Resistance movements also recruit for the armed component from existing military personnel, whether conventional forces or illegal/quasi-legal militias. Al Qaeda on the Arabian Peninsula, for example, recruited heavily from the ranks of those Saudis who fought in Afghanistan in the late 1990s. These men offered several advantages: they were trained in combat techniques, they had proven themselves as religiously committed, and they shared a common and strong bond of camaraderie with their fellow veterans. These attributes make for strong and reliable insurgents.[166] A second example is the "sobel" (soldier-rebel) phenomenon in Sierra Leone in which soldiers would join their rebel friends at night to share drugs and alcohol, periodically conduct joint raids on villages to steal property, and jointly run illegal diamond-mining operations.[167]

Professional forces, whether veterans, paid contractors, or defected national soldiers, can be force multipliers for poorly trained and equipped armed components in resistances by filling key roles like training and logistics, as well as serving in combat. Introducing air assets or advanced sniper teams are two examples from the Balkans and West Africa. There is potential risk in that their commitment is defined by the contract they entered.

Conversely, governments also resorted to the use of professional soldiers when their armed forces are poorly trained, undisciplined, or under-resourced, but they have sufficient wealth to hire professional soldiers. This led to curious scenarios, such as FARC insurgents serving as hired snipers to defend Colonel Muammar Gaddafi in November 2011 during the Libyan uprising and mercenaries who served together in Angola finding themselves supporting two different contracts and opposing each other a year later in Sierra Leone.[168]

The Underground[169]

The underground is the clandestine organization established to operate in areas denied to the armed or public components or conduct operations not suitable for the armed or public components. Bolanieves can consider this component as Sarca's special operations forces. They can operate covertly and clandestinely to coerce, subvert, and sabotage the government, and they can conduct operations that help sway the population in areas denied to Sarca. The ARIS program of work also produced a volume on undergrounds that can be consulted regarding this situation.[170] *The Captain of the ODA supporting Bolanieves and Sarca should consult these and other doctrine available to him.*

TC 18-01.1
A-3, A-4

ATP 3-05.1
2-16, 3-1

Recall back to Figure 2 that showed the range of organizational functions performed by an underground. The configuration of the components of a resistance depends on the group's operational requirements, which can depend on that state it occupies in its evolution. Take the Orange Revolution in Ukraine as an example. Experienced and highly effective organizers during the Orange Revolution in the Ukraine mobilized hundreds of thousands of people (often despite frigid temperatures) against the sitting government while simultaneously avoiding the use or provocation of violence. On November 22, 2004, the day after a fraudulent vote, approximately five hundred thousand people (many dressed in orange) gathered in Independence Square in Kiev and marched to the headquarters of the Ukrainian parliament while carrying orange symbols (e.g., orange flags). This scene was broadcast globally, sending an unambiguous message to the members of parliament who would vote a few days later to void the election results.[171]

Figure 4[172] depicts a time series component model of the Orange Revolution, which represents how the auxiliary subsumed the armed component and served essentially as a security element to protect prominent members of the political component from government attacks. The Yushchenko camp anticipated and prepared for violence. For instance, Yevhen Chervonenko led Viktor Yushchenko's personal security detail, which included fifty-five former military special operations and Interior Ministry security experts. Chervonenko claims that they had an "elaborate system of reconnaissance, intelligence, and physical protection."[173] However, the deciding factor was nonviolent political expression in large numbers with an international audience. The Orange Revolution, the resistance, did not engage in violence, and its armed component became less and less needed as the success of the public component increased. While the underground was initially prominent, the relatively rapid expansion of the Orange Revolution was almost entirely in the public component.[174]

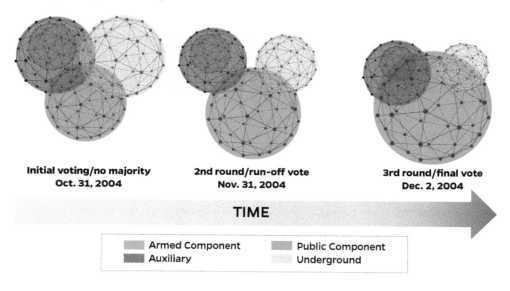

| Initial voting/no majority | 2nd round/run-off vote | 3rd round/final vote |
| Oct. 31, 2004 | Nov. 31, 2004 | Dec. 2, 2004 |

TIME

| Armed Component | Public Component |
| Auxiliary | Underground |

Figure 4. Time series component model for the Orange Revolution.

Target Populations for Recruitment[175]

The myth that only disaffected or unemployed people join insurgencies has been proven wrong. Resistance movements of all types recruit from all groups in society. The ideologies, propaganda tools, and recruiting methods may change from audience to audience, depending on their motivations and ways to consume information. Those motivations vary:

sense of duty, religious obligation, nationalism, hatred, despair, desire for vengeance, desire for personal gain, and more.

Some scholars think that resistance movements that develop past their early states occur in populations with a culture of radicalization. By this, they mean the culture in that society created a value system where participating in a resistance movement, including violent ones, is not discouraged, derided, or judged wrong. Instead, it is tolerated as normal or even celebrated. An example is Saudi Arabia, where the society tolerates Muslim men fighting in religiously motivated conflicts abroad, even if their behavior is illegal.[176]

A culture of radicalization can also develop out of harsh treatment by the government of suspected radical group members. Perceptions of victimization and injustice or other grievances can result from police crackdowns, poor conditions in prisons, and arbitrarily violating someone's person, property, and privacy. Examples of where this occurred include:

- The killing of Boko Haram founder Mohammed Yusuf in police custody in Northern Nigeria in 2009;

- The Serbian killing of popular Kosovo Liberation Army (KLA) leader Adem Jashrai and his family in Kosovo in 1998;

- El Salvadoran "death squads" targeting FMLN sympathizers in the 1980s; and

- The British Army's use of live ammunition against Irish protesters in Derry in 1972 ("Bloody Sunday").

Societal factors can also contribute to radicalization for recruitment, most notably unemployment and underemployment. However, while it is a strong contributing factor, it is not automatic that unemployed people join violent groups; wealthy and employed people join as well. Examples, though, of the unemployed joining a resistance includes the "lumpen" youth who joined the RUF in Sierra Leone and recently laid-off coffee plantation workers in Rwanda who were deliberately drawn into soccer clubs and indoctrinated with the concept of "Hutu Power."

Rural Populations[177]

It is important to note that recruiting in rural areas can be fruitful because the threat to the resistance is greater in the denser terrain than in rural areas. Governments tend to have more presence in urban areas, leaving a resistance more free to approach the rural population directly. Resistance movements are often direct and immediate when recruiting rural populations because they tend to be less educated, depending on the country. They emphasize opportunities for improvements in economic and security situations to these populations. Examples of this recruitment method can be found in the FARC, the FMLN, and MEND in Nigeria.[178] The FARC was successful recruiting youth in rural settings with Marxist propaganda about three square meals a day.[179]

RESISTANCE IN FOCUS: Viet Cong Rural Recruiting

The Viet Cong based much of its recruiting efforts in the rural communities of South Vietnam, in part because the government had little influence there. However, village recruiting, particularly in the Central Highlands of Vietnam, was not simply the result of opportunity; it was part of the overall objective of limiting and disrupting the reach of the government in Saigon. The creation and sustainment of a rural power base not only sustained the insurgency with a reliable source of manpower, but it also demonstrated the weakness of the American-backed regime.[180]

Urban Populations[181]

Rural settings may attract recruitment efforts, but resistance movements inevitably must move to urban areas where the majority of today's populations live. Recruiting in urban areas has a security tradeoff. It places members of the resistance closer to government personnel, but it also provides them opportunity to hide amongst the larger, denser population. Being more easily concealed is an attractive condition for recruitment because recruiters can recruit with less concern for their own security, and the potential members are able to support the resistance with less fear of exposure (if so desired).

RESISTANCE IN FOCUS: FARC Urban Recruitment

In the 1970s, the FARC had limited reach and impact on society because it remained largely a rural movement.[182] As the country continued to urbanize, however, leaders decided that they would expand operations into the cities. The opportunity came as poor urban workers began to protest against their living conditions and economic stagnation. The FARC secretariat quickly attached themselves to this grievance and represented the movement as that of the proletarian struggle against the imperialism and corruption of the government. It established student groups and civic action programs within universities and schools, and it used these platforms to persuade people to vote for left-wing politicians and agitate for reforms that would benefit the insurgency. The FARC also drew upon the growing urban population for recruitment into local militias and mobile guerilla armies. Leaders learned to adapt their recruiting methods to various target audiences. Whereas rural recruits were typically drawn into the insurgency with promises of basic necessities, urban youth responded more to strong ideological propaganda.[183]

Elites[184]

Socioeconomic and political elites join resistance groups for different reasons than lower class society members. Generally, elites join for ideological motivations and personal grievances. In contrast, lower class citizens join more commonly for incentives related to necessities: food, shelter, protection, or money. Another motivation for elites is if the government threatens or harms their interests or excludes them from the benefits of their elite status.[185] Otherwise, elites are often incentivized to support the government because it has been a source or contributor to their elite status. Recruiting elites can pose a security risk as their elite status may create a public profile that could draw attention to the resistance once recruited.

Women[186]

Resistance movements choose to recruit women for multiple reasons. The first is to replenish numbers lost during operations. Second, women can be effective operatives in areas where norms discourage close contact with women who are not family members. Finally, they can serve propaganda purposes by signaling modernism and friendliness to women's rights. The conflicting incentives for women who are recruited include the obvious dangers of joining and fighting in a resistance, such as getting arrested or killed. However, participation in a resistance movement can also provide an opportunity to undo patriarchal norms in the society.

The LTTE targeted women for recruitment as a means for siphoning strength from other Tamil resistance movements.[187] The ruthlessness of Eritrean female fighters during the insurgency against Ethiopia became legendary.[188] The FARC brought women into the movement and encouraged romantic relationships to strengthen recruitment and sustainment.[189]

Youth[190]

Recruiting children is politically volatile, but some resistance movements do so to replace lost members or gain new members that can evade detection. Those members are used for intelligence and courier tasks in urban settings, as well. Sometimes youth are recruited with the expectation of developing them in the resistance to eventually join the regular ranks. This is in contrast to those groups that develop entire units of youth.[191] Children from all walks of life can be recruited. One method is to use precursor groups or activities, such as student groups, athletic clubs, religious organizations, or refugee camps. These places provide opportunities to draw children into the group slowly as well as assess them for their utility. In these instances, the leaders of these groups perform some of the recruiting, but youth have been self-radicalizing through the various media with which they engage.[192] Other methods for recruiting children include persuading them with promises of food, shelter, security, and acceptance, or they can be kidnapped.

When a country has a so-called youth bulge, when the country's population has a high share of young people, the risk of resistance, whether riots, protests, or terrorism, can rise.[193] This dynamic usually arises from the tendency for young populations to possess beliefs, ideas, and demands that clash with or challenge the status quo established by the older generations.[194] Studies propose that youth bulges contributed to some historical resistance examples, including the European Revolutions of 1848, the rise of Nazism in Germany in the 1930s, and the American anti-war and civil rights protests (led by "baby boomers") in the 1960s. The researcher Henrik Urdal[195] examined a large historical dataset[196] and found a relationship between nations with a comparatively large percentage of young people (fifteen to twenty-four years old) and levels of smaller scale political violence. Using a separate dataset,[197] Urdal also found a relationship with levels of terrorism and rioting. This effect seemed to hold across different types of governance but seemed to be a greater risk factor in autocratic regimes.

Prisoners[198]

Recruiting in prisons takes advantage of a captive audience to increase the insurgency's ranks. The Korean War provides an example when the communists took over the prisoner-of-war camp Koje-do. In that case, the insurgents used persuasion, coercion, and violence to take control of large sectors of the prison population and eventually set up courts. They executed those convicted of crimes against the communists, warred against

anti-communist factions, and triggered armed intervention by the US Army. The incident served as propaganda against the West and remains a stunning example of how prisons can become breeding grounds for rebellion and violence.[199]

Today, prisoners are vulnerable to faith-based or ideology-based recruitment where inmates already recruited and indoctrinated convert other inmates to their brand of radicalization. These recruits can serve to recruit more prisoners, or upon release, they can operate for the insurgency. The dynamics in prisons sometimes yield the merging of religious influences and gang dynamics, resulting in conversions aimed at filling the ranks of various gangs or co-opting gang organizations into radical religious movements. Individual prisoners often turn to radical religions partly because of genuine spiritual convictions and partly for protection.[200]

Native Populations

Native populations can be recruited for the same reasons as any other group (money, food, promise of purpose, etc.), but their unique dynamic is that their indigenous identity can be politicized around a demand for rights and political influence.[201]

Bolanieves will have to decide the kinds of people and skills Sarca needs to succeed. The first task is finding those people, but then Bolanieves and his cadre will need to convince them to join Sarca. Some recruits will come for pragmatic purposes, while others for psychological ones. Sarca's recruiting efforts will need to be tailored to each population and even each individual. The factors previously addressed can help guide that tailoring, but the best judgment of the Sarca recruiter is the final decision maker.

External Support[202]

TC 18-01.1
3-16

In addition to managing the variety of actors within Sarca, Bolanieves will have to manage relationships with external actors. Sarca could receive assistance from the Estatian diaspora, whether individuals or businesses abroad. Alternatively, Bolanieves will be viewing the ARSOF soldier as an external state actor seeking to assist him and his resistance movement. He will consider his objectives, risks, and which US interactions are best for him and the resistance movement.

ATP 3-05.1
2-5, E-12

States sometimes choose to support a resistance inside another state. It might be because the external state benefits from weakening its rival, and the resistance can accomplish that. It could also result from a population of the external state that wants to support the resistance because of a connection such as ethnic identity.[203] Additionally, the state may

TC 18-01
2-6

be positioning itself to demand reciprocal assistance in some form. Alternatively, the resistance may seek state assistance because the resource and logistic demands, as well as its aim to remain self-sufficient to avoid debt. The NPA in the Philippines during the Ferdinand Marcos presidency was designed from the start to be self-sufficient. As the insurgency became more complex, however, the logistics requirements became greater. During 1971, the Communist Party of the Philippines established a permanent delegation in Beijing to coordinate support from the Chinese government.[204]

The types of provided support can be displayed in a two-by-two matrix using cells derived from US Army doctrine (see Figure 5).[205]

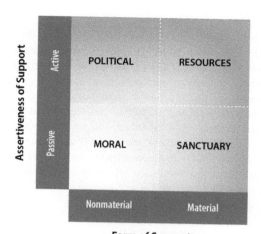

Form of Support

Figure 5. Types of external support.

The two categories represent forms of support (material or nonmaterial) and the assertiveness of the support (passive or active). Moral support is a nonmaterial form of passive support, such as sympathetic public statements or similar measures. Political support is active and nonmaterial, including diplomacy in the form of advocacy and symbolic actions to express support. Sanctuary is a material form of passive support by providing training sites, operational bases, protection from extradition, or other shields from adversary actions. Finally, the provision of resources (funds, weapons, food, advisers, training, foreign fighters, etc.) is active material assistance, the most involved type of resistance support offered by an external actor.

Foreign governments may decide to provide its support clandestinely to avoid attribution and provide plausible deniability. The Iranian Revolutionary Guard Corps (IRGC) operating in Iraq after the 2003 American invasion used this method to provide Shiite militias with materials to produce improvised explosive devices. Other potential external supporters include NGOs, diaspora, transnational crime groups, and individuals. Individuals can choose to provide support from outside the country, such as by raising money in the diaspora or from foreign communities. Political opposition to President Maduro of Venezuela receives funds from the Venezuelan diaspora in the United States. Other individuals can choose to join the conflict because of sympathy, conviction, or shared grievance against the government. This has been most notable with the foreign fighter phenomenon in ISIS.[206]

Businesses can also support a resistance by serving as a conduit for resources. For instance, a company could import contraband items under non-contraband labels. The companies involved would be paid for the goods and services to keep records clean. In 2010, a similar scenario emerged when thirteen shipping containers labeled "building supplies" were seized in the Nigerian port of Lagos and found packed with rocket launchers, mortars, explosives, and ammunition. Authorities remained unsure of whether the weapons—originally shipped from Iran—were destined for internal insurgent groups, such as the MEND or Boko Haram, or whether the weapons were en route to Gaza via West Africa.[207]

Bolanieves and Sarca

Resistance leaders must gain and maintain legitimacy, manage the components, recruit members, and negotiate external support. Bolanieves has to manage a wide variety of actors as a resistance leader. Likewise, the resistance will demonstrate a diversity of members and participants, and some form of culture, norms, or rules will be needed to govern them harmoniously. As Sarca grows, it should be thoughtful and careful about how it incorporates and governs populations that come under its control. The population can be a great asset or a great danger for Sarca. Sarca meanwhile will be challenged to maintain its legitimacy as the public component of the resistance. Finally, Bolanieves should not neglect the opportunities to leverage external support to the Sarca resistance. They represent valued actors for a resistance movement, and their support can range from money to messaging, arms, or diplomacy.

Questions

Arturo Bolanieves is the resistance leader that the ODA was tasked to support. In this section on actors, the reader learned about resistance leadership, shadow governments, inter-group competition, popular support, resistance components, fighting forces, underground elements, recruitment, and external support actors. To best prepare to support the Sarca resistance, the reader should further explore how this knowledge should apply to Bolanieves and the Sarca movement. A series of discussion questions follow that examine the content in the context of the Sarca narrative. The questions are scaled to the required level of reader knowledge: introductory, intermediate, or mastery. Those seeking an intermediate level of knowledge should demonstrate competency in both introductory- and intermediate-level questions. Those seeking a mastery level of knowledge should demonstrate competency in all three levels of questions. Finally, these questions may be used for individual analysis, group discussion, and/or instructor assignments.

INTRODUCTORY - BLOOMS LEVEL ONE

- Identify: What does Bolanieves have to think about when determining whether to pursue a shadow government or government in exile?

INTRODUCTORY - BLOOMS LEVEL TWO

- Identify and Categorize: What are the components of the Sarca resistance? How are they different from one another?

INTERMEDIATE - BLOOMS LEVEL FOUR

- Attribute and Differentiate: How can Bolanieves use those components?

 MASTERY - BLOOMS LEVEL FIVE

- Detect and Evaluate: What kinds of considerations should Bolanieves account for when exercising leadership?

- Detect and Evaluate: What kinds of recruiting methods and tools should the Sarca resistance consider?

CAUSES[208]

JP 3-05.1
B-1

ATP 3-05.1
1-7, 2-1, 2-4,
E-2

TC 18-01
2-1, 2-4

After establishing his leadership position and identifying segments of the population that could join Sarca, Bolanieves faces the challenge of understanding the many and varied motivations behind a resistance as it emerges and continuously evolves. No single factor or problem fully explains resistance by itself. Multiple different issues across many aspects of society can affect Sarca and its motivations; economic, political, ideological, religious, ethnic, and social issues may all play a role in Sarca's resistance. History, sociology, and politics could all help Bolanieves explain Sarca's motivating factors and root causes.

Bolanieves could first consider the problem of relative deprivation. In this case, the people of Estatu may feel entitled to reach for and achieve a certain quality of life, but the actual opportunities to succeed in reaching that life in Estatu are very limited and fall short. This failure could lead to conflict as people violently protest against the limitations and join Sarca's movement. For example, a sudden loss of job opportunities in Estatu or high inequality across different social groups in Estatu would both be cases of relative deprivation. To motivate Sarca's resistance, Bolanieves could bring together the people of Estatu who feel deprived of the ability to achieve economic success, political freedom, or other benefits and rights.[209] However, some researchers challenge this economic deprivation theory. One study found that supporters and members of terrorist groups are actually often better educated and more economically advantaged, not poor or lacking opportunity.[210] Additionally, historically economic inequality has not been significantly connected with causing violent conflict.[211] Knowing this, Bolanieves would also want to identify and assess other potential causes that motivate Sarca.

In Estatu's political arena, emerging opportunities for participation, such as breakdowns of traditionally powerful groups in the country and new paths to power, could motivate Sarca's actions. In this case, Bolanieves could leverage the new political opportunities to demand change and publicize Sarca's grievances and complaints.[212] Conversely, if Estatu's government used harsh oppression and violence against its people, more people might join Sarca if they started to believe there was no other choice but to fight back.[213]

Ethnic and religious identities in and around Estatu could also contribute to resistance and violence. If the government of Estatu mostly includes people from only certain ethnic groups, other people could feel excluded and disadvantaged, leading to resentment of the powerful group's status. Similarly, if Sarca primarily recruits members from a particular ethnic group, fear of a threat from or hatred of another group could further contribute to the problem in some cases.[214]

If religion plays an important role in Estatu, a nonreligious city government or the rising presence of a different religion in the city could lead resistance fighters to believe they are rightfully defending their religion from a threat. If Sarca had religious motivations or influences, the group could take on greater symbolic meaning.[215] However, Bolanieves should be aware that multiple studies suggest that ethnic and religious divisions are not usually primary causes of resistance by themselves.[216]

Bolanieves should consider another potential motivation to change the structure of Estatu's society. Warfare between social and economic classes, especially in the context of Marxist ideology or anti-colonial resistance, often falls under this social revolution motivation. In this scenario, Sarca might seek to change both the social and government structures of Estatu.[217] This is especially so if the state government lacks legitimacy.

Lack of Government Legitimacy[218]

Legitimacy of the government is an important factor in its ability to govern, especially in the face of challenges. A government only has legitimacy when it is seen to have both the right to rule and the ability to carry out expected functions of government. These are the most important factors affecting legitimacy:

- **Security**. People who experience threats to their physical safety often lose faith in their government. This is particularly true when threats are internal, from crime, insurgency, or terrorism, rather than external threats, which evoke a unifying reaction. (Not surprisingly, governments tend to blame internal security problems on "outside agitators" or external manipulation whenever they can). Terrorism attempts to undermine a government's legitimacy by undermining people's sense of security.

- **Justice**. Governments are expected to settle disputes fairly and quickly. Widespread corruption in the judicial system undermines legitimacy. Many countries with widespread corruption rely on alternate judicial systems, such as the Shura system in Afghanistan and adoption of Shari'a law in a number of states in northern Nigeria; these workarounds undermine the legitimacy of federal governments.

- **Economic needs**. Governments are expected to make sure people of the nation are fed and to meet their other basic needs, which could include fuel, roads and utilities, health care, education, and employment. Expectations for the services a government should provide vary widely between cultures and nations and are tied closely to prior conditions and conditions of immediate neighboring countries. Widespread corruption, by which employment, health care, and other services can only be obtained through bribes or connections, can undermine legitimacy (although judicious use of patronage can in some circumstances increase it).

- **Ideological legitimacy**. Cultures also have idiosyncratic expectations for what constitutes a legitimate government. Religious leaders may undermine a government by withholding sanction or declaring the government illegitimate. The Catholic Church in the past held such power over many European states (Henry VIII founded the Church of England because he could not obtain legitimization by the Roman Catholic Church). Modern-day Islamists often direct their most vehement criticism at secular leaders of Muslim nations who do not meet their standards for Islamic rulers. Nonreligious ideologies also matter; governments may forfeit legitimacy for violating strongly held ideals of freedom and democracy or other values that a population feels to be ideologically nonnegotiable.

Legitimacy is ultimately a subjective judgment in the eyes of the people. Regimes that provide poorly for their people may still enjoy popularity or acceptance among those people. However, exposure to information from outside may sometimes raise

questions about the government's legitimacy and lead to changes in how people see their government. Information and communication with the outside world are therefore important factors in determining legitimacy, and underperforming governments have good reason to try to control perceptions among a population. Attacking the government's legitimacy is regularly a central theme of the war of words between insurgents and the government.

Economic Rationale[219]

Economic hardship plays a significant role in resistance as a justification for violence or as a factor in a person's decision to join a resistance group. In broad terms, political violence is more likely to break out in countries with lower levels of economic development and less likely to appear in prosperous countries.

However, insurgencies do not spring up solely because of a population's anger about poverty or other similar deprivations such as lack of education, health care, or employment. Deprivation may lead individual poor people to participate in "bread riots" to demand basic necessities or to commit minor crimes, but it does not directly lead to organized, sustained insurgencies.

A similar theory focuses on relative deprivation, or the idea that the difference between the life people expect to live and the life that people can actually achieve motivates violent resistance. For example, the sudden loss of job opportunities or high economic inequality between the very rich and very poor are both cases of relative deprivation that could lead to political violence.[220] However, other research challenges this theory. One study found that supporters and members of terrorist groups are often better educated and more economically advantaged, not poor or lacking opportunity.[221]

As shown by these different theories and ideas, the economic factors in resistance are diverse and complicated. Poverty may lead young people to feel that they have fewer options in life and less to lose, which makes joining an insurgency a more attractive option. Additionally, poverty may increase lawlessness and violence, which undermines the government's legitimacy and authority because it cannot maintain order.

Political Rationale[222]

A country's system of governance is an important risk factor for resistance. However, what kinds of governments are the most at risk for violent insurgencies? It might be natural to assume that the most violent and repressive governments are most likely to have violent resistance, but the answer is actually more complex.

Generally, the most democratic governments are the least vulnerable to violent insurgency because there are many nonviolent opportunities for opposition, including elections, public protests, and free speech. Most potential resistance members realize that they have better and safer options than trying to take on the central government with force.

Highly repressive regimes are also less likely to experience violent resistance. The most repressive regimes prevent resistance groups from forming and resistance messages from disseminating. Additionally, these types of governments usually have powerful secret police that gather intelligence on potential resistance groups and crush them before they can grow in strength. Modern North Korea is an example of a highly repressive but stable regime.

Most countries fall somewhere in between full democracy and the most repressive dictatorships. These governments may allow opposition political parties but rig elections so that the ruling party is not truly challenged. They may restrict political freedom while allowing a lot of economic freedom. Similarly, they may restrict the media but otherwise allow relatively free Internet access.

When looking at these three kinds of states, one theory is that countries at each of the ends—the most democratic and the most repressive—are the most stable. Democracies allow nonviolent disagreements and protests so people are less likely to escalate to violence, while dictatorships completely crush all resistance. However, the middle of the road regimes with a mix of democratic and repressive policies may be the most unstable. These governments allow enough freedom of speech and assembly to allow opposition groups to form but are simultaneously repressive enough to use force against the groups. As a result, existing resistance groups may gain support to escalate violence against the government.

Ideological Rationale[223]

The crucial role of ideology in an insurgent or resistance movement cannot be overstated. An ideology grows out of discontent with the status quo; it is the intangible idea that gives rise to acts of defiance and rebellion. Ideology also plays a dual role in an insurgency in that it serves as the basis for recruitment and illuminates strategic direction.

While an organization rarely survives on ideology alone, "men who are participating in a great social movement always picture their coming action as a battle in which their cause is certain to triumph."[224] Successful movements often rely on a narrative for recruitment, legitimacy, and support that resonates with a deep cultural, ethnic, or historical myth/memory within the population.

Common to most underground movements is an ideology, a set of interrelated beliefs, values, and norms. Ideologies are usually highly abstract and complex and are more than a group of rationalizations and myths that justify the existence of a group; they can manipulate and influence the behavior of the individuals within the group.

These observations seem obvious. What is not so obvious is the decisive role leaders assume as they cultivate, develop, and evolve ideology during the course of a resistance. Their decisions and motivations regarding the specific ideological principles of the movement serve to characterize the movement's ability to appeal to the masses, and they both energize and constrain the progress of the movement's strategy.

Ideology evolves. It is rare for a movement's ideology to remain unchanged throughout the course of the struggle. It moves along a spectrum of exclusivity and inclusivity as leaders stake out the movement's position on politics, religion, social justice, etc. *Exclusive* ideologies aim at energizing a targeted sector of the population, helping the members of that population to define themselves in relation to those they oppose. *Inclusive* ideologies seek to unify various groups and encourage them to coalesce around the insurgency's main goal. Exclusive ideologies facilitate strategic focus because they embrace specific and dramatic goals. The disadvantage of exclusivity, however, is that the ideology does not appeal to a broad sector of the population. Inclusive ideologies embrace large portions of the population, but they suffer from multiple, vague, and often conflicting goals that make strategic focus problematic (see Figure 6[225]).

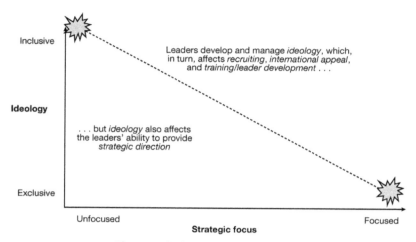

Figure 6. Ideology and strategic focus.

Yasser Arafat's leadership of Fatah and, later, the Palestine Liberation Organization (PLO) illustrates both the strengths and weaknesses of an inclusive approach to ideology.226 The most fundamental goal of the PLO was the destruction of Israel so that displaced Palestinians could return to their homeland. Beyond that single point of congruity, however, there were many competing ideas within the movement. Pan-Arabists viewed the unification of Arabs as the key to achieving the overall goal (the destruction of Israel) and agitated for the PLO to subordinate itself to the Arab leaders of surrounding states— primarily Egypt's Gamal Abdel Nasser. Communists insisted that the entire Palestinian conflict was a manifestation of the universal struggle against capitalism and imperialism. Islamists interpreted the conflict in theological and eschatological terms and pushed for religious revival as the means to victory. Confronted with these and other disparate ideas, Arafat welcomed them all, and an inclusive attitude led to the growth and sustainment of the movement.

The drawback, however, was that Arafat was under constant attack from leaders within his own organization. To them, he was not Arab enough, socialist enough, or Islamic enough. Not only did this inherent disunity foil his attempts to cement his control of the organization, but it also led to various subgroups "hijacking" PLO strategy. As factions sought to dominate both the headlines and the parent organization, leaders would sometimes engage in spectacular acts of terror or other violence. Arafat often found himself racing to keep up with events and trying to rein in recalcitrant colleagues. In this he was never fully successful.

Sendero Luminoso (Shining Path), the Maoist insurgency in Peru, developed an exclusive ideology rooted in the ethnic and class conflict within the country. The movement allied itself with the largely disenfranchised and impoverished indigenous population, and that ideology garnered immediate and widespread support within the local communities of the Peruvian highlands. However, this ideology did not resonate as strongly with other communities in the coastal plain or in the urban communities of Lima and other Peruvian cities. Oddly, Abimael Guzman, the leader of Sendero, chose to not reach out to other constituencies or to potential external sources of support. Instead, his ideology, and that of his followers, remained focused on the centrality of Guzman and the Maoist model he endorsed within Peru for addressing ethnic and class conflict. Consequently, the exclusivity of the Shining Path ideology served as a brake on the movement's progress, just as it initially helped to accelerate the movement's development in the early stages.3

Finally, the complete absence of a strong, unifying ideology (whether inclusive or exclusive) can severely limit the development, growth, and sustainment of an insurgency, especially when this ideological void is filled by personal motivation and ambitions. Insurgencies such as the FARC in Colombia, the RUF in Sierra Leone, and the MEND in Nigeria all started with pseudo-ideological foundations related to government repression and government control of resources but soon deteriorated into struggles between local insurgent leaders and their control over drug crops, diamond fields, and oil bunkering operations (respectively). In this environment, where individual aspirations usurp any strategic ideology, organizational cohesion quickly deteriorates.

The grievances of those in Estatu supporting Sarca and Bolanieves began under economic and political rationales, but as it grows, different members join for ideological reasons regarding ethnicity and language. The recruiting methods may change to reflect this, or the goals of the movement may evolve to make more members feel part of the group. The ODA would benefit from maintaining awareness of why people join and stay in Sarca and why they follow Bolanieves or disagree with him.

Religious/Ethnic[227]

From history, Bolanieves is aware that one of the most powerful causes of resistance is the marginalization or persecution of social identity groups.[228] In Estatu, identity groups based on religion and ethnicity could be especially important for uniting similar groups of people or creating societal divisions. As with many other countries that have peacefully coexisting religions and ethnic groups, diversity in Estatu does not automatically mean that resistance and conflict will break out.[229] However, when diversity combines with some form of economic or political exclusion, as Bolanieves witnessed in Estatu, there can be a strong motivation for resistance. If the government of Estatu broadly discriminates against, excludes, controls, or uses violence against a certain religious or ethnic group, people from that group may be more motivated to join Sarca because they have no other way to protect their rights. For example, the Estatu government's language law heavily impacts and discriminates against certain minority ethnic groups that speak other languages. Those ethnic minority groups would have a powerful reason to side with Bolanieves to regain their rights and recognition.

To understand the typical types and ranges of discrimination, it is interesting to look at the criteria for discrimination used by the ongoing Minorities at Risk (MAR) project.[230]

Criteria for ratings of government repression, political discrimination, and economic discrimination categories are listed in Table 1.[231]

Table 1. Code guidance for three discrimination categories from the MAR dataset.

Rating	Government Repression	Political Discrimination	Economic Discrimination
1	**Surveillance**, e.g., domestic spying, wiretapping, etc.	**Neglect/remedial polices** Substantial underrepresentation in political office and/or participation due to historical neglect or restrictions. Explicit public policies are designed to protect or improve the group's political status.	**Neglect/remedial polices** Significant poverty and underrepresentation in desirable occupations due to historical marginality, neglect, or restrictions. Public policies are designed to improve the group's material well-being.
2	**Harassment/ containment**, e.g., saturation of police/ military presence, militarized checkpoints targeting members of group, curfews, states of emergency	**Neglect/no remedial policies** Substantial underrepresentation due to historical neglect or restrictions. No social practice of deliberate exclusion. No formal exclusion. No evidence of protective or remedial public policies.	**Neglect/no remedial policies** Significant poverty and underrepresentation due to historical marginality, neglect, or restrictions. No social practice of deliberate exclusion. Few or no public policies aim at improving the group's material well-being.
3	**Nonviolent coercion**, e.g., arrests, show-trials, property confiscation, exile/deportation	**Social exclusion/ neutral policy** Substantial underrepresentation due to prevailing social practice by dominant groups. Formal public policies toward the group are neutral or, if positive, inadequate to offset discriminatory social practices.	**Social exclusion/neutral policy** Significant poverty and underrepresentation due to prevailing social practice by dominant groups. Formal public policies toward the group are neutral or, if positive, inadequate to offset active and widespread discrimination.
4	**Violent coercion**, short of killing, e.g., forced resettlement, torture	**Exclusion/repressive policy** Public policies (formal exclusion and/or recurring repression) substantially restrict the group's political participation by comparison with other groups. (Note: This does not include repression during group rebellions. It does include patterned repression when the group is not openly resisting state authority.)	**Exclusion/repressive policy** Public policies (formal exclusion and/or recurring repression) substantially restrict the group's economic opportunities in contrast with other groups.
5	**Violent coercion**, killing, e.g., systematic killings, ethnic cleansing, reprisal killings		

Social[232]

Social identity groups in Estatu are not limited to religion and ethnicity. People could join Sarca through any relationship or group that provides a sense of belonging or encourages them to participate in resistance. For example, the rural migrants who feel marginalized and excluded in Estatu could begin to question their place in urban society and seek out other people in Sarca with similar backgrounds.[42] *Social identities and relationships that Bolanieves might use for reaching people are professional connections from work and friendships.*

Study of the al Qaeda social movement identifies similar motives for joining. The study compiled biographies of four hundred al Qaeda-affiliated radicals from trial transcripts, press accounts, academic publications, and corroborated Internet sources. The organization was a bottom-up, self-organizing group with no centralized recruiting mechanism. Of those interested in joining, only very few were actually accepted. Sixty-eight percent joined because of pre-existing friendships with members, and 20 percent joined because of familial ties with members; in 98 percent of the cases, social bonds preceded ideological commitment.[233]

- **Multiplicity of motives**. Usually, more than one motive is present when a member joins. A combination of factors is cited; no one factor by itself causes resistance.

- **Personal and situational factors.** Most of the motives cited for joining relate to situational or personal problems and reflect the individual's immediate needs.

- **Belief in the cause or political reasons**. Only a minority admits that political reasons or sympathy with the ideology or organization relate to joining.

- **Propaganda and promises**. Few join because of propaganda or promises alone. These are apparently more effective when combined with situational factors.

- **Coercion**. Coercion alone is a small but important factor in joining.

- **Coercion with other positive incentives**. When combined with other positive incentives related to personal or situational factors, coercion yields a significantly large number of recruits.

- **Government persecution**. This factor appears to be a small but significant factor leading individuals to join the movement.

There was no evidence of coercion or brainwashing; individuals acquired the beliefs of those around them. In each case, the individual joined the jihad through human bridges (acquaintances, relatives, and imams) and not electronic or bureaucratic ones.[234]

Motivations of the Individual

One major challenge that Bolanieves faces in trying to determine causes of resistance is understanding individual people. It is easier for Bolanieves to look at the big picture of society in Estatu than it is to understand each individual, unique person. Bolanieves can think about societal issues and groups, such as government illegitimacy, economic hardship, and religion and ethnicity, from a broad perspective. However, when it comes to individual people, it would be impossible for him to know every single person's unique experiences and thoughts. People may join Sarca due to emotion or a new experience, such as witnessing or suffering through poor treatment by Estatu's government forces. Individual people can also change their minds or experience different thoughts or feelings quickly, which means Bolanieves cannot expect to know the personal motivations of every

member of Sarca. To help him think about this complicated topic of personal motivation for resistance, there are some common individual issues and experiences of which Bolanieves should be aware.

Personal Connection to a Grievance[235]

Identification with victims (actual or vicarious)[236] will influence an individual and perhaps encourage resistance. If a person witnesses harm to a close friend, family member, coworker, or even another citizen who happens to be physically close by, there can be a greater chance of joining in resistance. Any political or military action taken by the government against its people will have unintended consequences, including causing individuals to suffer physically, psychologically, financially, or in some other way. This suffering will be seen by other people and influence how they personally think and feel.

Shamil Baseyev's Riyadus-Salikhin reconnaissance and sabotage battalion of Chechen martyrs is often associated with employing female suicide operatives recruited from pools of women whose husbands were killed by Russian forces.[237] These "Black Widows" are often described as being vulnerable because of this personal tragedy. Superficially, this is an exemplar of the personal grievance mechanism. Reality, however, is more complex. The degree to which these individuals willingly participated is debatable. Baseyev's recruiters coerced some, and others felt the social pressure of marginalization from an insulated culture of strict Islamic mores; others still may have been acting out of a sense of grief-induced hopelessness (along a depressive continuum).

Vicarious Experience of Grievance[238]

A personal grievance need not be direct but can be experienced by proxy. This dynamic is particularly prevalent in modern recruitment strategies of radical Islamic groups, which emphasize victimization of Muslims at the hand of Westerners. Vicarious victimization can be experienced through self-study, media exposure, or accounts learned from members of the same social network. Al Qaeda's narrative, from Osama bin Laden's fatwas to Dr. Ayman Al-Zawahiri's speeches and their propagation throughout the information environment, continues to call for devout Muslims to rise up and serve the greater *umma* through jihad. The individuals with no direct contact to al Qaeda leadership or even operatives (sometimes referred to as self-radicalized or super-empowered) become adherents to the narratives of violent extremists and radicalized to the point of contemplating terrorist acts. There are several variants of these grievances, including grievances against governments, a hatred for the perceived erosion of fundamental values, disaffection from society, anger over unequal economic opportunities, the desire to belong to a cause larger than self, and a desire to make a name and prove oneself.

Vicarious grievances are most effective when supported by ideological frameworks articulating perceived problems, a vision of the future, and a prescription for action. Cases of individual radicalization to political violence (when the individual acts alone rather than as part of a group) are relatively rare.[239] In such cases, the individual is likely to associate with a larger intellectual community or social movement.[240]

Mechanisms of Recruitment[241]

It is important to note that the adoption of radical beliefs alone does not mean an individual will become violent; the transition from activist to violent radical is not inevitable. In addition, an individual need not personally suffer a transgression to seek out radicalization opportunities. Any individual with a degree of empathy, sufficient emotional vulnerability, and the opportunity to access informative materials could potentially succumb to this mechanism. However, there may be underlying factors that predispose one to vulnerability, but those factors have not been studied with sufficient rigor to generate a set of empirically determined criteria for susceptibility to radicalization. These risk factors and mechanisms discuss the methods under which and the reasons why an individual chooses to participate in violent radical behavior. Some radicalize because of a personal or political grievance whereas others do so because of social or environmental pressures. Examples of the application is included in Table 2,[242] where the mechanisms apply to Zawahiri.

Table 2. Radicalization mechanisms and their relevance to the Zawahiri case study.

Mechanism[243]	Relevance to Zawahiri
Radicalization due to personal grievance: Harm to self or loved ones can move individuals to hostility and violence toward perpetrators.	High: Zawahiri's close relationship with his maternal uncle (Sayyid Qutb's attorney)
Radicalization under threat: Threat or harm to a group or cause the individual cares about can move the individual to hostility and violence toward perpetrators.	Medium: Generalized predisposition to perceived threat indicative of intolerance of uncertainty (manifested both individually as well as generally on behalf of Egyptian Islamists toward the secular regimes of Gamal Abdel Nasser, Anwar Sadat, and Hosni Mubarak)
Small involvements in political conflict can create new forces that can move an individual toward radicalization.	High: Early days (1966) as a clandestine cell leader within Muslim Brotherhood faction provided sense of political identity
Radicalization through social networks: Love for someone already radicalized can move an individual toward radicalization.	Low: Zawahiri's radicalization resulted more from his admiration for the idealized, martyred Qutb than the social network argument put forth by Sageman and McCauley and Moskalenko
Radicalization by disposition: The attractions of risk taking and status can move individuals, especially young males, to radical political action.	Low: Zawahiri did not exhibit novelty- or sensation-seeking behaviors in childhood, adolescence, or adulthood; in fact, he tended to be more "bookish" than athletic or adventurous
Radicalization through isolation: Loss of social connection can open an individual to new ideas and new identity that may include political radicalization.	Medium: This is more of a perception emanating from an introversive tendency as both maternal and paternal sides of his family were well connected socially, academically, and politically
Discussion among like-minded individuals tends to move the whole group further in the direction initially favored.	High: Particularly so during the internment period subsequent to the Sadat assassination
Radicalization in competition for the same base of support: Groups are radicalized in competition with other groups.	High: Particularly so when comparing the Muslim Brotherhood, Egyptian Islamic Group (EIG), and EIJ (although more so EIG-EIJ) from the late 1970s through the 1990s

Mechanism[243]	Relevance to Zawahiri
Radicalization through condensation or splitting: The power of group dynamics is multiplied to the extent that group members are cut off from other groups.	High: Particularly during the period immediately after internment when Zawahiri and many EIJ leaders "escaped" to Peshawar and linked up with Abdullah Azzam and Osama bin Laden
Radicalization through jujitsu politics: Terrorists often count on government reactions to advance their causes.	Medium: This seems to have been a consideration in the Embassy operations; however, al Qaeda's organizational reasoning was biased by the 1993 incident in Mogadishu and thus it miscalculated the U.S. response to 9/11
Radicalization through hate: In protracted conflicts, the enemy is increasingly seen as less than human.	High: Particularly so when analyzing the content of Zawahiri's speeches/press releases; his abrasive negativism has become more pronounced
Radicalization through martyrdom: A successfully constructed martyr can radicalize sympathizers for the martyr's causes.	Medium: The salience of Qutb's martyrdom remains with Zawahiri; however, he has demonstrated lack of empathy in considering the human effect (e.g., surviving family members, innocents, etc.) of martyrdom operations instead focusing on the enemy—bin Laden on the other hand, seems to have displayed more empathetic reactions toward the families of both suicide operatives and those killed in combat against the Soviets

Bolanieves and Sarca

Many different experiences, beliefs, fears, goals, and hopes may motivate the people of Estatu to join Sarca in resistance. To better prepare Sarca for resistance, Bolanieves should therefore remember that it is important to not only understand the people of Estatu and the environment in which they live, but also their motivations. The American ODA also needs to keep the motivations and causes of resistance in mind when engaging with Bolanieves and Sarca because it may not have the ability to control or affect all of the potential motivating factors. It could be a delicate and difficult process to manage or direct people's motivations for the good of Sarca as a whole, especially if members and supporters demonstrate different motivators.

Shared motivations and causes could be a positive force for Sarca by giving people a reason to join the resistance and unite together. However, motivations and causes based on divisive factors across society could alternatively fracture or isolate the resistance. Additionally, because motivations can be very personal and based on individual experiences, Bolanieves knows that there may not be one single way to address motivations. He may have to unite both large groups of people with common views and individuals or small units who have different perspectives. When encouraging people to support Sarca, planning Sarca's strategy, and setting objectives, Bolanieves will have to consider all of these factors.

Questions

Bolanieves must understand the central causes for resistance in Estatu. As the reader learned in this section on causes, there are many important concepts upon which the ODA must be prepared to advise Bolanieves. Among these resistance-based concepts are government legitimacy; economic, political, and ideological rationales for resistance; ethnic/religious and social identities involved in a resistance; and individual motivations such as grievances and relational recruitment. It is important for the reader to examine this content by applying it to the Sarca resistance with the following discussion questions.

INTRODUCTORY - BLOOMS LEVEL ONE

- Identify: What kinds of factors are motivating Sarca's goals and the people who may want to join?

- Identify and Categorize: Are some motivating factors better for Sarca than others? In other words, will some motivating factors align better with Sarca's objectives, or could some motivations create risks for Sarca?

- Identify and Categorize: Could individual motivations play a role in Sarca, or are larger scale societal motivations more important?

INTERMEDIATE - BLOOMS LEVEL FOUR

- Attribute and Differentiate: How can Bolanieves shape these motivating factors, or are they outside his control?

- Attribute and Differentiate: How could different motivations and causes of resistance affect different segments of Estatu's society?

MASTERY - BLOOMS LEVEL FIVE

- Detect and Evaluate: How should Bolanieves approach account for different motivations?

ENVIRONMENT

Resistance does not exist in a vacuum—a group must operate within the environment around it. The environment in which Sarca and Bolanieves operate consists of external factors that not only shape Sarca's actions but are also shaped by Sarca's actions. Some of the environmental factors that Sarca can face include the national and local economies, social structures and values, the state and its organs and institutions, and technology, to name a few. Factors from the geography to the economic structure of a country affect a resistance group. Furthermore, the state actively responds to the resistance movement and shapes the environment with its own actions. The consideration and study of environmental factors are integral to the study of any social phenomenon. This section reviews several factors and characteristics believed to be formative or impactful on resistance according to existing research.

JP 3-05.1
IV-8

Physical Environment

The physical environment plays a significant role in resistance because it defines the places in which conflict occurs. For example, countries with mountainous terrain have a higher risk of violent resistance because mountains can provide safety to fighters.244 Physical

TC 18-01.1
C-1

geography intersects with social structures when looking at differences in urban and rural regions. Traditionally, insurgencies are based in rural areas where they can leverage the weak government presence in remote locations. Additionally, rural insurgents benefit from local knowledge, including the details of knowing people in individual villages.245

ATP 3-05.1
1-7, 2-5, F-19

Conversely, in emerging urban settings, a resistance group is more likely to struggle against the state's centralized power, influence, and support. As such, it is usually not able to control large amounts of territory as it would in a rural region. However, cities also provide benefits to a resistance group, such as high-profile targets, financial opportunities, and easier access to resources.246

TC 18-01
1-3, 2-5

Rural/Urban[247]

Rural terrains can provide protection to a resistance. For instance, the Afghani Taliban benefits from mountainous terrain that hinders surveillance and pursuit. Mountainous terrain also isolates villages, making it harder for the government to protect and easier for insurgents to influence or intimidate. Two studies found a correlation between mountainous terrain and civil war in which conflict is more likely in countries with mountainous areas.[248]

Dense forest can have a similar effect. The FARC in Colombia benefitted from hiding and organizing in the thick jungles of that country. The Viet Cong may have benefited similarly, despite American attempts to deforest sections of the country. However, a general statistical relationship between forest cover and adverse political events has not been demonstrated comparable to that with mountains. It could be that difficult terrain does not encourage insurgencies to develop; it could lead them to last longer by hindering government response.[249] There are examples of prolonged insurgencies without any particular geographic cover. For example, the IRA relied on the human terrain of Catholic enclaves in larger cities for safe havens and bases of operations.

Megacities

As populations from the rural provinces of Estatu moved into the urban centers, two cities became megacities, featuring wealthy downtowns, industrial zones, infrastructure (both formal and informal), and shanty towns. The populations of these megacities have two constituencies in Sarca and Ajust. Those living in the shanty towns and out of reach of public services have gravitated toward Sarca as fighting for their position by calling for more radical change. Middle class segments of the urban population, however, have more commonly supported the agenda put forward by Ajust for moderate reform that will still protect their position in society and the economy.

Urbanization, the process of people moving from rural regions into cities, affects resistance movements and groups in many different areas from recruitment and support to legitimacy to operations. This trend of urbanization is rapidly changing cities: megacities with more than ten million people and other growing urban centers present a new environment with their government structures, high concentrations of people, diversity, and economic inequalities. Megacities are also often critically important centers of government, economic growth, and business, which means "security and stability of the city has a direct impact on the security and stability of the nation."[250] Together, these unique characteristics provide both challenges and opportunities for resistance movements and groups in the urban environment.[251]

Studies have found many different complex connections and relationships between large cities and conflict. First, violence in the country as a whole and poverty in rural regions may drive a higher rate of urbanization as civilians are forced to migrate to cities to escape conflict or seek economic opportunity.[252] Once urbanization has caused growth in cities, one study showed that large urban population sizes and a high number of large cities in a country can then lead to more protests.[253] Similarly, another study supported the idea that cities enable more "coordinated public action" and "enhance the effectiveness of uprisings."[254]

Because urbanization is connected with increasing resistance, it is important to specifically understand how this appears and works in cities. Some cities, called fragile cities, are at particular risk for resistance movements because they fail to provide important services to the population.[255] For example, parts of Rio de Janeiro in the *favelas*, or slums, have long been neglected by the rest of the city, leading to violence and conflict in those neighborhoods with little loyalty to the government.[256] Resistance groups can take advantage of these failings in fragile cities by reaching out to marginalized rural migrants for support, recruiting dissatisfied urban youths, rallying people against corrupt government structures in cities, exploiting racial and ethnic tensions, and using black markets.[257] Furthermore, when cities cannot provide resources, resistance groups have the opportunity to actively and positively gain legitimacy by providing necessities such as housing or water.258 Some groups additionally integrate into the city and gain supporters by providing security and policing for the neighborhoods in which they operate.[259]

The density of massive megacities also benefits resistance groups by making it difficult for the government to collect intelligence or target resistance members. With millions and millions of people moving through a megacity, a resistance group can easily physically hide amongst the "clutter." The density and connectedness of megacities also allows resistance

groups to quickly communicate with people, receive supplies from around the world, or globally publicize an event such as an attack or protest.[260]

However, there are also constraints on building large resistance movements and groups in cities. Due to migration from around the country, cities typically have high levels of diversity across many different ethnic groups. This diversity can hurt and hinder efforts to organize people into one single movement – people may live together in one city and have grievances against the government, but they may be too divided along ethnic lines to organize together into a bigger movement. Instead, the city may simply have many smaller resistance groups that do not cooperate with each other.[261] Similarly, if a group is often involved in urban election-related violence, this type of violence tends to increase divisions and conflict among ethnic groups who support different political parties. As a result, the group may lose legitimacy and support based on ethnic identity throughout the city. Additionally, if a resistance group becomes involved in urban organized crime, it may lose support from civilians that had wanted the group to provide security or stop crime in their neighborhoods.[262]

When evaluating resistance movements and groups in large cities, it is important to understand both the benefits and advantages of urban resistance operations and the potential challenges. As resistance and conflict in cities increases with urbanization, groups will need to decide how to best operate in this environment.

Characteristics of the State

Because resistance interacts with the government, the government significantly shapes the environment in which a group must operate. Under a weak, unstable state with little ability to provide services to its people or control its territory, resistance and rebellion can flourish.[263] However, a stronger or more competent government has other options open to it. Governments can buy off elites and powerful local leaders in the country to ensure their support against a resistance movement. Government actions may also include Imposing harsh controls on civilian populations and using forceful measures to cut off resources for the resistance group.[264] In a different approach, other government responses may be to hold peace negotiations or make concessions to resistance group demands.[265] All of these potential state actions affect the resistance environment, whether by escalating the violence or opening new ways for resolving the conflict.

The state against which Sarca resists will both be part of the environment and determine the environment. It will be part of the environment by reacting to Sarca's actions and undertaking operations of its own against Sarca. The state's strength may be a determining factor in how it reacts, so Bolanieves will have to consider that in his calculus of when and where to execute different kinds of operations. Strong law enforcement and military could squelch violent protests, but use of force may not produce a good reaction if the protests are nonviolent. In that circumstance a strong police and military facing nonviolent protesters can present an image of the oppressor against the oppressed that Bolanieves might be able to use. The state can determine the environment by opening or closing physical and virtual spaces.

Another way in which the state can determine the environment is by the level of openness or closedness that it institutes for activities a resistance might undertake to convince the government to change policies. If the state is open and democratic, Sarca can have opportunities to engage in resistance peacefully and legally, as well as illegally. An open society can provide physical and communication space to Bolanieves to spread Sarca's message and to engage in resistance activities. However, the state can tighten its control over society and close physical and communication spaces for Bolanieves and Sarca to act. This will change the tactics that Sarca uses and can increase the risk Bolanieves' and Sarca components' actions bring.

Characteristics of the state can fuel or defuse a resistance movement's rationale or motivation. For instance, state unwillingness to accommodate any demands for change can fuel resistance. Similarly, failing to meet the population's needs can drive individuals to resist. In contrast, holding free and fair elections can defuse resistance, as can providing popular access to and involvement in governing institutions. Finally, the capability and capacity of state institutions responding to and countering the resistance will always be an integral factor in the environment of a resistance.

Justice System[266]

The legal contexts (local, national, regional, international, and even religious, in some communities) within which a resistance operates can be a fundamental factor, particularly in the analysis of resistance strategy, tactics, and the barrier to collective action. While many means of nonviolent public activism are legal and protected in Western and industrialized countries, the imposing legal structures of authoritarian and totalitarian countries can outlaw some forms of speech or association, a factor that could greatly impact participation, organization, strategy, and tactics. Authoritarian and totalitarian regimes can also enforce laws unevenly and use questionably legitimate charges and trials to impede a resistance, otherwise known as kangaroo courts. Recent examples also include shutting down access either to the entire Internet or to key websites, such as Facebook and Twitter, the Internet-based social messaging service. Conversely, as was discussed in the section on legitimacy, the failure of a resistance to administer a justice system acceptable to the public can undermine the resistance's efforts.

Social Structures[267]

Sarca's strategy and tactics will interact with the larger society around it - including its people, its structures, and its values. Sarca might choose to engage in activities that match and reflect society's values in order to build trust and support. If Sarca's goal is to upend traditional power structures in society, it would interact with social structures by challenging and breaking them. Bolanieves would want to think carefully about how he himself interacts with the social environment as a representative of Sarca to the larger population. He and Sarca will have to answer how it fits into the society.

JP 3-05.1
II-10

TC 18-01.1
C-2, C-3

The dominant social structures of the country, region, and participants can also play a key role in the shape and development of resistance movements, regardless of the movement's cause. Some key questions to consider include, how old or entrenched is the norm, and how would it impact perception of or participation in the resistance?

ATP 3-05.1

E-2, F-1, F-8, F-10

TC 18-01

1-3

Preexisting and emerging relationships among individuals, organizations, various social groups (social, class-based, religious, ethnic), and governments can be significant. An example of preexisting relationships shaping resistance movements is the role of Baathist military officers in the growth, organization, and rise of the Islamic State, which later became the most prolific insurgent terrorist group in Iraq, Syria, and elsewhere in the region.[268]

Social Identity Groups: Categorization and Salience

The social environment can be important in resistance movements because it impacts group dynamics and must be navigated. Commonly, individuals seek out joining groups when anxiety and conflict are higher or more prevalent. Identifying and understanding identity affiliations, that is groups formed based on identity, can inform directions groups may take. In the context of Sarca and Bolanieves, this information could aid decision-making about in what direction the resistance will evolve.

Identity Stability[269]

The notion of an identity's stability describes the reliability of a group's identity over time or in the face of challenge. For example, some identities can command commitment for only a short period of time. In contrast, other identities, like ethnicity, can last a lifetime. However, all identities are subject to change and redefinition. The measure is following the narrative surrounding the identity and determining the identity group's interests. Identity groups can merge or split. Splitting can occur from independent variables like geography or language, but also from leaders' efforts to pursue maximizing their influence.

Bolanieves may have to grapple with a shifting identity, but how would he determine where the group's identity is moving? Where does he look to for the group's narrative and its interests? What are the influences that could shape Sarca's identity?

Salience[270]

The idea of salience is the importance of an identity to an individual. For example, a sub-group of Sarca might share the identity of a policy position, but it may not be as salient, in other words as important, as the identity of being from a particular region. If those two identities come into conflict, salience becomes relevant because that subgroup would likely act to benefit its regional identity over its policy identity. An example that goes in the opposite direction, from smaller identity to larger, can be religious groups. Within the Catholic Church there is division regarding issues like the importance of the environment, divorce, and social justice. American conservative Catholics disagree with Pope Francis on these and other issues.[271] However, their larger Catholic identity may be more salient to the conservative American Catholics than their identity based on the issues.

Conflict[272]

Studies have shown that ethnic identity in Africa increases in its importance during election years because they are seen as competitions, or conflict, between ethnic groups.[273] This is an example of how identities can increase or decrease in salience depending on the circumstances. Professional or economic identity may not be important until land use issues come to the forefront.

An important takeaway is that identities can be re-imagined to reinforce cleavages, invoke historical divisiveness, and institutionalize conflict. For example, Protestants in Northern Ireland identified themselves with religion, specifically that of the Protestant Ascendancy and the Glorious Revolution of 1688, to evoke a narrative of Protestant domination and Catholic subjugation. Meanwhile, the Irish Republican Army may have been predominantly Catholic, but referred to itself as Irish and Republican instead of Catholic. They cast their opponents as British Loyalists. This created a narrative of an Irish Republic struggling against politically dominant British oppressors and their Protestant steeds.

In-Group and Out-Group Formation[274]

The identity issues posed above come into play when actors, whether leaders or disruptors, encourage the creation of in-groups and out-groups. In-groups form easily. Lab experiments found that psychologists could manufacture in-groups with anything, including arbitrary labels.[275] The important implication is that in-group members demonstrate biases toward other in-group members, for instance by giving them more of a resource or showing more empathy.

These inward biases can express themselves as outward discrimination. When out-groups are defined they are generally treated unfairly, particularly through the pseudo-justifications by using stereotypes. Sometimes in-group leaders will use hostility toward out-groups to build cohesion within the in-group. Divides can make reconciliation difficult. For example, in Sri Lanka the Sinhalese language majority was mostly Buddhist, but the Tamil language group included Hindus, Muslims, and Christians. In contrast, the shared religion between African-Americans and white activists during the Civil Rights Movement enabled more in-group cohesion.

Competition Between Groups[276]

Many other factors contribute to the resistance environment. The existence of multiple resistance groups with the same objectives may create competition for members, power, and influence. The different resistance groups must then find ways to operate within alliances or hierarchies.[277] Conflict length and duration also contributes to an understanding of resistance. Poverty, economic inequality, and some ethnic group tension can all lead to conflicts that last a long time, and the decrease in value of primary resources and outside military assistance to the resistance fighters can shorten the conflict.[278] Connecting the concepts of multiple resistance groups and duration, the existence of more groups may lead to a longer conflict when the different groups cannot agree on an end to the conflict. For example, they may have different demands for peace negotiations, which slows down the process.[279]

Intergroup dynamics may not play an important role when resources are plenty and interests do not conflict. However, competition over resources can highlight these differences and bring identities to the forefront. It can also push individuals to decide between competing identities within themselves. A particular area of competition has been positions in governance. The perception of favoring one group in the distribution of governance positions and powers can lead to the perception and belief that unfairness and corruption exists. *If Bolanieves fills his close leadership positions in Sarca only with people from a particular language or ethnic group, this can create in-group out-group tension*

because members of other language and ethnic groups can perceive those decisions as bias and a threat against their group. Another factor that should be considered by Bolanieves is the economy.

Economy[280]

Bolanieves could find funding for Sarca in natural resource extraction, but research has found that approach commonly leads resistances to become more interested in the resources and the resistance (and its leadership) is corrupted by this practice. Similar negative consequences can come if Bolanieves encourages raising money through extortion. Such approaches alienate the demographic environment around the resistance and can make them a liability, or even an enemy. Beyond Estatu, Bolanieves may also reach out to the Estatian diaspora to take advantage of the economic wealth and opportunity generated by Estatians working in and sending money back from other countries. All of these different economic challenges and opportunities can push Bolanieves to take Sarca in a variety of directions.

At the country level, the structure of the entire economy contributes to conditions for resistance and violence. Economies that depend on the export of primary resources – oil, diamonds, timber, and other natural resources – create financial opportunities for a resistance group. It should be noted that if a state becomes extremely wealthy from resource exports, such as Saudi Arabia, then that economic structure actually benefits the government and not the rebels. However, in most other resource economies, a group can extort money from those resource industries and use that funding to sustain its operations. Similarly, if a country has a large number of people working abroad and sending money home, a resistance group may be able to renew and re-ignite conflict with that monetary support.[281] Although these economic factors are not motivating resistance in terms of core objectives, they are providing the economic environment and financial means that help rebels.

A provocative theory argues that violent rebellions are more likely when there is a "primary commodity resource" that can be used to finance a rebellion.[282] Examples of resistance movements financed in this way would be the FARC, which is financed by cocaine trafficking, and Nigeria's MEND, which is financed with "bunkered" oil, and Angolan rebels, who are financed with "conflict diamonds." It can be difficult for resistance movements to sustain themselves financially with legitimate businesses and other revenue sources because of the resistance's covert nature or because the government makes it difficult as a counter-strategy. Accordingly, some will resort to criminal enterprises. The controversial theory noted above argues also that funding a rebellion through theft and smuggling valuable commodities makes radical rebellions more likely.[283]

This theory seems to align with the research saying that countries with abundant natural resources are at a higher risk for internal conflict.[284] In particular, when those resources are located inside the conflict region, internal conflicts tend to last longer.[285] A competing theory, however, asserts that abundant natural resources do not encourage populations to rebel and fight, but that abundant resources corrupt the government and lead to a weak state with poor policy decisions.[286]

Large diasporas living in more developed countries are also asserted as increasing the risk of internal conflict.[287] Diaspora populations living in wealthier countries can send more funds home. For example, Tamils living in North America were a significant source of funding for the insurgency in Sri Lanka, as well as the Kurdish diaspora living in Europe.[288]

Apart from valuable commodities, resistance movements can finance themselves through extortion, sometimes referred to as protection, depending on the viewpoint. This method fits well with those groups that have mobile armed forces. This method of funding often requires the extorted populations to be rural because the more expansive geography and sparse population enable safer freedom of movement by the resistance.

Financing resistance through exploiting resources and populations has been thought to incentivize the use of conflict to generate revenue. This means a shift to raising funds through illicit means instead of through popular support.[289] In these cases, shadow governments do not serve the populations but serve the resistance to extract resources and extort people more efficiently. These resistance movements begin blurring the lines between the rebels pursuing justice and the criminal networks seeking resources.[290]

One of the preeminent examples of this new insurgent, and the variation of insurgent tactics over the lifetime of an organization, is UNITA. UNITA was initially a legitimate opposition group driven by Maoist practices struggling to overthrow the kleptocratic and ethnically exclusive MPLA regime. The group sought greater democratic and ethnic representation, especially for the majority Ovimbundu.[50] Its initial strategies aimed at eroding the authority and legitimacy of the Angolan state. As the MPLA continued to survive, UNITA redirected its efforts to extracting resources, including ivory, timber, gold, and, particularly, diamonds, and wealth accumulation. Its strategy evolved, as one researcher and first-hand witness acerbically noted, into a guerrilla force "whose primary objective is inflicting unrelenting and indiscriminate suffering upon defenceless civilian populations while obliterating all infrastructures as a means to render the country ungovernable."[51] The discovery of diamond mines in areas under UNITA's control is partially responsible. The resulting wealth allowed the group to acquire a considerable cache of weapons and other supplies needed to continue its armed struggle. As it became apparent to the group that the MPLA could not be dislodged by either "ballots or bullets," UNITA instead focused on creating enough disorder in the country to continue its diamond-mining efforts. Through violence and intimidation, UNITA drove away rural populations to government-controlled urban centers to facilitate diamond extraction. The trend is apparent in other African countries such as Sierra Leone and the Democratic Republic of Congo in addition to Angola, where effective governance of civilian populations is increasingly regarded as unduly burdensome when groups like UNITA can instead "enrich themselves without the political and administrative costs of governing."[52]

Technology

The importance of technology for resistance groups has grown. It provides tools and spaces for Bolanieves and Sarca to spread their messages to various audiences at home and abroad, and to seek and acquire resources. States, however, can make it harder for Bolanieves and Sarca to use technology tools and spaces by controlling access to the Internet, for example. Popular access to, and the growing capabilities of, various

JP 3-05.1
I-17, III-13,
III-18, IV-8

ATP 3-05.1
F-17

technologies is a factor that can be examined as potentially directly formative on tactics and strategy, as well as indirectly on the shape or rationale of resistance movements. The Internet is an obvious technology that a resistance must use and navigate, but older and less obvious areas of technology are worth consider, namely manufacturing.

The Internet[291]

The properties of being inexpensive, decentralized, and anonymous make the Internet a favorable environment for resistance groups, but state governments are learning how to combat that advantage; access to the Internet has become a new arms race.[292] The relative low cost of spreading information has made it easier to reach larger audiences in terms of both geography and demography. The intentional redundancy built into the Internet makes it ideal for those avoiding censors and government controls. This decentralization also makes borders less restrictive for resistance movements, and it enables command and control across a wider network. Another battle in this new arms race is the ability to identify actors and attribute actions on the Internet. Anonymity has always been good cover for resistance movements, and the Internet provides opportunity to continue that.

Uses of the Internet[293]

The way resistance movements employ the Internet grows as quickly as those groups can creatively invent them. The list grows constantly. Accordingly, below are some categories of uses the resistance groups have used in the past to be illustrative but not exhaustive.

The ARIS volume **Resistance in the Cyber Domain**
provides a comprehensive study of cyber resistance.

Bolanieves will need to consider his risks and rewards of using online methods. For instance, do the populations he wants to enlist or convince get their information online, or do they still use radio, TV, or newspapers? Does that change for different demographics? Sarca will also risk its legitimate online efforts being tainted by online activities of its underground or armed component. The ODA will need to consider the amount of exposure versus gain for using online methods.

Publicity and Communications[294]

A resistance historically used handbills and newspapers and leaflets to spread their messages. They would write anonymously or with a fake name. Famous examples can be recalled from the American Revolution, but other resistance movements have used this method throughout history. They often depended on coded language to clandestinely communicate themes and messages under the close watch of the government they resisted. Today it is more common for a group to publicize and communicate online. However, the same risk is present: when one speaks one can be identified and targeted. Accordingly, depending on the message or content, resistance groups communicating online will continue to obfuscate who they are. One might consider, for instance, how the subversive messages of an underground component could endanger the legitimacy or safety of the public component if they became associated.

> **RESISTANCE IN FOCUS:O nline Publicity and Communications**
>
> The Tamil insurgency in Sri Lanka made particularly effective open use of the Internet for publicity through sites including Tamilnet.com[34] and eelam.com.[35] Support from the diaspora was critical for the Tamil cause, and the Tamilnet website provides a much faster and easier means of keeping information flowing to distant supporters than printed newsletters did previously. In Sri Lanka, the government suppressed stories about police abuse (newspapers often printed "blacked out" stories in protest) and denied foreigners, including journalists, access to Tamil areas in the north and east of the country. The militant insurgents (the Tamil Tigers) also prevented unfettered coverage and did not permit journalists to enter territories they controlled unless they were sympathetic to the cause. Underground websites including Tamilnet (which does not appear to have been closely tied to the Liberation Tigers of Tamil Eelam) were often the most reliable source of information on government/Tamil clashes during the latter years of that insurgency. More than one observer has noted that despite the violent content, Tamilnet maintained the detached tone of a Western news source. Stories followed journalistic conventions and generally did not mix facts with commentary or political rhetoric. Even in accounts of graphic torture, stories were carefully sourced and referred to "alleged" police misdeeds. This suggests that Tamilnet's target audience went beyond its supporters and that the site sought to reach a skeptical foreign audience including the press. By providing information in a credible format, the site maximized its chances of being used as a source by foreign media, thereby creating traceable credibility for the movement and bolstering its legitimacy.

Targeting the Enemy[295]

Online media can provide a potent avenue for messages targeting the enemy by undermining the enemy's messaging efforts. For instance, Hizbollah revealed on its website that when the Israeli Defense Forces returned a coffin home it contained not one body but multiple. Parents of Israeli soldiers then began consulting Hizbollah.org because it could have information about the conflict not provided elsewhere.[296] In this way a resistance can damage the legitimacy of the government and gain legitimacy and trustworthiness of its own.

Recruitment and Radicalization[297]

According to Rita Katz, director of the Search for International Terrorist Entities Institute Intelligence Group, "We know from past cases—from captured al Qaeda fighters who say they joined up through the Internet—that this is one of the principal ways they recruit fighters and suicide bombers."[298]

Producing videos of operations has become so important to recruiting that several groups have included a videographer on operational teams. The videos serve multiple functions. They attract attention to the group and excite followers. They provide imagery that serves as a narrative for potential recruits; they can imagine themselves in the group more easily. Repetitive images can lead viewers to believe success is common. Finally, they desensitize recruits to violence and make dehumanizing opponents easier.

Technology also facilitates contact during the recruitment process. At some point, recruits reach out to groups, and technology also enables recruiters to reach out to potential

recruits. The increasing ability of civilians to encrypt their communications also makes these communications increasingly secure and therefore a more viable option. However, the same anonymity and secrecy also enables government personnel to pose as recruits or supporters and infiltrate resistance groups. A report in 2010 about the Irish Republican Board featured invitations to marches, to support prisoners with letters, as well as links to online petitions.[299] The board also had a chat feature that facilitated viewers and visitors connecting with one another.

Training[300]

Insurgent groups are utilizing Internet platforms to train followers and members all over the world. Historic manuals like *The Terrorist's Handbook*, *The Anarchist's Cookbook*, and *The Mujahadeen Poisons Handbook* are available online. A more modern approach is exemplified by Abu Omar, a Palestinian bomb maker who had been employed in Iraq to teach foreign fighters how to make bombs and carry out roadside attacks. In an interview with the *New York Times*, he explained that he had worked with two cameramen to videotape his bomb-making classes for online instructional videos.[301]

Fundraising[302]

TC 18-01.1
C-3

National legislation prohibiting monetary and material donations to terrorist groups has led many resistance groups not to seek donations online. They, however, continue to sell items online. Selling is not donating. For instance, the 32 County Sovereignty Movement, a group associated with the Real IRA (RIRA) at one time joined Amazon.com's "Associates" program and received a cut from book sales when they redirected visitors to buy those books at Amazon. The company removed the IRA from the program when it learned about its connections to the insurgency.[303]

ATP 3-05.1
2-27

Command and Control[304]

The Internet can also facilitate command and control (C2). In leaderless models, groups may attempt completely decentralized C2, for example, by openly suggesting targets and tactics and expecting that self-managed sub-groups will engage them. The website irelandsown. net once published specific information related to Prince William's boarding school, including a suggested location for an attack.[305] In this case, the Internet disseminated information as command guidance in a manner in which the resistance understood to substitute C2 from higher. However, the state may be aware of such methods, so suggestions that obvious and open could alert law enforcement.

Other examples include Hizbollah and World Trade Organization (WTO) protests. Hizbollah has installed a dedicated fiber optic network parallel to Lebanon's cable television and Internet lines. When the government threatened to dismantle it, Hizbollah's political power was able to lead the government to retract its threat and keep the Internet-based C2 network in place.[306] In another example, protests against the WTO in Seattle pioneered the use of text messages and social media for coordination. Previously, the use of strategic movement of crowds had to be pre-planned, but modern technology has enabled flexibility with real-time decision-making and execution of adaptive C2.

RESISTANCE IN FOCUS: Iran

Internet and cell phone technology are thought by some to have played an important mobilizing role in the Iranian protests after the disputed 2009 elections, although this claim is controversial. The use of Twitter during these protests received a great deal of attention.[307] Twitter is a very flexible text messaging service that can be used either to broadcast to a large audience or to send personalized messages among friends, and the messages can be broadcast using either the Internet or SMS (cell phone based). It is clear that Twitter, along with other services such as YouTube, were closely monitored by people outside the country who wanted to follow events. Some authors have questioned whether Twitter played an important role in mobilizing and organizing the protests themselves.[308] On June 16, during these protests, the U.S. Department of State contacted Twitter to ask them to delay a scheduled server upgrade that might have disrupted Twitter traffic. Later, the Iranian government intentionally disrupted Twitter traffic by shutting down or throttling (slowing) both Internet and cell phone services in sections of Tehran.

Egypt

There is a clearer case to be made that the Internet played a role in mobilization of popular protests in Egypt, which forced the resignation of Hosni Mubarak in 2011. One group at the center of the movement was the 6th of April Youth Movement, whose main outreach mechanism was a publicly accessible page on Facebook. The group had organized earlier demonstrations on April 6, 2008, with minimal impact, but had continued to gather followers, mostly among younger and better-educated Egyptians. This group was also able to communicate with and learn nonviolent protest tactics from the Serbian student group Otpor.[309] The January 25 protests, however, were not preplanned; they were an opportunistic response to events unfolding in Tunisia. A protest was hastily scheduled for the nearest available holiday, which ironically was "Police Day." Such rapid, coordinated response requires open and accessible communication channels, which the Internet provided. Mubarak's government shut down almost all Internet access to the country on January 26 in an attempt to control the movement. This was done relatively easily by pressuring four major telecommunications providers in Egypt. The move was ineffective at dispersing the already-assembled crowds, however.

The Internet also facilitates using traditional media. For instance, protestors in Egypt wanted to keep a pamphlet (see Figure 7) [310] out of the hands of the government, which monitored Facebook and Twitter. Instead of distributing it with Facebook and Twitter, protestors provided instructions on the pamphlet to distribute it only by photocopying or emailing it. In this way, the Internet served as a method to spread a piece of traditional media, in this case a pamphlet, quickly to a wider audience.

خطوات التنفيذ

١- التجمهر مع الأصدقاء والجيران في الشوارع
السكنية البعيدة عن تواجد قوات الأمن.

٢- الهتاف باسم مصر وحرية الشعب (هتافات
إيجابية).

٣- تشجيع سكان العمارات للانضمام (بشكل
إيجابي).

٤- الخروج في مجموعات ضخمة إلى الشوارع
الرئيسية لجمع أكبر حشد ممكن.

٥- السير نحو المباني الحكومية الهامة (مع الهتاف
الإيجابي) للاستيلاء عليها.

1. Assemble with your friends and neighbors in residential streets far away from where the security forces are.

2. Shout slogans in the name of Egypt and the people's freedom (positive slogans).

3. Encourage other residents to join in (again with positive language)

4. Go out into the major streets in very large groups in order to form the biggest possible assembly

5. Head toward important government buildings –while shouting positive slogans– in order to take them over.

The page reproduced shows how the Egyptian protestors assembled groups outside of Tahrir Square, which allowed protestors to recruit local residents and aggregate people in the square more quickly and in a manner that was harder to prevent or disperse.

Figure 7. Instructions for crowd assembly from Egyptian protestors' pamphlet.

Communications[311]

Bolanieves will need to institute mechanisms for communicating effectively and efficiently within Sarca and to the broader population. They will need a way to share their ideas and important information, to coordinate activities, to tell its version of events, and to interact with local, regional, and international populations and governments. Without tools to communicate Sarca could die before it gets started by failing to make itself and its ideas known. Undoubtedly, Sarca has access to and capability to use the Internet, but there may instances where it is either not available or not the best option. For instance, Sarca's underground may need to contact and coordinate with its armed component. Traditional nontechnical means of communication may not want to be discounted because in today's technology run world an analog method could be the least traceable. Also in a world dependent on technology, analog means could be useful if power is cut or Internet is denied.

A resistance cannot operate without the ability for its different components (underground, armed, auxiliary, public) to exchange information, orders, intelligence, requests for assistance, and other messaging required for any organization. The need for security and secrecy, however, leads to the need for clandestine communications. A resistance's communications will start undisciplined and ad hoc, but as the resistance grows its communications methods will evolve to develop secure, redundant systems by using diverse means: face-to-face meetings, couriers, mail, dead drops, radio, cell phones, the Internet, and social media, to name a few. The communications system will need to continue to evolve as the government increases its response. The rapid advance of technology presents a new battleground where the resistance and government will continuously compete. Accordingly, the advantage in communications may alternate between the parties to the conflict.

Cell phone technology and social media have opened a new dimension in resistance communications. Evidence suggests that these technologies can benefit both the resistance and the government. They may enable clandestine operations,[312] but they also provide opportunity to intercept, monitor, and gather intelligence.[313] Urban centers provide resistance groups the most opportunity to use cell phones and the Internet, but both technologies are rapidly spreading into rural areas. The spread of these technologies and its declining cost to the consumer[314] disrupt government's traditional methods of controlling information.

RESISTANCE IN FOCUS: Resistance Use of Cell Phones and Social Media

The Orange Revolution in Ukraine that unfolded from November 2004 through January of the following year featured perhaps the first widespread use of the Internet to help foster revolution. Web postings, combined with the use of cell phones, bolstered ever-growing crowds protesting the rigged elections in Kiev. By using technology that could not be easily interdicted or controlled by authorities, the crowds organized demonstrations, sit-ins, and strikes to compel the government to annul the suspicious election results. The outrage felt in the streets of Kiev found an international audience through the new technology, and the result was the deposing of a tyrant in favor of Victor Yushchenko.

Four years later, popular resistance in Moldova capitalized on Twitter. Angered by perceptions of fraud in parliamentary elections, citizens erupted in demonstrations and rioting in April 2009. They used Twitter to incite unrest, provide updates on protesters' actions and the government's reactions, and appeal to the international community for help. The protesters used hashtags to group messages under popular headlines, such as "#pman," which stood for "Piata Marii Adunari Nationale," the name of the biggest square in Moldova's capital of Chisinau. The use of the messaging service was so influential in the unrest that the incident became associated with the so-called Twitter Revolution.[315]

Later that year in June, the Green Movement in Iran—an abortive attempt to overthrow the government of President Mahmoud Ahmadinejad—made effective use of Twitter and YouTube to garner international attention. The amateur filming of the shooting death of a young woman named Neda Agha-Soltan appeared on Facebook and YouTube and incited outrage both within Iran and around the world. Protesters even conducted denial-of-service attacks against government websites, prompting the Iranian government to shut down Internet access. As the massive unrest continued, the government also shut down or limited cell phone usage and reinstated Internet access with low bandwidth to try to prevent video footage from being used. The conflict saw both sides very determined to control cyberspace for their own purposes, and both the government and the protesters demonstrated growing technological sophistication and innovation in their attempts to thwart each other.

Mohammed Nabbous, a Libyan businessman and technologist, established an Internet television station that he named "Libya Alhurra" (Free Libya) in Benghazi in February 2011.

Able to thwart government attempts to shut down his broadcasts, Nabbous found a worldwide audience and contributed both to the growing insurgency within Libya and to international outrage and eventual action from NATO. He was eventually shot and killed in a gun battle, but his efforts helped propel the anti-Gaddafi forces to victory over the tyrannical regime.

Education

Bolanieves will need to consider the various levels of education that he should recruit. He may choose to recruit a well-educated group to effectively run the movement but it is possible that these individuals may not be the best recruitment candidates. Some successful resistance leaders (Che Guevara, Mahatma Ghandi, Martin Luther King Jr., Hassan Nasrallah, Abu Bakr al-Baghdadi) were well-educated through formal schooling, but others like Mao Tse-tung and Abu Musab al-Zarqawi had little to no formal schooling. In turn, educated may not be a byproduct of formal education. Mao, for example, was quite intelligent and well-read, but he lacked the formal education of some other resistance leaders.

It is also important for Bolanieves to consider recruiting educated specialists to perform key administrative functions. This form of targeted recruitment tends to emerge once a resistance movement matures to the point of bureaucratization and identifies specific needs to increase and/or expand their capabilities. For example, Osama Bin Laden saw the need for database administrators to support the Mujahedeen in Afghanistan in the late 1980s and recruited them. The Islamic State specifically recruited web developers, software engineers, and/or other specialized skills sets after Baghdadi's seminal Mosul speech.[316] In sum, recruiting a variety of well-educated leaders and targeting the recruitment of specialized skills will support the organizational development and capacity of the resistance movement.

History of Conflict in the Country[317]

Countries with a history of violence are more likely to experience violence in the future.[318] The same is true for countries whose geographic neighbors have experienced violence. There are both psychological and non-psychological reasons for this. The simplest cause may be the available supply of weapons and people trained to use them, either in-country or nearby. When one conflict ends or dies down, both weapons suppliers and soldiers may be unemployed and have few other skills; they may return to their home countries or cross borders as mercenaries. A second reason for the bleed-over of violence across borders may be large numbers of refugees or other displaced persons. These refugees may strain the resources of new areas, leading to violence. Or the refugees may hold claims on their prior land (such as displaced Palestinians) or have other grievances (e.g., lost relatives and friends) to be redressed with violence in a new location.

Bolanieves and Sarca

Bolanieves must be aware and keep track of the various environmental factors surrounding Sarca. Each time Sarca takes an action, including decisions not to act, it interacts with the different environments around it. Those interactions will lead to a feedback loop in which Bolanieves should participate because Sarca does not exist in a vacuum. Whether it is the social context in which Sarca is arguing its case, the physical geography where Sarca bases its operations, or the local economy's environment will be an influential factor. The environmental factors can also range from very simple to the complex. For instance, Sarca members will need to eat, drink, dress, and bathe. Bolanieves will be responsible for finding and securing a place where Sarca members can do this in relative safety. If Bolanieves does not accomplish this, then Sarca members could start leaving because its living environment is untenable. Bolanieves could negotiate for food and supplies from the local population, but if the state threatens the community and makes good on that threat, then Sarca will be forced to find new sources. Bolanieves could face this dilemma in rural and urban areas.

Megacities present complicated environment with social structures, physical terrain, and technological infrastructures with which a resistance movement must engage. Bolanieves and Sarca might represent one segment of society that is disliked by segments of society that dominate and run neighborhoods, impacting their transit routes, supply lines, and supply sources. This would also complicate Sarca's messaging as it tries to build shared resistance against the state across different groups with different ideologies or values. Sarca's values might trigger a rival resistance group to form and present a new challenge for Bolanieves. If Bolanieves permits a culture to grow within Sarca that violates social norms, the resistance can lose its popular support and become easier for the state to target. Alternatively, Sarca could leverage the state's violation of social norms in the city. The physical components of the megacity could provide multiple routes of ingress and egress but also limit Sarca's mobility if the state creates barriers that close off streets, underground tunnels, or other connective infrastructure. Finally, the megacity's technological infrastructure could provide Bolanieves and Sarca strong intelligence and communication capabilities, but if the state takes control of it, that technological infrastructure could become a vulnerability. If it becomes a vulnerability, Bolanieves and Sarca will need to develop alternative approaches.

Questions

Bolanieves and the Sarca movement are shaped by the environment of Estatu. In this section, the reader reviewed the importance of physical environment, state characteristics, social structures, economic factors, technology, education, and conflict history upon the creation of a resistance. By answering the following discussion questions, the reader can demonstrate how these factors can impact the Sarca movement.

INTRODUCTORY - BLOOMS LEVEL ONE

- Identify: What are some examples of environmental factors for the Sarca resistance? Is it limited to physical geography?

INTRODUCTORY - BLOOMS LEVEL TWO

- Identify and Explain: How might the level of openness of the society and state impact Sarca's strategy? Its tactics?

INTERMEDIATE - BLOOMS LEVEL THREE

- Incorporate: How does technology factor in to Sarca's environment for Bolanieves' planning?

INTERMEDIATE - BLOOMS LEVEL FOUR

- Differentiate: What actions of other resistance movements can Bolanieves ignore and which actions he must pay careful attention to?

- Identify and Differentiate: Why might some physical terrains be more or less advantageous for Bolanieves and Sarca?

MASTERY - BLOOMS LEVEL FIVE

- Detect: What important environmental factors would impact Sarca and its capabilities?

ORGANIZATION

Although Bolanieves has begun to identify members for Sarca and to understand the environment, it is clear to him that Sarca also needs a well-defined organizational structure to achieve the movement's strategic goals. Without good organization, the movement would simply be a jumbled collection of people with no leadership or plan and could fall apart quickly. To avoid that, Sarca's organization will have to bring its members together under his leadership to work toward a common goal. For example, if Sarca values media exposure and coverage, Bolanieves would want to develop an active and well-supported media team. However, if Sarca intends to affect the political process, Bolanieves may instead focus on improving public relations and creating a political wing of Sarca.

When looking at other aspects of organization, Bolanieves would have to reflect on his own leadership style, such as whether he wants to have a strict centralized system with himself at the top of the hierarchy or whether he wants to promote more equal relationships that are decentralized across many leaders. His style of leadership will shape Sarca's development, the experiences of the group's members, and ultimately how it carries out its actions. His leadership approach will also set the tone for Sarca's culture and the way all of its subordinate leaders and members interact. Additionally, Bolanieves will have to make decisions on Sarca's messaging and how the group communicates with the public. In order to spread its message and gain greater support for its larger goals, Sarca will need an effective way to reach out to other people. Bolanieves knows he has to give serious thought to all of these issues because most successful movements require effort and vision to evolve the group's organization, command and control, and messaging.

To exercise C2 over the many different participants in a resistance group, resistance leaders need an organizational structure. Ultimately, good organization is critically important for carrying out effective operations and achieving a group's objectives against the government.[319] Even when outnumbered or outgunned against a government, a resistance group can use strong organizational "cohesion and discipline" to overcome its disadvantages.[320]

Although organization in general is important to all resistance groups, it can look very different across individual resistance groups. Many factors, including strategy, objectives, historical background, and available resources, all help determine the organizational structure that best fits a group's needs. For example, if a group wants to lead a revolution and eventually replace the existing government, its structure should be inclusive of new members. It should also have broad administrative features, such as having a branch of the group working on running schools or hospitals to serve the people. That style encourages the public to support the group and trust that it is organized appropriately to govern the country in the future. However, a resistance group based on a specific identity, such as ethnicity, can exclusively organize its leadership, membership, and messaging around promoting that single identity. It does not need a complex structure to gain legitimacy or control other people outside the group.[321]

Movement Structures

The structure of a resistance movement can be defined as the system of relationships in the resistance movement, including how relationships are structured within individual groups and between groups in a larger resistance movement. Both the overarching movement and the individual groups within the movement have their own organizational structures. Sometimes the structures share similar features and characteristics, while other times one group can be very different from its partner groups and the movement as a whole. For example, the organizational structure of the Muslim Brotherhood in Egypt specifically is not the same as its partner groups around the Middle East and Africa or the broader Society of the Muslim Brothers.

Two of the foundational factors of organizational structure are level of formality (the strength of ties between the organizational nodes of the movement) and degree of centralization (hierarchical or networked authority). Adapted from the typology

proposed by Jurgen Willems and Marc Jegers[322] and presented in the ARIS volume *Conceptual Typology of Resistance* with permission, these two factors can be combined and categorized into four different types: formal-centralized, informal-centralized, formal-networked, and informal-networked (see **Figure 8**[323]).

In hierarchical organizations, one leader has authority over the other members and participants, usually due to the leader's control over information and other resources.[324] Alternatively, networked relationships mean actors have relatively equal power status with a "mutual exchange of information [or resources]."[325] Regarding formality, informal relationships tend to be flexible and based on trust or shared "culture, habits, and beliefs."[326] Formal organizations, on the other hand, have a more "rigid" structure "based on a legal system and/or a set of widely accepted rules."[327]

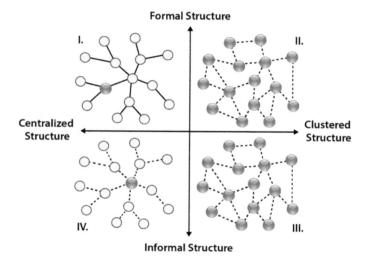

Figure 8. Movement structures.

Dynamics and Characteristics

Although resistance movements and groups usually have common ground and shared beliefs, there can still be sources of division in ideological, religious, social, ethnic, personal, or strategic differences. These dynamics can be examined through the strong or weak sources of division and commonality that the groups may have (see Figure 9).[328]

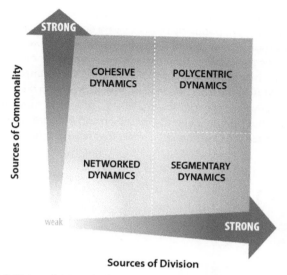

Figure 9. Types of dynamics in resistance movements or organizations.

Cohesive movements or organizations have strong shared beliefs and few divisions, creating more unity. Reversing those features, segmentary movements or organizations have few shared beliefs and many divisions, driving participants apart. Polycentric movements or organizations have both many commonalities and many divisions, which often means there are competing leaders and influences across all the different critical issues. Finally, networked organizations have weak shared beliefs and weak divisions, often leading to loose alliances of convenience. This dynamic can be seen when groups share a common enemy or have some similar beliefs, but are otherwise not strongly connected.[329]

There is no single organizational structure that is best suited for all groups under all conditions. A group must consider a number of major factors to decide the organizational style that will allow it to be most successful. Additionally, on the administrative side the underground must develop an effective organization in order to support its operational missions. This requires resistance groups to perform certain "housekeeping" functions to address problems and challenges.

Available resources and countermeasures employed by governments affect these organizational decisions and functions. As a result, there are many possible techniques and structures for organizing resistance movements and groups. For example, insurgencies in the modern world range from jungle tribes using drums for communication to Internet-savvy urban operatives leveraging the latest technology.

Foreign and Domestic Characteristics of Resistance Movements or Organizations

Resistance movements and groups can have foreign or domestic features in their organizational structures, which may affect recruitment, support, strategy, and many other factors (see Figure 10).[330] When a resistance group or movement is perceived as domestic and operates primarily within the given country, it is a domestic resistance. Although some domestic groups may have a few transnational activities, they are still primarily focused on the domestic issues and are popularly seen as being domestic. Conversely, a truly transnational organization or movement is actually perceived as foreign by the population even if it operates inside the country. Foreign resistance groups or movements are both seen as foreign and operate primarily outside the country. For example, from the point of view of the United States, the Irish Republican Army is a foreign resistance group, as it is both rooted and active in a foreign country. Finally, groups or movements that are perceived as domestic but primarily operate in foreign contexts are called displaced. The most notable example is a government in exile that has been forced out of its home country.

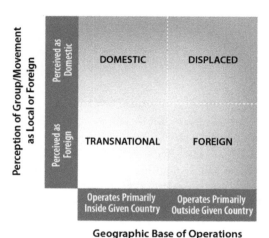

Figure 10. Types of foreign and domestic characteristics in resistance movements or organizations.

Command and Control

JP 3-05.1
III-1, III-34

When looking at the organization of a group, it is important to consider the C2 structures. One organizational theory for resistance groups categorizes a group as either integrated, vanguard, parochial, or fragmented. An integrated group has both strong central leadership at the top and good discipline within the locally-based lower ranks. On the opposite end of the spectrum, a fragmented group fails in both areas, with both weak central leadership and a lack of discipline at the local level. Vanguard groups and parochial groups fall in the middle of these two extremes. A vanguard group has effective top leadership, but struggles to implement the leadership's vision at the local level. Conversely, a parochial group enjoys influence and power at the local level, but the local units lack a strong centralized command at the top that unites all their smaller efforts. These different structures can impact the strength, effectiveness, and survivability of a group over time.[331]

TC 18-01.1
APPENDIX I

ATP 3-05.1
2-21, 2-27,
E-6

Another organizational theory focuses on the idea that the economic resources available to a resistance group shape the organization of that group. If a resistance group can profit from taking valuable resources such as diamonds, oil, or drugs, studies have argued that the group's organization tends to lack discipline and be at higher risk for disintegrating. This may happen because the large amounts of money involved attract members who primarily care about material gain and the money is not used to fund the group's core mission. Conversely, a group with few economic resources must recruit members based on social connections, shared beliefs, and common goals. A group with members who join for these ideological reasons benefits from strong organizational discipline and cooperation.[332]

Pyramid	Equal Interactions	Edge Structure
Centralization has implications for command and control and is worth examining. A classic military unit has a very strict hierarchy, with clear lines of authority, often drawn as a pyramid. Authority is established by one's level and position in the hierarchy.	On the other hand, network structures rely on personal relationships, reputations, and connections to decide authority among people who are equals.	A third option called an "edge" structure has clearer vertical lines of authority and position as in a hierarchy, but is also designed to distribute more authority to individuals and be more flexible as in a network.[333]

Hierarchy, network, and edge structures have different strengths that resistance groups have to consider. Examples of important questions related to the choice of command structure are:

- How important is speed of response? Hierarchical command structures almost always suffer from delays as requests move up and down a chain of command. Meanwhile, network systems typically gain speed but sacrifice reliability and quality control. The speed of competitors or enemy forces and the time window of opportunities drive this decision.

- How important is unity of command? Hierarchical command structures maximize consistency and enable crucial coordination of military, political, and communications actions.

- How important is efficiency? Hierarchical structures maximize efficiency by centralizing systems such as training, and enforcing consistency across the group. However, hierarchies can be increase bureaucracy, thereby increasing time and money.

- Are there cultural reasons to favor centralization? Hierarchies may be preferable when an organization's membership strongly favors it. For example, if a resistance movement recruits heavily from ex-military personnel, military-style organization may be easy to implement. This might also be the case in national cultures that have strong expectations for the roles of leaders and followers.[334]

None of these considerations and trade-offs are set in stone. It is possible to have fast-adapting hierarchies or efficient networks due to well-developed practices, competent leadership, or other factors that affect a specific group. However, these considerations help provide a framework for comparing a centralized hierarchy with a decentralized network.

Centralized and Decentralized Structures

In practice, Bolanieves can develop a balance between centralized and decentralized command and control for Sarca in order to take advantage of both organizational structures. To benefit from centralized strategic decision-making, Bolanieves can issue orders for tactical objectives and recommend activities that he believes can best accomplish the objective from Sarca's central command location in Estatu. If Bolanieves has special assignments for Sarca members, he can also send his own special representative to Sarca's individual units to supervise the operations directly. Furthermore, Bolanieves would have central authority to call for mass demonstrations, strikes, and other mobilizing actions as he sees fit. This allows Bolanieves to measure how quickly Sarca's participants respond to his orders and how many people mobilize for Sarca's causes. However, with such centralized power and importance, Bolanieves would need to have plans to transfer authority or reestablish the chain of command in the event that he is captured or killed.

Yet, to also benefit from decentralization, Bolanieves has the option to grant individual units the authority to devise their own plans for carrying out his orders. Since Bolanieves is often physically located in one central command location, he usually does not know precisely how many members belong to Sarca's individual units in other areas or the specific identities of those members. Furthermore, when working on local issues that he is not familiar with, Bolanieves has found it helpful to allow Sarca's individual local units to make independent decisions with only general guidance from him.

Centralization of Administrative Functions[335]

Resistance movements and groups that exist for a long period of time generally centralize administrative activities in the command. Activities such as fundraising, supply purchases, intelligence analysis, and new recruit security checks may be better performed by the central command, not by the individual units who have fewer resources.

The central command may also be located in a physically safer place than the individual units so that members can meet openly and discuss plans and procedures without fear of being captured or of having records fall into the hands of government security forces. For example, in the Philippines, the Communists had an intelligence analysis and planning command safely located in guerrilla-held territory. Similarly, during World War II, governments that fled from other European countries centralized their operations in England.

Decentralization of Units[336]

However, decentralization also has its own security benefits as the government or other adversaries cannot easily identify the resistance group members or target one single centralized command. In this case, the individual members may not know the real names of their fellow members. If the members operate as an intelligence unit, they may never even come in contact with each other and may only communicate with a leader through intermediaries. Decentralized units also avoid direct contact so if one unit is compromised its members cannot inform on anyone else.

To further reduce the possibility of its members being discovered, the underground decentralizes and disperses its units over widely separated geographic or territorial areas and groups. This extends the government security forces so that they cannot concentrate on any single area or group. Additionally, functions, roles, and duties may be duplicated across multiple different units or networks of units so that there are backup units if some are compromised.

Essentially, a decentralized organization and many of its activities are based upon a "failsafe" principle: if one element fails, there are few serious consequences for the resistance group as a whole. In general, this type of effective decentralization requires two factors: communications technology and highly trained and educated resistance members. First, information technology allows faster, more widespread, and more efficient communication between decentralized units in networks. Second, when intelligent and capable members are available, it is easier to train those members to adapt, coordinate, and optimize actions without direct management.

Evolution and Growth of Organizations[337]

A key factor in an insurgency's success is the adaptability of its leaders and the flexibility of its strategy and ideology.[338] For example, recruiting tactics must change over the course of an insurgency. During the early stages, leaders seek to carefully select, investigate, and approach potential fellow insurgents. During the middle stages of an insurgency, leaders usually have to expand the recruiting effort in order to fill out its membership. It is during this transition period that some revolutionary movements fail while others succeed, and the question often comes down to the organization's ability to find new sources for recruitment and support. During the latter stages of an insurgency, recruiting is characterized by the momentum of the movement. A successful insurgency that is able to either take power (replacing the former government) or achieve political, legal, or quasi-legal status will normally expand recruitment operations.

Ideology serves two purposes in an insurgency: it serves as the basis for recruitment, and it guides strategic direction. Ideology unifies a resistance movement and provides a common perspective from which members can see their environment. An insurgency's ideology can be based on exclusivity or inclusivity as leaders establish the movement's beliefs on any number of social, political, and/or operational issues.[339] Exclusive ideologies define the resistance by contrasting it with the government and set the resistance group apart from other parts of society. Inclusive ideologies, conversely, seek to unify groups and encourage them to come together for a common goal.

Resistance group organizational structures may evolve in response to a changing security environment or to reflect the increasing legitimacy of a movement. The degree to which an insurgency recognizes these internal or external changes and adapts appropriately correlates with longevity. Although restructuring does not come without its costs (for example, the highly ideologically oriented may disapprove of a more inclusive recruiting strategy and thus may discontinue their association with the movement), overly rigid organizations are unlikely to enjoy success.

Messaging[340]

JP 3-05.1
I-16, III-5, III-19,
IV-8, B-3

TC 18-01.1
2-25,
APPENDIX G

ATP 3-05.1
2-27, 3-3,
3-9, 4-2

TC 18-01
1-10, 2-18

Messaging is also an important factor in the organization of a resistance group because it helps with recruiting new members and communicating with the civilian population. To share its message, a resistance group needs to be organized in terms of both its infrastructure and the approach it uses for shaping the message. On the infrastructure side, religious spaces, community centers, social media platforms, and other open spaces offer public forums for resistance messaging to reach potential new members. As a next step, private homes, hidden locations, and restricted social media groups provide opportunities for sharing radical or violent messages underground. Together, these spaces form an organized network through which a group can spread its message.[341] For shaping the message, some groups rely heavily on a single popular leader to create a united identity, while others such as Islamic State have a broad media strategy across multiple issues.[342]

Since a resistance movement is full of competing actors, motivations, and goals, narratives are especially important tools for turning these many different parts into a united story and message.[343] Traditionally, militaries have focused on the impact of kinetic operations on conflict outcome. Studying narratives helps highlight the social and political dimensions of conflict that often remain overlooked when conflict is limited to a purely force-on-force manner. Both the government and the resistance movement seek to influence key members and supporters in ways that favor their political objectives. Narratives affect all of human experience, whether in the social or political realm or at the individual or group level. Therefore, it is important to pay special attention to the role narratives play in resistance — how to mobilize people to participate in organized political support or action. As discussed in previous sections, grievances such as political exclusion, economic hardship, discrimination can all potentially motivate resistance. However, the existence of these issues alone does not always cause resistance by itself. Messaging and narratives can help overcome the many difficulties resistance movements face in mobilizing others to join and support their goals.

For example, narratives can be used to provide legitimacy to government security forces and their actions by creating a positive story and message.[344] A persuasive narrative may help the government justify its use of force and explain why its citizens should support it. On the opposite side, a resistance group can shape its narratives and messages to the public to argue that it should be the legitimate government and to gain sympathetic support. Narratives can also take advantage of culture or other beliefs to craft messages that resonate meaningfully with local supporters.[345] Above all, resistance movements need to leverage narratives to persuade their audiences of the necessity and effectiveness of taking collective action to mobilize and resist in support of the strategic goals. As a result, understanding these narratives and their uses helps with influencing desired outcomes in conflict.

Messaging of Resistance Movements or Groups[346]

Because narrative messaging and media exposure play a significant role in the support for a resistance group, Sarca and Bolanieves would need to communicate with the following groups to some extent:

- *Internal supporters. Sarca needs to communicate internally to spread news that may be suppressed by the government, support Sarca's ideology, provide encouragement, and reinforce loyalty.*

- *External supporters. In Estatu and beyond, Sarca relies on networks of supporters, ranging from local residents, whose main contribution may be forgetting what they have seen when questioned by police, to international sympathizers, who may provide money to Sarca or advocate to foreign governments to support Sarca. Sarca's use of media and messaging will help to preserve this support and encourage sympathy from outsiders.*

- *Non-sympathetic audience. Terrorist groups, in particular, target media at external audiences that do not support them. In this case, the group usually wants to intimidate and terrorize outsiders and gain publicity for the group. Bolanieves would have to consider whether negative messaging is an approach that Sarca would want to employ. He may potentially be advised that using a messaging tactic often associated with terrorists could hurt his ability to gain more support.*

- *The enemy. Sarca could potentially use external communications to demoralize or mislead its enemy combatants. For example, Sarca could learn from the FMLN in El Salvador, which organized a letter-writing campaign that encouraged resistance supporters to write letters to soldiers urging them to desert the military.*

As part of this messaging to different parts of society, Bolanieves and Sarca have several options for media and communication. Most often, resistance movements want to appear united and strong, which would require Bolanieves to create and enforce a united message for all of Sarca's members and activities. A single strong message would show unity and cohesion of the group. If Bolanieves fails to create a shared message that unites the group, he might be faced with conflicting messages from other Sarca members that contradict his official message.

However, a united message is not the only option for Sarca. If Bolanieves does not want to try to impose a single message and wants to avoid potential conflict, he could instead welcome diversity of opinion among Sarca's members. In this context, Bolanieves would work with members to coordinate a message that everyone can debate and finally agree on together. Alternatively, Bolanieves could allow an open forum for Sarca members to voice their different opinions and messages freely.

Finally, once Bolanieves has identified an audience and created the message, Sarca would need a method to carry out distribution of that message. Sarca could use combinations of many different methods to reach out to people: face-to-face conversations, indirect contact, mass public announcements, and private messages can all be adapted for use in different situations.[347] Sarca might use traditional media like newspapers or invest in radio and television broadcasts. Additionally, Bolanieves would need to strategize the best way for Sarca to use the Internet for communications and other important resistance activities.

Narratives[348]

Insurgent groups often employ narratives as a means of communicating grievances, goals, and justifications for their actions within a story-like framework. A narrative has three distinct elements: (1) actors and the physical, social, and informational environment within which they operate; (2) events across time; and (3) causality, with cause and effect attribution.[349] Narratives provide a way to contextualize and justify grievances against the government. Narratives also frame a struggle and tie grievances to specific goals and actions.

Different types of movements will employ different types of narratives that align with their goals. In another volume in the ARIS series,[350] insurgent movements were classified into five types, depicted in the : Revolution to Modify the Type of Government, Revolution Based on Identity or Ethnic Issues, Revolution to Drive Out a Foreign Power, Revolution Based on Religious Fundamentalism, and Revolution for Modernization or Reform (see Table 3[351]).

Table 3. ARIS dataset.

Type of Movement	Group
Revolution to Modify the Type of Government: Common narrative themes are class-based arguments, ideological alternatives to the existing government, and the illegitimacy of the government.	New People's Army (NPA)
	Fuerzas Armadas Revolucionarias de Colombia (Revolutionary Armed Forces of Colombia, or FARC) and the Ejército de Liberación Nacional (ELN)
	Sendero Luminoso
	Iranian Revolution of 1979
	Frente Farabundo Martí para la Liberación Nacional (Farabundo Marti National Liberation Front, or FMLN) of El Salvador
	Karen National Liberation Army (KNLA)
Revolution Based on Identity or Ethnic Issues: Common narrative themes are the existence of distinct cultural or ethnic identities, cultural preservation, unequal treatment of certain groups, and self-determination for different groups.	Liberation Tigers of Tamil Eelam (LTTE)
	Palestine Liberation Organization (PLO)
	Hutu-Tutsi genocides
	Ushtia Çlirimtare e Kosovës (Kosovo Liberation Army, or KLA)
	The Provisional Irish Republican Army (IRA)
Revolution to Drive Out a Foreign Power: Common narrative themes are the desire for independence, the need for reform, and the illegitimacy of the occupying power.	Afghan mujahidin
	Viet Cong (VC)
	Chechen Revolution
	Hizbollah
	Hizbul mujahidin (HM)
Revolution Based on Religious Fundamentalism: Common narrative themes are claims of religious scholarship and interpretation, religious symbology, and the extreme illegitimacy of the government.	Egyptian Islamic Jihad (EIJ)
	Taliban
	al Qaeda (AQ)

Type of Movement	Group
Revolution for Modernization or Reform: Common narrative themes are demands for political inclusion and calls for reform in a specific policy or issue area.	Movement for the Emancipation of the Niger Delta (MEND)
	Orange Revolution of Ukraine
	Revolutionary United Front (RUF)
	Polish Solidarity

Traditional Media[352]

Handbills and newspapers have been important tools for resistance groups for centuries, and they remain so, even as new media replaces them. The two have different purposes: handbills are used for short, often time-dependent and highly localized events; newspapers are aimed at somewhat broader parts of society and broader issues.

As an example of connecting these forms of media with methods of distribution, face-to-face hand delivery of traditional handbills and newsletters seems to be a key to their effectiveness. In the Philippines, Malaya, and Korea, handbills were passed secretly from person to person by hand or by chain letter. Giving a handbill thus implied a proof of confidence, an honor, and a privilege. In fact, it was reported that people saw, read, and remembered more of the handbills handed to them personally than those received by indirect mass distribution.

Global Broadcast Media[353]

Technological changes in broadcast media – which means radio and television before the Internet – have been impacting insurgency groups for at least a century, with particularly dramatic changes around the development of satellite television in the 1980s. Broadcast media provide insurgents with immediate access to large audiences in a way that is more engaging than traditional media. Although it has some limitations, particularly with the requirements for expensive and vulnerable infrastructure, the rise of international broadcast media brought many changes. It not only changed the way insurgent groups publicized themselves, but also changed their targets, their methods, and their goals as well.

The Irgun, a small terrorist offshoot of the Haganah paramilitary organization that was part of the Zionist movement to create a Jewish homeland, was one of the first to recognize and exploit the opportunities international broadcast media provided.[354] The most successful attack Irgun undertook was small but effective because of the gruesome, symbolic images that accompanied it: they publicly hanged two British sergeants in retaliation for the execution of three Irgun terrorists.

Additionally, the hijacking of TWA flight 847 in June 1985 and subsequent hostage taking represented a low point in the media's unwittingly publicizing of attention-seeking terror groups.[355] Hizbollah gunmen hijacked the flight on June 14 with the purpose of exchanging hostages for a group of associates imprisoned in Israel. Over the next several days, the hijackers took the plane back and forth between Algiers and Beirut, releasing non-American passengers along the way and killing one American Navy diver. The crisis became the subject of constant attention by the three major U.S. television networks. "During the 17 day crisis, while Americans were held hostage in Beirut, nearly 500 news segments—an average of 28.8 per day—were broadcast by the 3 major U.S. television networks . . . and their regularly scheduled

programs were interrupted at least eighty times over those 17 days with special reports or news bulletins."[356] The drawn-out nature of the crisis created more media exposure than a single attack or simpler hostage-taking event might have.

From these examples, insurgent groups aspiring to broadcast media coverage could learn lessons for managing the media:

- **Go where the coverage is**. Broadcast media coverage is much easier to gain in urban areas, and the largest cities are the most media saturated.

- **Guarantee access to the media**. Savvy insurgent groups may go out of their way to develop relationships and guarantee access. Former Chechen insurgent leader Shamil Basayev was particularly proactive; he openly courted the media, frequently gave interviews from his command post or living quarters, and had correspondents as guests in his home.

- **Images matter**. A small event with memorable video or imagery may have a greater effect than a larger operation conducted away from cameras.

- **Follow news cycles and provide a sustained trickle of news over time**. Broadcast media thrive on events that are drawn out over time. Media-savvy insurgent groups can sustain attention by providing a steady stream of developments or new information rather than a single rush of information.

Insurgent-Owned Broadcast Media[357]

To avoid the difficulties of managing externally controlled broadcast media, resistance groups have occasionally set up and run their own broadcast media sources. The Farabundo Marti National Liberation Front (FMLN) in El Salvador, Sendero Luminoso in Peru, and the Contras in Nicaragua all used radio to broadcast propaganda aimed both at sympathizers and the neutral population. The FMLN actually operated two stations, including one that temporarily switched from shortwave broadcast to FM and operated from atop the Guazapa volcano outside of the capital, San Salvador. This location presented an excellent broadcast location but was also very vulnerable to attack, requiring a large commitment of manpower to protect the facility. As can be seen from this experience, setting up actual broadcast facilities presents considerable logistical challenges and gives the adversary a fixed, high-value asset that can be attacked.[358]

One of the more successful resistance-run broadcasts is Hizbollah's Al-Mansar television station. Al-Mansar is primarily dedicated to promoting Hizbollah's point of view but is also notable for its variety of programming. Besides news, it broadcasts documentaries such as "My Blood and the Rifle," about Hizbollah's guerilla fighters, and "In Spite of the Wounds," dedicated to individuals who have been injured while fighting against Israel. Even supportive audiences may not be interested in talk formats that present only repetitive, ideological rants. Insurgent media is subject to the same demands for high-quality production and "immediacy, exclusivity, and drama" as other media.

Communication Network[359]

The emergence of the Internet as a globally accessible communications network has changed and will continue to change, the equations for insurgent communications and messaging. Several aspects of the Internet make it particularly valuable to resistance movements and groups:

- **Inexpensive**. Newsletters, historical information, and press releases can be made accessible worldwide for a few dollars a month. Furthermore, groups can cheaply and quickly stream audio or video around the world.

- **Decentralized**. The Internet was developed by the U.S. military to be a communications network that was resistant to disruption at any one node. This decentralized property is a perfect match for modern, stateless insurgencies such as al Qaeda.

- **Anonymous**. The Internet was developed without strong identity verification measures. It is easy to use a fake identity and there are many options for anonymous activity.

The most important current uses of the Internet for undergrounds and insurgencies fall into the following categories.

	Publicity and Communications. Publicity, international media relations, and reports on resistance operations or government abuse are all part of resistance on the Internet. The Internet also helps recruitment, especially from distant locations. Furthermore, more traditional media benefit from Internet distribution. A twenty-six-page pamphlet with instructions for protestors played an important role in the Egyptian revolution and was distributed in either print or pdf format from person to person.
	Targeting the Enemy. A less common goal of Internet communications, but one that still exists, focuses on terrorizing or manipulating the opponent.
	Recruitment and Radicalization. Videos of successful terrorist attacks, guerilla missions, and extreme graphic violence are popular features of sites focused on recruitment. Producing these videos is important enough that a number of violent groups, including Hizbollah, the Chechen resistance, and Al Qaeda, routinely include a videographer as an essential part of an operational team. These videos serve several functions. First, they attract attention and excite passions of sympathizers, particularly young males who may be recruited to perform these types of actions. Second, they create repetitive mental imagery, allowing recruits to imagine themselves as successful operatives. Third, they begin the process of desensitizing recruits to violence and dehumanizing opponents.
	Training. A variety of insurgent groups are experimenting with use of the Internet as a channel for training in operational techniques. Self-training manuals such as The Terrorist's Handbook, The Anarchist's Cookbook, and The Mujahadeen Poisons Handbook are available online. However, some skills such as bomb-making are complex and difficult to learn alone, so online self-training is probably more effective for simply updating already-trained operatives with new information rather than for training absolute novices.

Fundraising.

The first generation of insurgent websites included explicit appeals for online donations; however, subsequent legislation preventing fundraising for terrorist organizations forced this activity underground. Aboveground websites sometimes make money by selling souvenirs and may imply that the money will support the insurgent cause.However, financial transactions are easier to track than other kinds of information that flow over the Internet, making online fundraising more difficult for insurgents than simple Internet recruitment or publicity.

Command and Control.

The Internet can also facilitate command and control. Mass protests sometimes rely on text messages and Twitter to mobilize supporters, share information on issues such as police presence, and publicize the movement. As an example of Twitter's potential influence, on June 16, during Iranian election protests, the U.S. Department of State contacted Twitter to ask them to delay a scheduled server upgrade that might have disrupted Twitter traffic. Later, the Iranian government intentionally disrupted Twitter traffic by shutting down or slowing both Internet and cell phone service in sections of Tehran.

Organization Theories and Membership

JP 3-05.1
IV-1, III-29, B-3

Membership Strategies[360]

In addition to deciding leadership and structure, Bolanieves is responsible for determining the type of members Sarca will recruit. Sarca will need to recruit members to grow, but Bolanieves knows that to be successful Sarca also needs to think about the way that membership affects the organization. Bolanieves can set high barriers to membership to limit Sarca to only elite members or he can open up membership to more people by having low barriers. He will also have to make decision on whether new participants are integrated into the core membership or used in front organizations (see Figure 11).[361]

TC 18-01.1
2-41, C-4

ATP 3-05.1
2-7, 2-24,
3-8, 4-4, E-4,
E-10, F-14

In many resistance movements, recruitment is chaotic and varies widely across the movement, meaning it does not always fit into a perfect framework. However, this is still a good starting place for Bolanieves to think about the organization of recruitment and membership for Sarca.

TC 18-01
2-7, 2-13,
2-16, 2-18

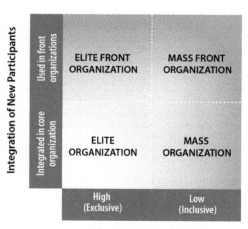

Figure 11. Types of membership strategies in resistance organizations.

Types of Organization

Organizational structure varies with the organizational theories of the resistance or the revolutionary leaders. As discussed earlier in this section, a group's organization should align with the strategy it is pursuing. For example, if a group wants to carry out very complex guerrilla warfare that requires high levels of physical fitness or weapons skills, it would likely need high, exclusive standards for membership. Conversely, if the group wants to mobilize mass protests and marches it would be more effective to have an inclusive membership that welcomes as many people as possible. There is no single answer for the best way to organize a group since every group is different, but this chart provides a way to think about the options and the effect on the group.

Mass Organization[362]

When leaders conclude that a large number of people are necessary to overcome the power of the governing authority and its instruments of force, they may opt for mass organization. Membership is open to anyone who wishes to join, and the objective is to recruit as many people as possible. For the LTTE in Sri Lanka, the attempt to mobilize the entire population in the territory it controlled led it to create in 1999 a policy for a "Universal People's Militia" that would impose military training on anyone over the age of fifteen.[363]

One disadvantage of this organizational structure is the loose security measures associated with it. The members are usually not practiced in security precautions, and the identities of underground members are easily obtained through loose talk and careless, overt actions. However, organizations of this type have managed to minimize the threat of informers primarily through the public sympathy for the movement and through the use of terrorism, as was the case of the Provisional IRA and its practice of "knee-capping" informants. Another disadvantage of mass organization is in the command and control structures, as the large number of members may lack training and discipline. It is then difficult to organize united action against the government.

Elite Organization[364]

The theory here is that a small elite organization can make up in skill and discipline what it lacks in size and that at the proper moment, a small militant group can accomplish more in one blow than a large mass organization can accomplish over a prolonged period of time. The membership in a movement such as this is small, and each individual is carefully screened and tested before he is permitted to join. Once a member, he is subjected to intensive training and discipline to develop the skills necessary for clandestine work. This type of organization usually works toward a coup d'état, or a revolution from the top. In a police state, where the mechanisms of internal security are extensive, this is the most common form of resistance. The disadvantages of this type of organization can include that it must remain relatively inactive while waiting for the proper moment, and inactivity usually works against a movement because its members may lose their enthusiasm, as well as small numbers can limit the types of actions they can undertake.

Elite-Front Organization[365]

Communist insurgents have historically worked from this type of organizational theory. Recruitment is very selective, and the core party itself does not expand rapidly. Instead, a

"front" organization is created that claims to seek some popular objective such as liberation or independence. Within the front movement, Communists organize military and civilian groups and take leadership positions. If the front group fails, the core Communist resistance is not damaged either organizationally or by reputation because it is the front group and not the Communists who lose the insurgency. On the other hand, if they are successful, the Communists are in firm control of the revolutionary organization.

Internal Governance[366]

The internal governance of a resistance organization relates to several concepts. Command and control, which has already been discussed in depth, fundamentally shapes the nature of authority and governance in the resistance group. However, in addition to command and control, other factors directly contribute to governance. First, disciplinary measures and rules enforce the objectives of internal governance on members. Second, organizational culture affects member behavior within the group.

Discipline and Rules[367]

Internal discipline may include oaths; rigid codes of conduct; standing orders and standing operating procedures; operation orders; military manuals; internal organization documents on issues such as command structure and authority; and penal or disciplinary codes.[368] Another instrument for internal governance is a founding charter, which more generally addresses the goals and vision of the resistance and is written for both internal members and the wider public.

Organizational Culture[369]

Resistance groups are composed of individuals who must collectively coordinate their efforts toward the achievement of shared, common goals. Therefore, it is worth looking at how resistance members interact and the type of group culture they develop.

Various studies created a framework that examines a group's acceptance of culture dissonance, or cultural differences and disagreements, and the antagonism, or hostility, of relationships between group members (see Figure 12).[370]

First, an organizational culture of rivalry exists when cultural differences are accepted but relationships are hostile. This results in a culture characterized "by strong rivalry" where "members believe that it is necessary to prove their superiority."[371]

Second, organizations have a culture of dominance when there is both a lack of acceptance of cultural differences and hostile relationships between various types of groups, cultural and otherwise. In this case, members hold the "belief that they are superior" to others. Dominance cultures also usually make cultural beliefs and expectations one of the most important factors in deciding the group's actions.[372] Because of the fundamental nature of resistance and the groups that practice it, the vast majority of resistance organizations and movements should theoretically have cultures of dominance.

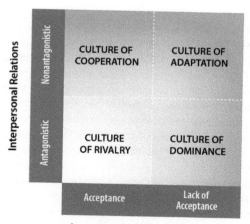

Figure 12. Types of organizational cultures (Sikorski and Sułkowski).

Third, in a culture of adaptation, the organization remains unaccepting of cultural differences, but relationships are not hostile. Adaptation cultures place significant weight on the quality of interpersonal bonds and similarities, but also tolerate uncertainty and often look to the future.[373]

Finally, organizational cultures of cooperation (likely the least common organizational culture among resistance groups), have both the acceptance of cultural differences and non-hostile relationships. As such, they have more "harmony" and avoid of "conflicts and rivalry." This includes employing democratic management styles that value personal bonds and communication under "equality" and "respect for differences."[374]

Environmental factors may significantly influence how the culture of a resistance organization develops. Additionally, the organizational structure of the group often affects or is affected by the organizational culture of the resistance group. For example, lack of trust due to security necessities can lead to dominance cultures, as the group wants members to conform to group requirements for cultural and security reasons. *Bolanieves will need to balance the need to retain operational security with empowering members of the movement to engage within the movement itself.*

Bolanieves and Sarca

After considering all of these aspects of organization, Bolanieves has many decisions to make on the type of structure, leadership, messaging, governance, and culture he wants to develop for Sarca. The type of authority he chooses to establish, centralized or decentralized, could have large effects on Sarca operations and functions. After establishing his authority, Bolanieves also needs to consider the internal culture that Sarca will promote among its members. Interactions and acceptance of different people and perspectives would create a very different atmosphere than a more hostile and exclusionary environment. There are also questions for Sarca's messaging because messaging is crucially important for recruiting members, gaining supporters, and highlighting Sarca's positions and goals. Bolanieves' use of different types of media and distribution methods could determine who Sarca can reach in Estatu and where the message can spread. Sarca's organization affects all components from the top-level structure of the group to the individual members to the people of Estatu. Ultimately, his decisions will help determine Sarca's in pursuing its strategic goals.

Questions

The reader now understands the dynamics of organizational features on the capacity of a resistance movement. Using the following discussion questions, explore components of the movement's structure, C2 (including communications), organizational theories and membership, and internal governance. Examine how these factors will, in particular, be important for Bolanieves and Sarca movement.

 INTRODUCTORY - BLOOMS LEVEL ONE

- Identify: Who should Sarca target with messaging?

 INTERMEDIATE - BLOOMS LEVEL FOUR

- Differentiate: What types of media will be most effective, engaging, safe, secure, and distributable for Sarca?

- Attribute: Does Bolanieves want Sarca to be accepting of different viewpoints or be more exclusive among its member beliefs? What would be most effective for achieving Sarca's objectives?

MASTERY - BLOOMS LEVEL FIVE

- Critique: In what ways can Bolanieves enforce internal discipline for Sarca and create a group culture?

- Use Criteria for Evaluation: How should Bolanieves make a decision on whether to be a centralized, hierarchical leader or a decentralized leader who shares authority with other Sarca commanders?

ACTIONS

The act of resistance can manifest in either violent or non-violent strategies and employ a wide variety of tactics within those overarching strategies. Once decided, a resistance group's chosen actions define the nature of the movement and the impact it has on the government.

It is important to acknowledge that in some cases a resistance group is not in control of the actions of all its members. If a group suffers from weak leadership or top leaders are killed in targeted strikes, violence could escalate as lower ranking members are empowered to potentially follow personal incentives for attacking and harming people with little oversight from official leaders.[375] However, in other cases, a group has the ability to explicitly evaluate the political utility and propriety of engaging in violence or remaining non-violent to achieve its goals.[376] In this way, it can plan its resistance tactics and organize its other activities, such as fund-raising and training, in accordance with its desired strategy.

In a democracy, violence may not be necessary since there are peaceful sociopolitical vectors through which people can gain representation or participate in government, and in a heavily repressive dictatorship violence may be unsuccessful against powerful government security forces.[377] Additionally, violence can limit opportunities for a group to obtain change, particularly when violence leads the government to refuse to negotiate or make concessions on principle, as often occurs with terrorist groups.[378] As such, non-violence is often a reasonable strategy with both pragmatic and moral advantages.[379] In particular, non-violent movements create a more appealing environment for mass participation by lowering the barriers to entry – fewer physical fitness requirements or moral challenges in attracting people to join – and can then leverage that broad support to achieve desired outcomes.[380] Within this non-violent framework, a resistance group can benefit from monetary donations,[381] use unique tactics such as subversive humor,[382] and even attend classes taught by groups that have conducted successful non-violent campaigns.[383]

However, violence is still a viable, powerful option that can be an effective means to quickly exert change on a weaker regime,[384] intimidate political candidates and voters,[385] or fight for influence in a highly competitive political arena crowded with numerous factions.[386] It can also provide the means for a group that feels unjustly relegated to a low status to aggressively fight for higher status against a dominant rival.[387]

Occasionally, violence even becomes an attractive force for its own sake, as a group can celebrate sacrifice and glorify violent acts in its efforts to recruit new members.[388] Violence can further extend to other functions, such as opening new vectors for fund-raising by enabling threats of violence for extortion payments or involving a group in lucrative drug trafficking.[389]

Tactics

JP 3-05.1
I-13 TO I-19,
II-11, IV-2

Once Sarca has members, supporters, and an organizational structure, it will be time for Bolanieves and Sarca to act. Resistance requires action and Bolanieves knows Sarca will have to take that step. However, before carrying out acts of resistance, Bolanieves must decide on and shape the tactics that Sarca will use. Sarca's actions can be legal or illegal, and violent or nonviolent (see Figure 13).[390] Bolanieves must think about the variations and combinations of violence and legality to decide what is best for Sarca.

TC 18-01.1
2-33, 2-34,
2-58, A-3,
A-8

In the category of legal nonviolent resistance, rightful resistance tactics are similar to conventional political and activist efforts. Sarca can make use of these tactics when needed or when they would be effective, such as encouraging a protest or strike in Estatu, but these tactics alone would not necessarily qualify as resistance.

ATP 3-05.1
2-1, CHPT 3,
E-8

The vast majority of violent resistance tactics that Sarca would use are illegal. If Sarca's resistance eventually progressed to the point of looking more like traditional interstate war, Sarca's actions could be recognized as legal under international laws of war. However, in general, most of Sarca's resistance tactics would continue to be illegal under domestic laws within the country.

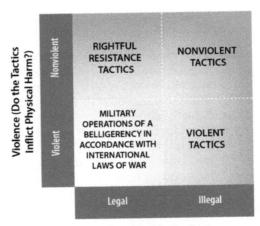

Figure 13. Types of resistance tactics.

Violent Tactics[391]

When focusing in on use of physical violence, Bolanieves must consider the lethality of the tactics Sarca is willing to use. Bolanieves would expect lethal violent tactics to result in deaths, while he would intend for nonlethal violent tactics to only result in some harm or damage.

Bolanieves could decide to take the path of paramilitary operations and guerrilla and insurgent groups, including small-arms and light-weapons combat and the use of explosive mines and improvised explosive devices, and mortar and rocket attacks. He could also authorize targeted killings and assassinations of Sarca's enemies. Other resistance movements willing to use lethal violent tactics, often at an asymmetric disadvantage in numbers and resources, may resort to terrorism.

Bolanieves also has nonlethal violent options for Sarca's actions. Nonlethal violent tactics include violent but nonlethal riots and mobs that Sarca could organize, as well as various forms of nonlethal crime and intimidation, such as extortion and kidnapping. Sexual violence is another tactic that applies to this group. With nonlethal tactics, it is important for Bolanieves to remember that some actions intended to be nonlethal, such as protests, can become lethal if they escalate into greater levels of violence.

Escalation of Violent Actions[392]

Besides moral justification, groups also escalate their violent actions over time as they individually and collectively desensitize themselves to violence. Many law enforcement organizations have employed a staged approach to assess this mechanism. The Seven-Stage Hate Model, depicted in Figure 14,[393] comprises the following.

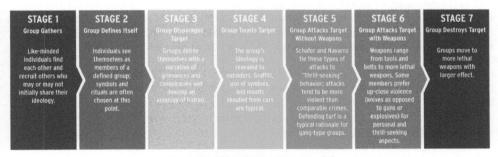

Figure 14. Seven-stage hate model.

The personal story of Lars, a former member of Norway's right-wing extremist National People's Party, illustrates the process of one person working through these stages.[394] Lars, who would later be imprisoned for bombing a mosque, began his involvement with no particular hatred toward Muslims or other groups targeted by the National People's Party. Instead, he began as a lonely and disconnected teenager in Oslo. He contacted the party after seeing a bumper sticker and was unaware of their political views; he was invited to gather with other young people at a social event (Stage 1). After becoming involved socially, he became exposed to the group ideology of hatred. The ideology at this point began to be a part of identity (Stage 2) but not yet a matter of political urgency. Gradually, he began to take part in small acts of aggression against opportunistic targets, such as small shops owned by Pakistani and Indian immigrants. Taunting (Stage 4) took the form of surveillance

and putting glue in the door locks at night. Smashing shop windows was another small escalation (Stage 5). Only after these lines were crossed was Lars encouraged, indirectly, to make an attack with some dynamite stolen from a construction site (Stage 6). He intended to commit only property damage in this attack, but several people were injured. Presumably Lars might have escalated to more lethal attacks had he not been arrested and undergone an ideological transformation in prison.

Thresholds of Violence[395]

JP 3-05.1
III-24

Violence is a double-edged sword for the resistance and the government. Both sides need to engage in violence to win, but both sides are also competing for the support and sympathy of the population. "On the one hand violence is needed to fight the other side and perhaps deter individuals in the population from supporting the other side, but on the other hand it can turn the population against the source of that violence."[396] Scholars have

ATP 3-05.1
E-13

supported this common sense idea with the equivalent response model.[397]

The equivalent response model (see Figure 15)[398] simply explains that there are a lower and upper threshold to the level of violence used. The lower threshold is the minimum amount of violence or force necessary for effectively responding or harming your opponent. Act below that threshold and it either has no impact on the adversary, or it makes the actor look weak and lose support of the population. The upper threshold is the maximum amount of violence or force that can be used before the actor loses popular support either because the violence harms the community or because it brings a response from the adversary that harms the community. Accordingly, to use violence effectively a resistance and a government must operate in the zone in between the lower and upper thresholds. Crucially, these thresholds are determined by the communities and are constantly changing.

Accordingly, Bolanieves needs to stay up to date about how the populations feel and perceive the amount of force and violence being used, both by Sarca and the government. That requires an advanced intelligence capability and continuous assessment. Misreading the level of acceptable violence can prove damaging to Sarca even if its operation successfully destroys government assets.

Speaking of the use of violence by the IRA, Darby noted:

> On the evidence of the IRA's use of legitimate targeting, its denials of unwanted casualties, its exclusion of certain groups from attack and its care to anticipate internal criticism, it is clear that the IRA is aware of the limits of its own community's tolerance. The need to maintain the tolerance has been a major restraint on its escalation of its campaign of violence towards a more genocidal indiscriminate slaughter. The instruments for measuring the community's toleration are not precise ones. The limits are often defined only when they are breached, and the community indicates by the means of communication at its disposal that the violence has gone too far.[399]

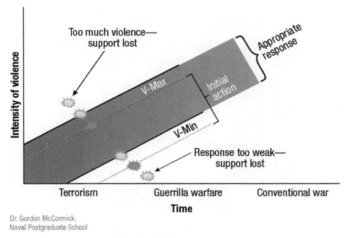

Dr. Gordon McCormick,
Naval Postgraduate School

Figure 15. Equivalent response model.

Attribution of Violent Actions[400]

The attribution of resistance actions is a critical strategic decision, particularly for violent movements that might seek to either take credit for successful strikes against opponents or avoid blame for potentially unpopular operations or mistakes. With attribution, the resistance group chooses whether to publicize its actions or not. However, the group cannot control how much the general public or opponent knows if information is exposed in other ways. This results in four scenarios for attribution of violent actions: clandestine operations, exposed operations, public operations, and suppressed or ignored operations (see Figure 16).[401]

First, clandestine operations are those in which the role of the resistance organization is successfully concealed from the public and opponent. Suspicions about the resistance group's involvement may exist, but the group does not openly take credit for the action and may actively deny involvement.

Exposed operations are those in which the resistance tried to conceal its role in a given action but was exposed by its opponents or other external actors such as journalists. This scenario can lead to blame for the consequences of the action, the prosecution of participants for their roles, or negative propaganda against an operational failure.

Public operations are those in which the resistance group readily and publicly accepts attribution for its actions. Usually the group will either openly identify as a participant or claim attribution for the action.

Finally, suppressed or ignored operations are those in which the resistance group wants to publicize and announce its role in a given action, but that attribution is overshadowed. Knowledge of the group's role is then suppressed or credited to another group.

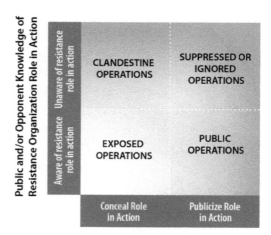

Figure 16. Types of action attribution

Nonviolent and Rightful Resistance[402]

In his book The Politics of Nonviolent Action, scholar Gene Sharp presented a thorough accounting of the types of non-violent resistance, which became widely known as his 198 methods.[403] There has been no effort here to differentiate between particular methods as either legal (rightful resistance) or illegal (nonviolent tactic), as this categorization will differ for every country or city based on local laws and environments.

Although exhaustive when originally written in 1973, the advent of the Internet and the widespread availability of innovative information technologies have dramatically changed the face of resistance movements and created a vast number of completely new tactics. For the thorough and effective analysis of modern cases of resistance, there is a glaring need to expand Sharp's methods to include both methods of cyber protest and noncooperation and methods of nonviolent cyber intervention.

However, his methods are still relevant for many other aspects of resistance that still remain important to resistance groups and movements and their members and supporters. These non-violent and rightful resistance actions are still open for people to join and contribute their support for pressuring the government. Sharp's methods of nonviolent action can be found in the appendix for further exploration. Next, this section will discuss broader themes that help with thinking about and understanding all of these different actions.

Sharp's key theme that shapes these 198 methods of non-violent resistance is that political power is not derived from the qualities of those in positions of authority. Rather, the power of any state is derived from the consent of the governed, and the people have the moral and political authority to take the power back. Essentially, leaders lack power without the consent of the people they govern. Since the government usually holds the monopoly on the use of force, nonviolent methods are the ideal means for the people to impose their will on the state.[404] The arsenal of the passive resister contains a number of weapons of nonviolence. One reason these weapons may be effective is that the government forces may not know how to cope with nonviolence. Police and soldiers are trained to fight force with force but are usually "neither trained nor psychologically prepared to fight passive resistance."[405]

Actions of passive resistance may range from small isolated challenges to specific laws to complete disregard of governmental authority, but the techniques of nonviolent resistance have been classified into three general themes: attention-getting devices, noncooperation, and civil disobedience. These three themes take the different approaches that resistance can use, and organizes and unites them under these themes that describe the level and effect of resistance. For example, Sharp's action number eight of "communicating with slogans, caricatures, and symbols" is a different action from number fifty-four of "turning one's back to renounce" something. However, both could be for the purpose of attention-getting and publicizing the resistance movement's goals. Similarly, noncooperation could have many different types of actions, but they are all united by the common intent of refusing to cooperate correctly with the government's wishes and throwing a wrench into the government's plans.

Attention-Getting Devices[406]

Passive resistance in the early stages usually takes the form of actions calculated to gain attention, provide propaganda for the cause, or be a nuisance to government forces. These actions force the authorities to choose between allowing such activities to continue and taking the risk that the resistance will gain influence, or imposing harsh punishment on people who are engaged in a nonviolent and seemingly harmless activity.[18] Attention-getting devices include demonstrations, mass meetings, picketing, and the creation of symbols to bring attention to the resistance and educate the public about the goals of the resistance. Symbols can include martyrs, religious leaders, flags, and certain symbolic actions, such as during World War II when the King of Denmark would ride his horse through the capital city of Copenhagen despite the Nazi occupation. Other unique attention-getting actions involve the use of humor to attract supporters and joke about the government or the use of nuisance activities to annoy government forces, such as when Algerian children would publicly spit on French soldiers.

Noncooperation[407]

Techniques of noncooperation call for a passive resister to perform normal activities in a purposefully different way, but not so that police or government can make accusations of breaking ordinary laws. Activities such as "slowdowns," boycotts of all kinds, and various forms of disassociation from government are all examples of noncooperation. There are numerous examples of noncooperation in the anti-Nazi resistance movements, including workers in shipping departments of Nazi factories addressing shipments to the wrong address or conveniently forgetting to include items in the shipments. Feigned sickness was also widespread.[408] In Yugoslavia, railroad workers used a particularly effective noncooperation technique: during an Allied air raid, they deserted their jobs and, after the raid, they stayed away for twenty-four hours or more because of "feigned fear." This seriously delayed railway traffic.[409] As a result, these acts of noncooperation harmed the Nazi war effort while appearing simply to be honest mistakes.

Noncooperation is a principal tool of passive resistance and has been shown to be most effective in disrupting the normal processes of society and challenging a government—all in a way that is difficult for the government and its security forces to challenge. Many individuals altering their normal behavior only slightly can still add up to a society behaving most abnormally.

Civil Disobedience[410]

Mass participation in deliberately unlawful acts is considered civil disobedience. This is perhaps the most extreme weapon of passive resistance. Although it usually involves misdemeanors and other minor crimes, the boundary between those small crimes and potential serious crimes can be considered the dividing line between nonviolent and violent resistance. Forms of civil disobedience include the breaking of specific laws, such as tax laws (nonpayment of taxes), traffic laws (disrupting traffic), and laws prohibiting meetings, publications, free speech, and so on. Civil disobedience can also take the form of certain kinds of strikes and walkouts, mass resignations, and minor destruction of public or private property.

For example, in Palestine, after the Haganah raided the British and hid in a nearby village, passive resistance by the Jewish population was effective in preventing their capture. When the police began a search, people vigorously refused them entrance to their homes, stopping only short of using weapons. Additionally, sirens would alert villagers to the British arrival in an area, prompting villagers to rush into that area and flood it with people in order to confuse the British in their search for the resistance fighters.[411]

Civil disobedience is a powerful technique, but to be effective, it must be exercised in large numbers. There is a calculated risk involved - breaking the law automatically justifies punishment by the government and security forces. However, the more massive the scale on which civil disobedience is organized, the less profitable it is for the government to carry out punishments. For example, Gandhi led so many millions of people in the breach of law that it proved impractical, if not impossible, for the British to jail all offenders. As the jails became impossibly full, Gandhi's position in making demands on the government significantly increased.[412]

Organizers of passive resistance are selective about the laws that are to be broken. The laws should be related in some manner to the issues being protested or the demands being made. Examples are Gandhi's selection of the salt tax in India, which was considered a hardship tax on the peasants and representative of unjust British rule and the civil rights sit-ins in the United States, which were directly related to discrimination in public places. Finally, hacktivism, or hacking for a political purpose, brings methods of civil disobedience to cyberspace.[413] Hacktivist tactics include numerous evolving techniques such as denial-of-service (DOS) attacks, automated e-mail bombs, and computer viruses and worms.

Normative Factors[414]

One method by which leaders of passive resistance movements secure widespread legitimacy is by cloaking their movement and techniques in the beliefs, values, and norms of society—those things people accept without question.

For example, the clergy led the earliest stages of the Norwegian resistance against the Nazi occupation. The religious leadership of Norway turned public opinion against the Nazis by invoking the voice of the church and refusing to cooperate in religious affairs with the Nazi occupation.[415] Because the institutions of religion were held in high esteem, and because the clergy appealed to religious values, the Nazis never were able to break the church's resistance.

Mystical Factors[416]

Rare or extraordinary factors such as charisma play an important part in mobilizing public opinion in a passive resistance movement. Gandhi's leadership of India's independence struggle verged on the mystical. Thousands of villagers from rural India, who perhaps could not be touched or aroused by any modern means of communication or organized population pressure, were mobilized into action by Gandhi's fasts and his religious mystique.

Consensual Validation[417]

The technique of "consensual validation"—in which the simultaneous occurrence of events creates a sense of their validity—is often used to unite public opinion. For example, if demonstrations take place at the same time in diverse parts of a country, the resistance cause appears to be valid and right simply because many people are involved. Ostracism, or social exclusion and shunning, is frequently used to apply social pressure on individuals not participating in the passive resistance campaign.

Undermine Military and Security Services[418]

A primary strategy of insurgent forces is to seek to undermine the authority and influence of the opposing military and security services. Highlighting and bringing attention to abuses committed by the government often turns the population against the government and increases support for the insurgency.

In the absence of abuse, or in situations where abuse by government security or military organizations has not recently occurred, insurgent groups may spread false reports about new abuses or, in some cases, conduct abuses themselves but blame the military or security apparatus. In an extreme scenario, that became a violent strategy, an insurgent group can conduct atrocities against the population and then blame these actions on the governing military force, as the RUF rebels did in Sierra Leone when they performed "false flag operations" while wearing Sierra Leone Army uniforms during some of their raids and attacks on villages.[419]

Economic Degradation[420]

Deliberate degradation of the economic capabilities of a country or government reduces its financial stability and creates hardships for the general population. This often leads to popular backlashes against the government. In Nigeria, where the country's economy is depends on oil revenues, the MEND periodically targeted the oil industry in order to force the Nigerian government to give in to its demands.

Removal of Dangerous Persons[421]

Some resistance groups may believe that certain people in the government or society pose a potential risk to the insurgency because of their role in active countermeasures or ability to undermine the resistance's influence. In these situations, nonviolence may beget violence, whereby the resistance may cross the threshold of violence when deciding to remove the person through kidnapping, intimidation, or murder.

Undermine Political Authority and Morale[422]

A central approach for undermining the government is to carry out actions that weaken the political authority of this government. This includes actions such as a resistance group establishing a shadow government to provide services to the population or holding its own elections independent of the official government.

Organizational Subversion[423]

The ability of a resistance movement to influence or control key organizations in a country can shape the strategy and outcome of the insurgency. For example, in El Salvador and Northern Ireland, where the Catholic Church is very influential, the ability to obtain support from priests and nuns provided a degree of legitimacy to the insurgencies that were taking place.

Intelligence[424]

To perform many of the actions, organization, and functions discussed in this book requires gathering intelligence about the adversary, its own members, and the larger populations. Other intelligence targets and subjects include political developments, lucrative targets for attack, defectors, social dynamics, and criminal activity. The information and insight gathered from intelligence will support Bolanieves' decision-making and Sarca's tactics and strategy.

Resistance movements usually build intelligence networks out of the other preexisting social, political, and messaging networks. Additionally, because the group membership commonly comes from the areas in which they operate, they have the advantage of knowing the human and physical terrain, whether rural or urban. Supporting the population incentivizes those preexisting networks to participate in intelligence. For example, the communist NPA in the Philippines won the loyalty of the people with economic advocacy and opportunities for democratic organization. As a consequence, local populations provided accurate, timely intelligence concerning government operations and countermeasures.[425]

Intelligence operations also take place outside the country in populations sympathetic to the resistance for purposes of logistics, procurement, and knowing international attitudes. For example, the LTTE maintained more than fifty offices and cells in foreign countries with large numbers of Tamil expatriates. Canadian intelligence discovered that the LTTE had communication hubs in Singapore and Hong Kong to facilitate its weapons procurement activities, with secondary cells in Thailand, Pakistan, and Myanmar and front companies in Europe and Africa. From these locales, LTTE operatives coordinated purchases and shipments from Asia, Eastern Europe, the Middle East, and Africa.[426]

JP 3-05.1
II-6

TC 18-01.1
A-8

ATP 3-05.1
2-27, 3-38

TC 18-01
2-19

Military Intelligence

To increase the effectiveness of operations and reduce the risk to the armed component, resistance groups need timely and accurate intelligence. Resistance groups, however, typically do not have the kinds of intelligence methods and tools that governments do, so they rely on infiltrating society and building networks of operatives and supporters. The Viet Minh manual referred to auxiliary members who collected intelligence as popular antennae. One example is the Vite Minh's use of children playing near Japanese and later French bases to gather information that untrained children could easily gather, such as troop movements and timing, as well as guard systems. *If Sarca and Bolanieves pursue this tactic, they will need to learn how to ask children the right questions and how to convince them to participate. Likewise, Sarca will want to gather that information from children in a manner that does not endanger the children so as not to alienate the community and lose popular support.*

If a foreign government is supporting the resistance, intelligence can be one form of that support. Military advisors or companion forces can provide targeting information or give technical direction for intelligence gathering on the resistance's own. Most resistance members, after all, will commonly lack experience in intelligence because they come from diverse backgrounds. If foreign government forces are not able to be present with the resistance group, they can also provide manuals that the resistance can use to learn on their own. For instance, during World War II the Soviet Union distributed detailed booklets, such as the *Guide Book for Partisans*, in regions under German occupation. The following excerpt from a passage in this manual is a typical instruction:

> If you happen to encounter troops . . . do not show that you observe the enemy . . . ascertain the colour of their headgear, their collar braid, and the figures on their shoulder straps. If they have questioned the inhabitants about something, try to find out what the Fascists have asked.[4277]

Communications technology that the government uses can be a source of intelligence if the resistance can intercept messages or capture the hardware, such as radios. For example, the Karen National Liberation Army in Burma captured VHF radios during operations and used them to gather information about the Burmese military's operations and movements. Another source can be industry or other civilian entities with knowledge of infrastructure or buildings like factories. If the resistance targets infrastructure or government facilities, those who operate in them, built them, or keep records about them can provide key information for sabotage operations. That intelligence should also include which targets will inflict the most damage. These sabotage operations might be used to hinder government operations or to interfere with the government's ability to provide services and thereby undermine its legitimacy. The FARC and Sendero Luminoso practiced this approach.

An example from World War II shows how intelligence can be collected by multiple components of a resistance and used by its military forces. Prior to the blowing up of a Norwegian heavy-water plant being operated by the Germans during World War II, the preliminary reconnaissance was done by a Special Operations Executive agent parachuted into Norway. Details about the factory's equipment were obtained from a Norwegian scientist in London. Other data, perhaps about the guard system and access to the equipment, apparently were supplied by underground workers in the plant.

Political Intelligence

Resistance groups need to know the political state of affairs and the direction social and political dynamics are developing. Recall that this is key to staying with the thresholds of violence. *It is also critical to deciding on Sarca's tactics and strategy.* If it moves in the opposite direction from the popular political direction it risks losing support and effectiveness. The Orange Revolution in Ukraine provides a very good example. The ability to rapidly acquire and distribute nonpartisan election data on the Internet, radio, and television enabled the resistance to target their messaging to populations in the districts where the voting was rigged. Providing clear evidence quickly mobilized individuals and garnered international support.[428]

Part of political intelligence is not only the attitudes of society, but the morale of the adversary's forces. For example, Polish civilians who worked in the postal service during German occupation read and photographed mail sent to German soldiers, providing an estimate of troop morale. Knowing that information can enable the resistance to tailor its messaging to that audience to undermine their effectiveness or sow discord in their ranks.

Fundraising

To achieve its objectives and carry out operations over long periods of time, Sarca must fund-raise and obtain money. Sarca cannot do anything significant without money. Bolanieves knows that sustaining and growing a movement into something that will lead to change requires time, patience, and above all, money. As a result, one of Bolanieves key resistance functions is raising money, and he has many options for how to obtain that money. His decisions on fund-raising tactics could have a direct impact on the nature, ideology, and strategy of Sarca.

Sarca may need money to meet the following expenses: the salaries of full-time Sarca members; the purchase of materials, such as Internet access, for propaganda publications; the purchase of explosives and other supplies for sabotage; aid to families who shelter refugees; aid to the families of Sarca members who have been captured or forced to flee; and money to families of suicide bombers or other "martyrs." Money is also often needed for bribery since Sarca may need to pay money to key officials in Estatu to obtain their protection or silence. Bribery also plays a part in the gathering of intelligence if Sarca needs to buy information.

Finally, if Bolanieves wants to carry out social outreach work and shadow government activities, such as providing school and hospital services to people in Estatu, Sarca will need additional money to fund that work. Just as legitimate state governments struggle with the rising cost of medical care, unemployment insurance, food aid, housing subsidies, and pensions, Sarca could also end up struggling to provide similar services in an attempt to undermine the government, care for people in their areas of control in Estatu, and provide a cover for illegal and violent activities. Aware that these activities are expensive and require sustained and reliable income, Bolanieves has to consider how he will fund-raise and who he will work with for fund-raising.

External Sources of Money[429]

Foreign Governments. Often an underground is aided by an outside sponsor, usually a government. Much of the money used by the anti-Nazi Belgian resistance of World War II, for example, came from franc reserves in London released by the British government. The Viet Cong's resistance against the government of South Vietnam and its American allies was funded by both China and the Soviet Union. Some external sponsors, such as Colonel Muammar Gaddafi in Libya, supported a number of different insurgencies. Foreign governments extend support to undergrounds for several reasons. The most important is that the activities of the resistance often contribute to the defeat of a common enemy.

Non-State Actors. In addition to governments, friendship societies or quasi-official aid groups may channel funds to a resistance movement. Perhaps the best known of the latter was the Jewish Agency, which, during the Palestine revolution, had offices or representatives in every part of the Western world. In the run-up to the Israeli War for Independence, Palestinian Jews obtained critically needed financing from fellow Jews throughout the world, especially in Europe and the United States. Open appeals for money were made in newspapers and lectures and at charity balls and other social events.[430] Similarly, the main source of overseas funding for the NPA in the Philippines during the Ferdinand Marcos administration was from humanitarian organizations, including a number of European churches, and radical groups in Europe.

Cash in the Local Currency. Aid is often given in the form of cash in the local currency, which has the advantage of being easily exchanged for goods or services. The main problem is the physical transfer of the money. Usually this is handled by a front business organization, through diplomatic channels, through clandestine couriers, or by infiltrated agents.

Substitute Currency. Hard currency, such as U.S. dollars or British pounds, is sometimes given to a resistance group when the sponsoring government lacks adequate amounts of the local currency. Hard currency makes a good substitute because it is easily exchanged on the black market for local currency or goods.

Counterfeit Money. One other way to finance a resistance movement is through counterfeit money. Since resistance groups usually lack the necessary facilities and technical skills to counterfeit money, the main effort is generally carried out by friendly governments.

Online Fraud. Insurgencies increasingly use illegal online operations to steal money or goods. Techniques include credit card and online banking fraud. In some cases, insurgents purchase stolen credit card or bank account numbers and passwords from criminal organizations and then use that information to withdraw money from compromised accounts or to buy goods directly. This avenue of obtaining funds illegally features an ongoing conflict between insurgents exploiting vulnerabilities in global computer networks and various government and international organizations attempting to fix those vulnerabilities and shut down online fraud through technical means, legislation, and enforcement.

Parallel Financial Systems[431]

Islamic history and culture gave rise to an innovative and effective approach to financing insurgency as practiced by members of the Muslim Brotherhood and al Qaeda. Hasan al-Banna, the founder of the Muslim Brotherhood, viewed finance as a critical weapon in undermining the infidels and reestablishing the Islamic caliphate. To do so, he believed Muslims must create an independent Islamic financial system that would parallel and later overtake the Western economy.[432] Al-Banna's successors set his theories and practices into motion.

In 1962, the Muslim Brotherhood convinced the Saudi Arabian king Saud bin Abdul Aziz to launch a global financial joint venture that established numerous charitable foundations across the globe. This joint venture became the cornerstone of the Brotherhood and was used to spread Islam, and later to fund terrorist operations, worldwide. In 1978, Saudi Arabia backed another Brotherhood initiative, the International Islamic Relief Organization (IIRO), an entity that has been implicated in funding organizations such as al Qaeda and Hamas.

Furthermore, most Muslim nations collect mandatory Islamic charity (zakat) of approximately 2.5 percent from Muslim institutions and companies.[433] Zakat is intended to go to those who are less fortunate. However, the Brotherhood determined that those engaged in jihad against the enemies of Islam are entitled to benefit from the charitable offering.[434]

Internal Sources of Money[435]

Noncoercive Means 	**Gifts.** Voluntary financial gifts from wealthy individuals and, occasionally, from commercial enterprises have constituted a good source of income for many resistance groups and are easier to hide from security forces. For example, money that comes as a cash gift will not leave a trail through the banking system.
	Loans. The resistance group may also borrow funds. If the resistance group can borrow in the name of some established authority such as a government-in-exile, it is more likely to receive a favorable response than if a loan is sought in the name of an aspiring underground whose trustworthiness for later repayment may be in doubt. In addition, if an underground has access to some form of collateral, such as oil or diamond fields, they may be able to secure funding, weapons, and other needed assets in exchange for granting access to the resource. The RUF in Sierra Leone obtained funds and weapons from Liberia and Libya in exchange for diamonds and access to mines.[436]
	Embezzled Funds. A resistance group may obtain funds embezzled from government agencies, trade unions, businesses, and nongovernmental organizations. For example, in Somalia, drought relief funding and supplies were intercepted by Al Shabaab to support their network.[437]
	Sales. The sale of various items through door-to-door canvassing or through "front" stores may provide money.

	Robberies.
	To bring in money, resistance groups frequently resort to robberies. The Hukbalahap in the Philippines,[438] for instance, was able to collect funds by staging train robberies. However, robberies are risky for a resistance that wants political power because they may hurt the reputation of the resistance and make it look like an illegitimate criminal group.
	Kidnapping and Hijacking.
	The practice of kidnapping to collect a ransom has been conducted by insurgent groups across the globe, ranging from the FARC in Colombia, to the Taliban in Afghanistan, to al Qaeda in the Islamic Maghreb (AQIM) in Northern Africa, to MEND in Nigeria. These organizations utilize elaborate networks of middlemen and negotiators to exchange their captives for funding.
	Forced "Contribution".
Coercive Means	Although undergrounds usually do not rob the public so as to avoid alienating the population, they sometimes coerce individuals into making donations under the tacit threat of reprisals. Aggressive application of this technique is usually reserved for targeting wealthier people. OAS in Algeria demanded predetermined amounts of money to be taken from wealthier professionals, but allowed people with less wealth to only give what they wanted.
	Taxes.
	Taxes may be imposed against the general public in areas where resistance administrators can collect taxes with the backing of nearby military units. Many different things can be taxed for revenue. For example, the Taliban taxed the heroin drug economy, collecting a 20 percent tax from opium dealers as well as the drug transporters.[439]
	Narcotics and Black Market Trade.
	Modern insurgencies have increasing connections to the illegal drug trade throughout the world. The burgeoning industry of supplying marijuana, cocaine, methamphetamine, heroin, and other drugs offers opportunities for financing that most underground leaders find too lucrative to ignore.

Although extortion and kidnapping sustained the FARC for many years, growing the "little guerrilla army" required a corresponding growth in funding. To do this, the FARC reluctantly became involved in the narcotics trade. Initially, both Manuel Marulanda and Jacobo Arenas were opposed to *las drogas* for ideological reasons. In the long run, however, pragmatism won the day. The estimates of FARC financing obtained through narcotics run from at least $30 million annually to as high as $1.5 billion.[440]

It is important to recognize that when resistance groups become involved in the drug trade or other black market activities, it tends to impact the organization's core ideology and strategy. With the new drug trade came money and corruption for the FARC. Some of the FARC in coca-rich areas began to live as drug lords with gold jewelry, fancy cars, and other luxuries. This created dissent in the ranks as FARC members who stayed true to the guerrilla life realized others were living as gangsters.

Ultimately, finances are the lifeblood of an insurgent or revolutionary movement. Normally such organizations obtain financing through a combination of internal and external sources. The nature of the movement's fundraising tends to affect the organization, in some cases despite its founding ideology.

Furthermore, how the movement handles acquired funds tends to characterize the organization in the eyes of the wider civilian population. Insurgencies that distribute money to impoverished citizens gain favor as the champions of the underprivileged. Conversely,

leaders who fall into patterns of corruption tend to discredit their organizations. This could be a concern for American ODA operators if resistance leaders have other corrupt financial interests or decide to use risky fund-raising methods.

Finally, finances need to be used to further the goal of the resistance movement by enabling resistance actions. The purpose of fund-raising is to pay for things such as supplies, member incomes, member family support, and training. Training is an especially important function to fund since it prepares new members to fully participate in the movement and enhances the skills of existing members.

Training[441]

Training remains one of the core functions of an insurgent underground and that is true for Sarca as well. Through the training process, Bolanieves will select, evaluate, and develop recruits to join Sarca's forces. Additionally, Bolanieves will want to take advantage of the Internet and the privatization of security operations to improve Sarca's training program. Previously, resistance groups faced a problem of lacking access to training materials, but now Sarca can quickly and easily find training information on many useful hard skills: weapons, explosives, guerrilla tactics, surveillance, communications, and so on.

Beyond the basic resistance training, Bolanieves knows that insurgent training is very different from conventional military training when it comes to ideological preparation of Sarca members. Bolanieves must replace each Sarca member's previous loyalty to the government with an allegiance to Sarca's ideology. This type of training includes immersion in propaganda, whether religious or political. A recruit's mastery of and devotion to Sarca's ideology may ultimately help Bolanieves determine the recruit's potential for advancement within Sarca.

Given the nature of Sarca as a resistance group acting against the government, Bolanieves will have to plan and prepare for clandestine training operations to avoid detection. Sarca's clandestine training most often aims at training individual recruits and very small units, because dealing with larger units would compromise security. Similarly, Bolanieves wants Sarca's training to focus on the opening minutes of an attack, rather than sustained land combat operations. Finally, Bolanieves will have to deal with time requirements for training because clandestine training tends to take a long time if it is interrupted by government forces in Estatu or needs to take place in small pieces to stay hidden. Conversely, training in less controlled environments, such as those enjoyed by al Qaeda in Afghanistan, allows for more intensive and continuous training all at once.

Even after initial training, Bolanieves puts a premium on adapting to lessons learned from Sarca's operations. He reviews Sarca's battles, acts of sabotage, terrorist attacks, and other operations—whether they succeeded or failed— to better understand mistakes and best practices. Later, Bolanieves takes those lessons learned to improve training techniques and prepare for future operations.

Bolanieves also finds it helpful to establish rules on "do's and don'ts." In general, he thinks it is often easier to tell Sarca members what not to do than what to do.[442]

In addition to training dedicated Sarca members for violent resistance operations, Bolanieves may want to prepare other passive resisters for nonviolent actions such as noncooperation and civil disobedience. These actions may not require hard skills training such as weapons training, but Bolanieves knows that nonviolent resistance still involves organization, solidarity, and other forms of training. To achieve this nonviolent training, Bolanieves has several options. He could model Sarca's training after Gandhi's nonviolent actions, which were based on a moral creed and included a code of conduct and oath for volunteers. Another option would be training Sarca's nonviolent resisters to withstand violence and physical abuse without responding with more violence.

Training Infrastructure[443]

Training camps are the center of terrorist and insurgent training throughout the world. As described in numerous first-hand accounts, the camps provide an environment of isolation, focused skill building, and indoctrination that can mass produce deadly and committed warriors.

Al Qaeda maintained secret training camps in Afghanistan and Bosnia that were later exposed and destroyed. But these well-known examples are in fact typical of similar facilities in every corner of the globe. The Bekaa Valley in Lebanon has long hosted training camps for both Hizbollah and the Palestine Liberation Organization (PLO), while the Tamil Tigers of Sri Lanka based several training sites in the remote north of their country and Jemaah Islamiyah provided weapons and explosives training in Indonesia.

Once placed in a training camp, Hizbollah recruits received training and instruction in weapons, explosives, ambush techniques, infiltration, intelligence, and myriad other subjects, including psychological warfare. Hizbollah and IRGC agents paid close attention to actual combat operations, sifting through lessons learned in order to strengthen subsequent attacks.[444]

Al Qaeda's training regime, like that of many other terrorist groups, puts a premium on religious indoctrination, which al Qaeda considers to be infinitely more important than the development of military skills. The exact ideology taught, however, differs from camp to camp, based on the cultural context of each particular insurgency. In camps supporting ethnic-based insurgencies, for example, the ideology focuses more on the history and mythology of the subject's ethnicity and how it has been wronged. Other camps that develop jihadists for the restoration of the Caliphate emphasize jihad as a religious duty.[445]

Training camps in safe locations can evolve into highly effective institutions for training terrorists. Al Qaeda's camp at Darunta, near Jalalabad, Afghanistan, was one such location and typifies the smaller facilities. Only about a quarter-square mile in size, it consisted of a tunnel complex, four sub-camps, each with a different purpose, and a defensive system of trenches and outposts. The entire complex was camouflaged. Within the camp, al Qaeda ran a chemical training laboratory and a guerrilla training center. The Taliban owned a part of Darunta, and Pakistani terrorists operating in Kashmir ran the fourth sub-camp. Investigation of the abandoned site revealed extensive training and indoctrination materials—many in English, and much of it downloaded from the Internet.

Used by Secretary of Defense William S. Cohen and Gen. Henry H. Shelton, U.S. Army, chairman, Joint Chiefs of Staff, to brief reporters in the Pentagon on the US military strike on a chemical weapons plant in Sudan and terrorist training camps in Afghanistan on August 20, 1998[446]

Figure 17. Photograph of the Garmabak Ghar Terrorist Training Camp, Afghanistan.

Training Online[447]

The information age introduced a new avenue and method for training. Previous mention of the Internet's use for training demonstrates how it provides access to knowledge. Prior to the advent of the Internet, access to information sources on weapons, explosives, tactics, and other resistance methods was limited. Today, anyone can download a manual that instructs him or her how to conduct illegal attacks and other operations. Insurgent groups also use the Internet, however, to host training exercises that can combine motivational and operational aspects.

Online resources for insurgent and terrorist training include both motivational and operational information. Most often, these two categories are combined into a single document because the psychological preparation of a student is deemed to be equally important to the development of hard skills. Motivational information includes psychological, sociological, political, or religious components.

Hizbollah, under the direction of its senior leaders, developed a video game called "Special Force," in which players experience a simulated operation against Israeli soldiers based on real-life events (see Figure 18).[448] The game was released in 2003 and allowed players to conduct "target practice" against Israeli political leaders. Thousands of copies of the game were sold in the Middle East, in the United States, and throughout the world. Through the publication of a game, Hizbollah was able to export both its ideology and a form of skill building that would prepare youngsters to one day assume the role of jihadist. Hizbollah copied this training technique from American supremacist groups that offer, on their websites, similar games focused on racial hatred. These games allow players to kill Jews, black people, or other targeted groups in "first-person shooter" formats.[7]

Figure 18. Screenshot from "Special Force."

An important emerging area of online insurgent training is the ever-growing community of hackers. Thousands of new websites emerge annually that offer instruction and tools for hackers. While such sites offer little motivational information, they are replete with operational know-how, tips, tricks, and "best practices." Visitors to such sites can learn detailed techniques for conducting denial of service attacks, stealing passwords, overloading websites, and probing networks for vulnerabilities. They can also download tools for encryption, programming, and data manipulation to facilitate their efforts. Islamic jihadist groups all over the world have devoted resources to encouraging their followers to conduct cyberterror attacks and providing training and tools to assist them.

Training Process

Training is central to the success of an insurgency. The most successful and long-lived movements treat this key function as a major area of concern and focus for leadership. The experience of the Provisional Irish Republican Army is instructive as an example of how an insurgent organization plans, organizes, and conducts training.

RESISTANCE IN FOCUS: The Provisional Irish Republican Army

The IRA organized a training department under its general headquarters with the responsibility to maintain all training resources and facilities. They conducted training in three areas: new recruit training, operational skills training, and intelligence/counterintelligence/security training. During new recruit training, the emphasis was on motivational information—i.e., what it means to be a Republican and the history of Irish resistance against the British occupation. The other two phases of training focused on the necessary hard skills to conduct operations and to protect the security of the organization.

New recruits were required to attend training sessions about once per week during their first three months in the organization. The sessions included lectures and discussions about member duties, the history of the organization, the rules concerning military engagement, and how to resist interrogation. During this period of initial training, the recruit was also evaluated as to his potential for service and his risk to the security of the organization.

The IRA learned to emphasize rigorous training and instruction in hard skills—weapons, explosives, and urban and rural tactics. Since unsophisticated attacks by impulsive and unskilled youths led to arrests, interrogations, and political failure, training was considered highly important. Similarly, inexperience with weapons and explosives caused numerous accidental deaths among the insurgents, emphasizing the need for a military training program. The IRA put recruits into covert training camps where they learned to shoot and maintain weapons, employ demolitions, and other basic skills. Due in part to the requirement for secrecy, the average IRA insurgent's training took about six months.

Before the advent of the Internet, it was difficult for insurgent leaders to get access to training resources. IRA operatives solved this deficiency by recruiting former military members, obtaining printed military manuals, and in some cases sending members to pursue education opportunities that they could use in later insurgent activities. In the 1970s, IRA leaders had to devote resources to producing written materials to support training. This resulted in, among other products, the infamous *Green Book*, which included both ideological and operational information for potential members.

These efforts paid off in better operational performance. Better-trained insurgents began to operate collectively instead of individually, giving them the ability to stand their ground in skirmishes with government forces. Resistance marksmanship improved, and British casualties increased.

Beyond the general training of recruits in weapons and tactics, IRA leaders also sought to improve performance in bomb making, sniping, logistics, and intelligence. Specialists in these areas would occasionally come together to receive training and pass on lessons learned with the intent of improving safety, security, and performance in battle.

Since weapons ranges—especially those designed to handle mortars, explosives, and other large weapons—tend to be noisy and hard to conceal, the IRA used remote locations throughout Ireland, including abandoned farm houses, unused beaches, and woods. In one case, they used a beach for mortar fire using dummy (i.e., nonexplosive) shells. In other cases, they positioned their live-fire ranges near army training facilities so that their gunfire noise would not attract attention. Recruits were often not told the exact location of the camps where they trained in an attempt to prevent the authorities from discovering and shutting them down. The IRA also turned to other sympathetic groups based in foreign countries for training support, such as support for using training camps in Libya.

Bolanieves and Sarca

When considering actions to take, Bolanieves faces a critical question on Sarca's use of violent and nonviolent resistance options. A decision to use violence, especially lethal violence, sets the tone for the movement and could affect the lives of Sarca members and the people of Estatu in a significant way. Nonviolent resistance also has its own important considerations, such as how to prepare people to withstand abuse and other effective actions. In both cases, whether Sarca chooses violence or nonviolence, Bolanieves knows that Sarca should concentrate on training its members to be most effective with its actions. Bolanieves may have to find ways to hide training areas from Estatu government forces for physical training or learn to use online training resources to quickly reach more Sarca members. Finally, resistance operations, training, supplies, and all other actions require money. To sustain the movement, Bolanieves will need to engage in fundraising, but there are many different options and approaches in this regard as well. Bolanieves may want to reach out to external and foreign donors to support Sarca's cause. Additionally, the earlier question of violence or nonviolence could also affect how Bolanieves thinks about fundraising. If he accepts violent resistance actions, he might also approve of using threats to extort money or kidnappings for ransom. Criminal activities is an option for Sarca to make money. In all of these ways, Sarca's actions will affect the people of Estatu and will show a certain image to the public—either violent or nonviolent. Bolanieves' decisions on training and fundraising will further ingrain that image for Sarca.

Questions

A resistance movement is often defined by the actions that are attributed to it. The reader now understands how the concept of a threshold of violence will influence the movement's decision to employ violent or nonviolent tactics. In turn, the reader examined the importance of intelligence, fundraising and internal support mechanisms, external financial support, and the role of training camps, programs, and online studies. These factors are essential actions of a resistance movement, and the reader should explore this knowledge in the context of the Sarca narrative with the following discussion questions.

INTRODUCTORY - BLOOMS LEVEL ONE

- Identify and Compare: What options should Bolanieves consider for training? What does each option provide him? Is online training a useful option for Sarca?

INTRODUCTORY - BLOOMS LEVEL TWO

- Identify and Explain: If Bolanieves wants to remain nonviolent, which actions are most effective for Sarca's goals?

INTERMEDIATE - BLOOMS LEVEL FOUR

- Differentiate and Deconstruct: If he authorizes violent resistance, would he willingly take lethal resistance actions? What are the different effects for the ODA and US objectives?

- Differentiate: For funding, which voluntary, nonviolent or violent, and coercive options would work best for Bolanieves and Sarca?

MASTERY - BLOOMS LEVEL FIVE

- Critique and Evaluate: What issues should he and the American ODA team consider for relying on foreign donors for money, using criminal activities, engaging in threats for payment, or carrying out other fundraising efforts? What are the critical components of external support for Sarca?

- Detect and evaluate: How should Bolanieves decide on the use of nonviolent or violent resistance to achieve Sarca's objectives? Which factors are critical to determining the threshold of violence to achieve Sarca's stated objectives?

CONCLUSION

With all of the decisions Bolanieves must make for Sarca and its growing resistance movement, he needs to carefully consider all of the factors, issues, and areas of opportunity. The actors that will support Sarca and provide its membership base need to be identified. Causes and motivations of resistance for those supporters become equally important to understand when forming Sarca into a movement. Outside of the people of Sarca, Bolanieves recognizes that the environment around Sarca and its supporters in the city of Reseau will affect the movement. Then, once Sarca motivates supporters and an understanding of its environment, Bolanieves needs to organize his leadership and the people's support into an operational group. Finally, Bolanieves should decide the actions, operations, and sustainment measures Sarca will employ.

These are difficult and complex questions for Bolanieves. However, if Sarca wants a chance to change the government of Reseau and successfully bring greater representation to the marginalized groups, Bolanieves will have to make difficult decisions on preparing Sarca for resistance. However, Bolanieves is not the only one with big questions to consider. If the United States is tasked with supporting Bolanieves and providing advice to help him succeed, there are other questions to answer.

How can the United States help Bolanieves with his decisions on organizing and growing Sarca? What guidance can it give him to help him consider different options? As the ODA helps Bolanieves, one of the first phases to consider is preparation. At this stage, the causes of resistance and the environment surrounding the resistance are particularly important to understand. Establishing the legitimacy of the resistance leaders and the goals of the movement within this environment sets the foundation for the next phases. Because the United States already made contact with Bolanieves and is working with him in Reseau, the next phase is organization. Organization is critical to becoming an effective and sustainable group that can conduct operations. Organizing resistance actions includes many seemingly smaller details, such as logistics and fundraising.

After initial organization, Sarca will need to recruit, train, supply itself, and prepare for real operations. Planning for operations could include advising Bolanieves to decide on the actions to take, the targets to pursue, and the most effective Sarca operation to employ. Once decisions are made and Sarca starts growing into an active resistance, Bolanieves can employ his forces to start achieving Sarca's strategic goals. Throughout this entire process, Bolanieves should consider his role in command and control. Finally, the United States should pursue achieving its own objectives and see Bolanieves and Sarca successfully become the legitimate government of Reseau.

Whether the mission is counterinsurgency, foreign internal defense, or UW, the object of the ARSOF soldier's profession is the phenomenon of resistance. Understanding resistance as a concept empowers the ARSOF soldier to maximize his or her expertise and experience when working with or against the resistance as a living entity on the ground. This text seeks to guide the ARSOF soldier through the basics of resistance, as well as provide frameworks, theories, and concepts he or she can use in confronting the questions, issues, and decisions that need to be answered, addressed, and made in the field. While the phenomenon of

resistance undoubtedly continues to evolve, it is built on the history that comes before each new case, and there is no new case completely unique from those that came before. The frameworks, theories, and concepts in this text all derive from that history, and they can be found in more detail in the volumes created by the ARIS program. This text introduced and explained those frameworks, theories, and concepts to the reader. It is up to the ARSOF soldier to marry this material and the understanding it provides with his or her training, expertise, and experience to execute his or her missions without equal.

APPENDIX: METHODS OF NONVIOLENT ACTION[449]

Methods of Nonviolent Protest and Persuasion

Fomal Statements

1. Public speeches
2. Letters of opposition or support
3. Declarations by organizations and institutions
4. Signed public statements
5. Declarations of indictment and intention
6. Group or mass petitions

Communications with a Wider Audience

7. Slogans, caricatures, and symbols
8. Banners, posters, and displayed communications
9. Leaflets, pamphlets, and books
10. Newspapers and journals
11. Records, radio, and television
12. Skywriting and earthwriting

Group Representations

13. Deputations
14. Mock awards
15. Group lobbying
16. Picketing
17. Mock elections

Symbolic Public Acts

18. Displays of flags and symbolic colors
19. Wearing of symbols
20. Prayer and worship
21. Delivering symbolic objects
22. Protest disrobings
23. Destruction of own property
24. Symbolic lights
25. Displays of portraits
26. Paint as protest
27. New signs and names
28. Symbolic sounds

29. Symbolic reclamations
30. Rude gestures

Pressures on Individuals

31. "Haunting" officials
32. Taunting officials
33. Fraternization
34. Vigils

Drama and Music

35. Humorous skits and pranks
36. Performances of plays and music
37. Singing

Processions

38. Marches
39. Parades
40. Religious processions
41. Pilgrimages
42. Motorcades

Honoring the Dead

43. Political mourning
44. Mock funerals
45. Demonstrative funerals
46. Homage at burial places

Public Assemblies

47. Assemblies of protest or support
48. Protest meetings
49. Camouflaged meetings of protest
50. Teach-ins

Withdrawal and Renunciation

51. Walk-outs
52. Silence
53. Renouncing honors
54. Turning one's back

The Methods of Social Noncooperation

Ostracism of Persons

55. Social boycott

56. Selective social boycott
57. Lysistratic nonaction
58. Excommunication
59. Interdict

Noncooperation with Social Events, Customs, and Institutions

60. Suspension of social and sports activities
61. Boycott of social affairs
62. Student strike
63. Social disobedience
64. Withdrawal from social institutions

Withdrawal from the Social System

65. Stay-at-home
66. Total personal noncooperation
67. "Flight" of workers
68. Sanctuary
69. Collective disappearance
70. Protest emigration (hijrat)

The Methods of Economic Noncooperation: (1) Economic Boycotts

Actions by Consumers

71. Consumers' boycott
72. Nonconsumption of boycotted goods
73. Policy of austerity
74. Rent withholding
75. Refusal to rent
76. National consumers' boycott
77. International consumers' boycott

Action by Workers and Producers

78. Workmen's boycott
79. Producers' boycott

Action by Middlemen

80. Suppliers' and handlers' boycott

Action by Owners and Management

81. Traders' boycott
82. Refusal to let or sell property
83. Lockout

84. Refusal of industrial assistance

85. Merchants' "general strike"

Action by Holders of Financial Resources

86. Withdrawal of bank deposits

87. Refusal to pay fees, dues, and assessments

88. Refusal to pay debts or interest

89. Severance of funds and credit

90. Revenue refusal

91. Refusal of a government's money

Action by Governments

92. Domestic embargo

93. Blacklisting of traders

94. International sellers' embargo

95. International buyers' embargo

96. International trade embargo

The Methods of Economic Noncooperation: (2) The Strike

Symbolic Strikes

97. Protest strike

98. Quickie walkout (lightning strike)

Agricultural Strikes

99. Peasant strike

100. Farm workers' strike

Strikes by Special Groups

101. Refusal of impressed labor

102. Prisoners' strike

103. Craft strike

104. Professional strike

Ordinary Industrial Strikes

105. Establishment strike

106. Industry strike

107. Sympathetic strike

Restricted Strikes

108. Detailed strike

109. Bumper strike

110. Slowdown strike

111. Working-to-rule strike

112. Reporting "sick" (sick-in)

113. Strike by resignation

114. Limited strike

115. Selective strike

Multi-Industry Strikes

116. Generalized strike

117. General strike

Combination of Strikes and Economic Closures

118. Hartal

119. Economic shutdown

The Methods of Political Noncooperation

Rejection of Authority

120. Withholding or withdrawal of allegiance

121. Refusal of public support

122. Literature and speeches advocating resistance

Citizens' Noncooperation with Government

123. Boycott of legislative bodies

124. Boycott of elections

125. Boycott of government employment and positions

126. Boycott of government depts., agencies, and other bodies

127. Withdrawal from government educational institutions

128. Boycott of government-supported organizations

129. Refusal of assistance to enforcement agents

130. Removal of own signs and placemarks

131. Refusal to accept appointed officials

132. Refusal to dissolve existing institutions

Citizens' Alternatives to Obedience

133. Reluctant and slow compliance

134. Nonobedience in absence of direct supervision

135. Popular nonobedience

136. Disguised disobedience

137. Refusal of an assemblage or meeting to disperse

138. Sitdown

139. Noncooperation with conscription and deportation

140. Hiding, escape, and false identities

141. Civil disobedience of "illegitimate" laws

Action by Government Personnel

142. Selective refusal of assistance by government aides

143. Blocking of lines of command and information

144. Stalling and obstruction

145. General administrative noncooperation

146. Judicial noncooperation

147. Deliberate inefficiency and selective noncooperation by enforcement agents

148. Mutiny

Domestic Governmental Action

149. Quasi-legal evasions and delays

150. Noncooperation by constituent governmental units

International Governmental Action

151. Changes in diplomatic and other representations

152. Delay and cancellation of diplomatic events

153. Withholding of diplomatic recognition

154. Severance of diplomatic relations

155. Withdrawal from international organizations

156. Refusal of membership in international bodies

157. Expulsion from international organizations

The Methods of Nonviolent Intervention

Psychological Intervention

158. Self-exposure to the elements

159. The fast: Fast of moral pressure, Hunger strike, Satyagrahic fast

160. Reverse trial

161. Nonviolent harassment

Physical Intervention

162. Sit-in

163. Stand-in

164. Ride-in

165. Wade-in

166. Mill-in

167. Pray-in

168. Nonviolent raids

169. Nonviolent air raids

170. Nonviolent invasion

171. Nonviolent interjection

172. Nonviolent obstruction

173. Nonviolent occupation

Social Intervention

174. 174.   Establishing new social patterns

175. 175.   Overloading of facilities

176. 176.   Stall-in

177. 177.   Speak-in

178. 178.   Guerrilla theater

179. 179.   Alternative social institutions

180. 180.   Alternative communication system

Economic Intervention

181. Reverse strike

182. Stay-in strike

183. Nonviolent land seizure

184. Defiance of blockades

185. Politically motivated counterfeiting

186. Preclusive purchasing

187. Seizure of assets

188. Dumping

189. Selective patronage

190. Alternative markets

191. Alternative transportation systems

192. Alternative economic institutions

Political Intervention

193. Overloading of administrative systems

194. Disclosing identities of secret agents

195. Seeking imprisonment

196. Civil disobedience of "neutral" laws

197. Work-on without collaboration

198. Dual sovereignty and parallel government

ENDNOTES

1. Bloom, B. S. (1956). Taxonomy of Educational Objectives, Handbook I: The Cognitive Domain. New York: David McKay Co Inc.; Anderson, L. W. & Krathwohl, D.R., et al (2001) A taxonomy for learning, teaching and assessing: A revision of Bloom's taxonomy of educational objectives. New York: Longman.

2. This section was excerpted from the ARIS volume Understanding States of Resistance. W. Sam Lauber, et al., Understanding States of Resistance (United States Army Special Operations Command, Fort Bragg, NC, 2015).

3. ATP 3-05.1, Unconventional Warfare, Headquarters, Department of the Army (Washington, D.C., September 2013).

4. ARIS, Understanding States of Resistance, (United States Army Special Operations Command, Fort Bragg, NC, 2015).

5. US Department of the Army, "Insurgencies and Countering Insurgencies," FM 3-24, May 2014, 4-8.

6. Jonathan Christiansen, "Four Stages of Social Movements: Social Movements and Collective Behavior," Research Starters Academic Topic Overviews (Ipswich, MA: EBSCO Publishing, 2009).

7. Lyford P. Edwards, The Natural History of Revolution (Chicago: University of Chicago Press, 1927), 23-25.

8. James Chowning Davies, "The J-Curve and Power Struggle Theories of Collective Violence," American Sociological Review 39, no. 4 (1974): 607-610; and James C. Davies, "Toward a Theory of Revolution," American Sociological Review 27, no. 1 (1962): 5-19.

9. Rex Hopper, "The Revolutionary Process: A Frame of Reference for the Study of Revolutionary Movements," Social Forces 28, no. 3 (1950): 271- 272.

10. David J. Danelo, "Exploring the Phases of Contemporary Resistance," in ARIS, Special Topics in Irregular Warfare: Understanding Resistance (Fort Bragg, NC: United States Army Special Operations Command, 2015) 11-13.

11. ARIS, Casebook on Insurgency and Revolutionary Warfare, Volume II: 1962-2009 (Fort Bragg: US Army Special Operations Command, 2012), 645-672.

12. Hopper, "The Revolutionary Process," 272-275; Christiansen, Four Stages of Social Movements, 3, and Crane Brinton, The Anatomy of Revolution (New York: Vintage Books, 1965).

13. Christiansen, Four stages of Social Movements.

14. Maurice Jackson et al., "The Failure of an Incipient Social Movement," The Pacific Sociological Review 3, no. 1 (1960): 35-40.

15. Hopper, "The Revolutionary Process," 272-275.

16. Ibid., 273; Christiansen, Four Stages of Social Movements 3.

17. Christiansen, Four stages of Social Movements, 3.

18. Edwards, Natural History of Revolution, 38; Jessop, "Reviewed Work: The Natural History of Revolution," 130.

19.　Brinton, Anatomy of Revolution.

20.　Danelo, "Exploring the Phases of Contemporary Resistance," 11-13.

21.　ARIS, Casebook on Insurgency and Revolutionary Warfare, Volume II, 2012, 625-644.

22.　Edwards, Natural History of Revolution; Brinton, Anatomy of Revolution, Meadows, "Sequence in Revolution."

23.　Hopper, "The Revolutionary Process;" Christiansen, Four Stages of Social Movements.

24.　Edwards, Natural History of Revolution, 98.

25.　Brinton, Anatomy of Revolution; Hopper, "The Revolutionary Process," 275-277.

26.　Paul Meadows, "Sequence in Revolution," American Sociological Review 6, no. 5 (1941):_707-709.

27.　Danelo, "Exploring the Phases of Contemporary Resistance."

28.　ARIS, Casebook on Insurgency and Revolutionary Warfare, Volume II, 293-328. The Provisional IRA was established at the conclusion of the December 1969 Army Convention after a two-third vote ended the IRA's policy of abstentionism (not assuming elected seats in British legislative institutions such as Westminster Parliament). Those who remained were called the "Officials" and supported an electoral strategy. Those who walked out became known as the "Provisionals" or "Provies." This split was reflected at Sinn Fein's 1970 Ard Fheis where a similar motion split the movement. The Provisionals later ended their own policy of abstentionism in 1985/6.

29.　Christiansen, Four Stages of Social Movements.

30.　Meadows, "Sequence in Revolution."

31.　Hopper, "The Revolutionary Process," 275-277.

32.　Danelo, "Exploring the Phases of Contemporary Resistance," 11-13.

33.　ARIS, Casebook on Insurgency and Revolutionary Warfare, Volume II, 409-442.

34.　W. Sam Lauber, "Understanding States of Resistance: Pocket Guide," ARIS Publication, July 2019.

35.　Tarrow, Power in Movement, 209.

36.　Ibid., 190, 207-208.

37.　ARIS, Casebook on Insurgency and Revolutionary Warfare, Volume II, 2012, 381-409.

38.　Ibid., 207-208.

39.　Hopper, "The Revolutionary Process," 277-279.

40.　Frederick D. Miller, "The End of SDS and the Emergence of Weatherman: Demise through Success" in Waves of Protest: Social Movements since the Sixties, ed. Jo Freeman and Victoria Johnson (Lanham, MD: Rowman & Littlefield Publishers, 1999), 303.

41.　Ibid.

42.　Tarrow, Power in Movement, 209.

43. Ibid., 54, 127, 189-190.

44. ARIS, Casebook on Insurgency and Revolutionary Warfare, Volume II, 2012, 293-327.

45. Miller, "The End of SDS," 306-307.

46. ARIS, Casebook on Insurgency and Revolutionary Warfare: Volume II, 2012, 625-644.

47. Miller, "The End of SDS," 305

48. Ibid., 307-308.

49. Jackson et al., "The Failure of an Incipient Social Movement," 40.

50. Ibid.

51. Ibid.

52. Ibid.

53. Miller, "The End of SDS," 305.

54. Ibid.

55. Christiansen, Four Stage of Social Movements, 4.

56. Patrick G. Coy and Timothy Hedeen, "A Stage Model of Social Movement Co-Optation: Community Meditation in the United States," The Sociological Quarterly 46, no. 3 (2005): 411, 413-426.

57. John J. Macionis, Sociology, 9th ed. (Upper Saddle River, New Jersey: Prentice Hall, 2003), 619.

58. Hopper, "The Revolutionary Process," 277.

59. Edwards, Natural History of Revolution.

60. Tarrow, Power in Movement, 206.

61. Stacy Keogh, "The Survival of Religious Peace Movements: When Mobilization Increases as Political Opportunity Decreases," Social Compass 60, no. 4 (2013): 561-578.

62. Christiansen, Four Stages of Social Movements, 6.

63. Traci M. Sawyers and David S. Meyer, "Missed Opportunities: Social Movement Abeyance and Public Policy," Social Problems 46, no. 2 (1999): 188.

64. Verta Taylor, "Social Movement continuity: The Women's Movement in Abeyance," American Sociological Review 54, no. 5 (1989): 762.

65. ARIS does not set intelligence requirements. It is educational material. The questions in this section prompt the reader through possible inquiry about the relevant group. The questions in this section do not constitute and should not be interpreted as setting intelligence requirements.

66. US Department of the Army, Unconventional Warfare, Army Technical Publication 3-05.1 (Washington, DC: Headquarters, Department of the Army, 2013), at 5-2.

67. This section is adapted from Human Factors and Undergrounds in Resistance. ARIS, Human Factors Considerations of Undergrounds in Insurgencies, (United States Army Special Operations Command, Fort Bragg, NC, January 25 2013), 89-108; ARIS,

Undergrounds in Insurgent, Revolutionary, and Resistance Warfare, (United States Army Special Operations Command, Fort Bragg, NC, January 25, 2013), 24.

68.   Jerrold M. Post, The Psychological Assessment of Political Leaders: with Profiles of Saddam Hussein and Bill Clinton (Ann Arbor, MI: University of Michigan Press, 2003).

69.   Yossi Shain, The Frontier of Loyalty: Political Exiles in the Age of the Nation-State (Ann Arbor, MI: University of Michigan Press, 1989). See also Balam Nyeko, "Exile Politics and Resistance to Dictatorship: The Ugandan Anti-Amin Organizations in Zambia, 1972-79," African Affairs 96, no. 382 (January 1997): 95-108.

70.   ARIS, Human Factors, 91 et seq.

71.   Bernard M. Bass, "Two Decades of Research and Development in Transformational Leadership," European Journal of Work and Organizational Psychology 8, no. 1 (1999): 9–32.

72.   Philip M. Podsakoff, Scott B. Mackenzie, Robert H. Moorman, and Richard Fetter, "Transformational Leader Behaviors and Their Effects on Followers' Trust in Leader, Satisfaction, and Organizational Citizenship Behaviors," Leadership Quarterly 1, no. 2 (1990): 107–142.

73.   Gary Yukl, Angela Gordon, and Tom Taber, "A Hierarchical Taxonomy of Leadership Behavior: Integrating a Half Century of Behavior Research," Journal of Leadership & Organizational Studies 9, no. 1 (2002): 15–32.

74.   ARIS, Human Factors, 92 et seq.

75.   Jay A. Conger and Raabindra N. Kanungo, "Toward a Behavioral Theory of Charismatic Leadership in Organizational Settings," The Academy of Management Review 12, no. 4 (1987): 637–647.

76.   Ibid.

77.   Abimael Guzman was the undisputed leader of Sendero Luminoso. This physically unremarkable man, rarely seen by Sendero members apart from the highest leadership, employed an extraordinary capacity for persuasion and organization to create a cult-like organization whose members literally revered him as a god in many cases. For the Sendero members, Guzman was shrouded in mystery—a charismatic, almost hypnotic leader who held the one true vision of the future and the means to achieve it. In their minds, he was almost superhuman, and his commands were obeyed without question or hesitation. He demanded and received absolute devotion. Indeed, Guzman saw himself as a "revolutionary Moses who will lead his followers across a river of blood into the Maoist promise land of communism." Sendero believed that Peru was the epicenter of a world revolution and that ultimate victory depended on absolute obedience to Guzman, the leader of the world revolution. In one sense, the near deification of Guzman ensured unparalleled organizational unity and clarity of vision. (Ron Buikema and Matt Burger, "Sendero Luminoso," in ARIS, Casebook on Insurgency and Revolutionary Warfare, Volume II: 1962–2009, (United States Army Special Operations Command, Fort Bragg, NC, January 25 2012), 58–59.)

78.   Post, Psychological Assessment.

79.   Conger and Kanungo, "Charismatic Leadership."

80.   ARIS, Casebook on Insurgency and Revolutionary Warfare, Volume II. (United States Army Special Operations Command, Fort Bragg, NC, January 25, 2012).

81.   This portion was taken and adapted from ARIS, Undergrounds in Insurgent, Revolutionary, and Resistance Warfare, (United States Army Special Operations Command, Fort Bragg, NC, January 25, 2013), 10, 24.

82.   Chuck Crossett and Dru Daubon, "ETA: Euskadi Ta Askatasuna" (working paper, The Johns Hopkins University Applied Physics Laboratory, Laurel, MD, 2009).

83.   ARIS, Undergrounds, 24 et seq.

84.   Ron Buikema and Matt Burger, "Farabundo Marti Frente Papa La Liberacion Nacional (FMLN)," in ARIS, Casebook on Insurgency and Revolutionary Warfare, Volume II: 1962–2009, (United States Army Special Operations Command, Fort Bragg, NC, January 25 2012).

85.   Petter Nesser, "Jihad in Europe: Recruitment for Terror Cells in Europe," in Paths to Global Jihad, eds. Laila Bokhari, Thomas Hegghammer, Brynjar Lia, Petter Nesser, and Truls H. Tønnessen (Kjeller, Norway: Norwegian Defence Research Establishment, 2006), 10.

86.   1985 interview with Yuri Bezmenov, posted by MHadden88, "Bezmenov on Marxists," YouTube, uploaded October 5, 2008, http://www.youtube.com/watch?gl=US&hl=uk&v=dE38dLxapVo.

87.   ARIS, Human Factors, 107.

88.   Jenna Jordan, "When Heads Roll: Assessing the Effectiveness of Leadership Decapitation," Security Studies 18 (2009): 719–755.

89.   Ibid.

90.   ARIS, Undergrounds, 131 et seq.

91.   Ian S. Spears, "States-Within-States: An Introduction to Their Empirical Attributes," in States-Within-States: Incipient Political Entities in the Post-Cold War Era, eds Paul Kingston and Ian S. Spears (New York: Palgrave Macmillan, 2004), 15-34.

92.   Zachariah Cherian Mampilly, Rebel Rulers: Insurgent Governance and Civilian Life during War (Ithaca, NY: Cornell University Press, 2011).

93.   Ian Spears, "States-within-States: An Introduction to their Empirical Attributes," in States-within-States: Incipient Political Entities in the Post Cold War Era, ed. Paul Kingston and Ian Spears (New York: Palgrave Macmillan, 2004), 28.

94.   ARIS, Undergrounds, 138 et seq.

95.   Rosenau, "Patterned Chaos in Global Life," 2–5.

96.   Nelson Kasfir, Dilemmas of Popular Support in Guerrilla War: The National Resistance Army in Uganda, 1981–86 (Hanover, NH: Dartmouth College, 2002), http://www.yale.edu/macmillan/ocvprogram/licep/6/kasfir/kasfir.pdf.

97.   Spears, States-within-States, 15–34.

98.   Nelson Kasfir, "Guerrillas and Civilian Participation: The National Resistance Army in Uganda, 1981–86," Journal of Modern African Studies 43, no. 2 (2005): 86.

99.   Kasfir, "Guerrillas and Civilian Participation," 279–280.

100. People's Movement for the Liberation of Angola–Labor Party or the Movimento Popular de Libertação de Angola–Partido do Trabalho.

101. Alan Cowell as quoted in Spears, States-within-States, 21.

102. Ibid., 20.

103. Timothy P. Wickham-Crowley, "The Rise (and Sometimes Fall) of Guerrilla Governments in Latin America," Sociological Forum 2, no. 3 (1987): 482.

104. ARIS, Undergrounds, 144 et seq.

105. Spears, States-within-States, 22-23.

106. ARIS, Undergrounds, 133 et seq.

107. Tony Addison and Syed Mansoob Murshed, The Fiscal Dimensions of Conflict and Reconstruction (Helsinki: United Nations University, World Institute for Development Economics Research, 2001), 5.

108. Spears, States-within-States, 25.

109. James B. Love, Hezbollah: Social Services as a Source of Power (Hurlbert Field, FL: JSOU Press, 2010), 1; Spears, States-within-States, 26.

110. Love, Hezbollah, 21.

111. Ibid., 26.

112. This case study is taken from the ARIS volume Undergrounds in Insurgent, Revolutionary, and Resistance Warfare. ARIS, Undergrounds, 146-148.

113. Zachariah Cherian Mampilly, Rebel Rulers: Insurgent Governance and Civilian Life during War (Ithaca, NY: Cornell University Press, 2011), 115.

114. Ibid., 118-119

115. Ibid., 119-120.

116. Ibid., 120-123.

117. Mampilly, Rebel Rulers, 123-127.

118. This case study is taken from the ARIS volume Undergrounds in Insurgent, Revolutionary, and Resistance Warfare. ARIS, Undergrounds, 148-149.

119. Mampilly, Rebel Rulers, 123-127.

120. Ibid., 182. The RCD initially attempted to co-opt what was left of state institutions in their efforts at governance but eventually realized these institutions were "incapable of being resuscitated."

121. Ibid., 190-208.

122. Ibid.

123. Ibid., 191.

124. ARIS, Undergrounds, 131 et seq.

125. Lotta Harbom and Peter Wallensteen, "Armed Conflicts, 1946–2009," Journal of Peace Research 47, no. 4 (2010): 702.

126. Harbom and Wallensteen, "Armed Conflicts," 501.

127. Harbom, Melander, and Wallensteen, "Dyadic Dimensions of Armed Conflict," 704.

128. Ibid.

129. Chuck Crossett and Summer Newton, "The Provisional Irish Republican Army: 1969-2001," in ARIS, Casebook on Insurgency and Revolutionary Warfare, Volume II: 1962-2009 (Alexandria, VA: U.S. Army Publications Directorate, in press).

130. ARIS, Undergrounds, 149 et seq.

131. ARIS, Undergrounds, 149 et seq.

132. Nelson Kasfir, Dilemmas of Popular Support in Guerrilla War: The National Resistance Army in Uganda, 1981–86 (Hanover, NH: Dartmouth College, 2002), 272, http://www.yale.edu/macmillan/ocvprogram/licep/6/kasfir/kasfir.pdf.

133. ARIS, Undergrounds, 149 et seq.

134. Kasfir, Dilemmas of Popular Support in Guerilla Warfare, 273. Kasfir observed similar difficulties in the NRA's management of the governance activities in its territories.

135. Andrew Silke, "Rebel's Dilemma: The Changing Relationship between the IRA, Sinn Fein and Paramilitary Vigilantism in Northern Ireland," Terrorism and Political Violence 11, no. 1 (1999): 81. The military and political wing of the PIRA had reasons for disliking the necessary, but troublesome, governance activities associated with curbing criminal behavior. The military wing thought they brought ill repute to the movement and wasted resources. For members of the political wing, in addition to tarnishing the movement, they also made it difficult to gain political support among more moderate populations.

136. Ibid., 84.

137. Jeremy M. Weinstein, Inside Rebellion: The Politics of Insurgent Violence (Cambridge; New York: Cambridge University Press, 2007), 176–177.

138. Kasfir, "Guerrillas and Civilian Participation," 284-285.

139. Weinstein, Inside Rebellion, 178-180.

140. ARIS, Human Factors, 35 et seq.

141. Human Factors, 6; Undergrounds, 172.

142. Figure adapted from ARIS, Human Factors, 36.

143. The ARIS program has published two volumes specifically on the underground component of resistance movements. Information about the other components can be found throughout volumes one and two of the Casebook on Insurgency and Revolutionary Warfare. Very little space in the literature is devoted to analyzing the component of the auxiliary as a subject of its own, but some resources for information on the auxiliary include: David Kilcullen. "The Evolution of Unconventional Warfare." Scandinavian Journal of Military Studies 2, no. 1 (June 2019): 61–71. DOI: http://doi.org/10.31374/sjms.35; Chalmers A. Johnson, "Civilian Loyalties and Guerrilla Conflict," World Politics 14, no. 4 (July 1962): 646-661; Nelson Kasfir. "Guerrillas and Civilian Participation: the National Resistance Army in Uganda, 1981–86." The Journal of Modern African Studies 43, no. 2 (2005): 271–96. doi:10.1017/S0022278X05000832; Shane Joshua Barter. "Unarmed Forces: Civilian Strategy in Violent Conflicts." Peace & Change

37, no. 4 (2012): 544-571. doi:10.1111/j.1468-0130.2012.00770.x. Additional resources for information on the armed component include: Moore, Cerwyn, and Paul Tumelty. "Foreign Fighters and the Case of Chechnya: A Critical Assessment." Studies in Conflict & Terrorism 31, no. 5 (2008): 412-433; Tezcur, Gunes Murat. "Ordinary People, Extraordinary Risks: Participation in an Ethnic Rebellion." American Political Science Review 110, no. 2 (May 2016): 247-264; Wiegand, Krista E. Bombs and Ballots: Governance by Islamist Terrorist and Guerrilla Groups (London: Routledge, 2016); Wood, Reed M., and Jakana L. Thomas. "Women on the Frontline: Rebel Group Ideology and Women's Participation in Violent Rebellion." Journal of Peace Research 54, no. 1 (2017): 31-46. Finally, additional resources on the public component include: Allison, Michael E. "The Transition from Armed Opposition to Electoral Opposition in Central America." Latin American Politics and Society 48, no. 4 (2006): 137-62. doi:10.1111/j.1548-2456.2006.tb00368.x.; Bhasin, Tavishi, and Maia Carter Hallward. "Hamas as a Political Party: Democratization in the Palestinian Territories." Terrorism and Political Violence 25, no. 1 (2013): 75-93; Manning, Carrie. "Armed Opposition Groups Into Political Parties: Comparing Bosnia, Kosovo, and Mozambique." Studies in Comparative International Development 39, no. 1 (March 2004): 54-76; Wiegand, Krista E. "Reformation of a Terrorist Group: Hezbollah as a Lebanese Political Party." Studies in Conflict & Terrorism 32, no. 8 (2009): 669-680; ARIS, Undergrounds, 149 et seq.

144. Leonard Weinberg, Ami Pedahzur, and Arie Perliger, Political Parties and Terrorist Groups (London; New York: Routledge, 2009).

145. Ibid.

146. Ibid.

147. Ibid.

148. Weinberg et al., Political Parties and Terrorist Groups.

149. Veronique Dudouet, From War to Politics: Resistiance/Liberation Movements in Transition (Berlin: Berghof-Forschungszentrum für Konstruktive Konfliktbearbeitung, 2009), 47-48.

150. Chuck Crossett and Summer Newton, "The Provisional Irish Republican Army: 1969-2001," in Casebook on Insurgency and Revolutionary Warfare, Volume II: 1962-2009, ed. Chuck Crossett (Alexandria, VA: U.S. Army Publications Directorate, in press).

151. Bairbre De Brun, The Road to Peace in Ireland (Berlin: Berghof-Forschungszentrum für Konstruktive Konfliktbearbeitung, 2008), 14-15.

152. Mimmi Soderberg Kovacs, "When Rebels Change Their Stripes: Armed Insurgents in Post-War Politics," in From War to Democracy: Dilemmas of Peacebuilding, ed. Anna K. Jarstad and Timothy D. Sisk (New York: Cambridge University Press, 2008).

153. Matthew Hoddie, "Power Sharing in Peace Settlements: Initiating Transition from Civil Wars," in Sustainable Peace: Power and Democracy After Civil Wars, ed. Philip G. Roeder and Donald Rothchild (Ithaca, NY: Cornell University Press, 2005), 138, fn. 1.

154. Kovacs, "When Rebels Change Their Stripes," 138-139. UNITA eventually went back to armed struggle, however.

155. This section is taken from ARIS, Undergrounds, 153 et seq.

156. Dudouet, From War to Politics, 39.

157. Ibid.

158. As quoted in Kiyoko Ogura, Seeking State Power: The Communist Party of Nepal (Maoist) (Berlin: Berghof-Forschungszentrum für Konstruktive Konfliktbearbeitung, 2008), 41.

159. Ibid., 41-42.

160. Dudouet, From War to Politics, 39.

161. ARIS, Undergrounds, 27 et seq.

162. Bryan Gervais and Jerome Conley, "Viet Cong: National Liberation Front for South Vietnam," in Assessing Revolutionary and Insurgent Strategies, ed. Chuck Crossett (Laurel, MD: The Johns Hopkins University Applied Physics Laboratory, 2009), 36-38.

163. John Horgan, "From Profiles to Pathways: The Road to Recruitment," Foreign Policy Agenda 12, no. 5 (2007): 24-27.

164. Michael J. Deane and Maegen Nix, "Liberation Tigers of Tamil Eelam (LTTE)," in Assessing Revolutionary and Insurgent Strategies, ed. Chuck Crossett (Laurel, MD: The Johns Hopkins University Applied Physics Laboratory, 2009), 49.

165. Judith Burdin Asuni, "Understanding the Armed Groups of the Niger Delta," (working paper, Council on Foreign Relations, New York, September 2009), 7. One survey of members of MEND found that many of the young members were drug users—and some drug dealers—with limited education and no economic resources, so they were completely dependent on their leaders for financial support, food, and shelter.

166. Thomas Hegghammer, "Militant Islam in Saudi Arabia: Patterns of Recruitment to 'Al-Qaida on the Arabian Peninsula,'" in Paths to Global Jihad, eds. Laila Bokhari, Thomas Hegghammer, Brynjar Lia, Petter Nesser, and Truls H. Tønnessen (Kjeller, Norway: Norwegian Defence Research Establishment, 2006), 23, 28-29.

167. Jerome Conley, "The Revolutionary United Front (RUF), Sierra Leone," in ARIS, Casebook on Insurgency and Revolutionary Warfare, Volume II: 1962-2009.

168. Robin Yapp and Sao Paulo, "Female Colombian Snipers 'Fighting to Defend Col Gaddafi in Libya,'" The Telegraph, April 14, 2011, http://www.telegraph.co.uk/news/worldnews/africaandindianocean/libya/8451467/Female-Colombian-snipers-fighting-to-defend-Col-Gaddafi-in-Libya.html; author's interview with personnel involved in the Sierra Leone and Angola operations, South Africa, August 2010.

169. ARIS, Human Factors, 290 et seq. The ARIS program has published two volumes specifically on the underground component of resistance movements. Information about the other components can be found throughout volumes one and two of the Casebook on Insurgency and Revolutionary Warfare. Other resources for information on the auxiliary, armed component, and the public component include...

170. ARIS, Undergrounds in Insurgent, Revolutionary, and Resistance Warfare, (United States Army Special Operations Command, Fort Bragg, NC, January 25, 2013), available at: https://www.soc.mil/ARIS/books/arisbooks.html.

171.   Jerome M. Conley, "Orange Revolution (Ukraine): 2004–2005," in Casebook on Insurgency and Revolutionary Warfare, Volume II: 1962–2009, ed. Chuck Crossett (Alexandria, VA: U.S. Army Publications Directorate, in press).

172.   ARIS, Human Factors, 292.

173.   Conley, "Orange Revolution (Ukraine): 2004-2005).

174.   Conley, "Orange Revolution (Ukraine): 2004-2005).

175.   This section is taken and adapted from Undergrounds in Insurgent, Revolutionary, and Resistance Warfare. ARIS, Undergrounds, 27 et seq.

176.   Thomas Hegghammer, "Militant Islam in Saudi Arabia: Patterns of Recruitment to 'Al-Qaida on the Arabian Peninsula,'" in Paths to Global Jihad, eds. Laila Bokhari, Thomas Hegghammer, Brynjar Lia, Petter Nesser, and Truls H. Tønnessen (Kjeller, Norway: Norwegian Defence Research Establishment, 2006), 23, 28–29.

177.   ARIS, Undergrounds, 28 et seq.

178.   Mauricio Florez-Morris, "Joining Guerilla Groups in Colombia: Individual Motivations and Processes for Entering a Violent Organization," Studies in Conflict and Terrorism 30, no. 7 (2007): 626.

179.   Stephen Phillips, "Fuerzas Armadas Revolucionarias de Colombia—FARC," in Assessing Revolutionary and Insurgent Strategies, ed. Chuck Crossett (Laurel, MD: The Johns Hopkins University Applied Physics Laboratory, 2010), 26.

180.   Bryan Gervais and Jerome Conley, "Viet Cong: National Liberation Front for South Vietnam," in ARIS, Assessing Revolutionary and Insurgent Strategies (Laurel, MD: The Johns Hopkins University Applied Physics Laboratory, 2009), 36–38.

181.   ARIS, Undergrounds, 29 et seq.

182.   This case study is taken from Undergrounds in Insurgent, Revolutionary, and Resistance Warfare. ARIS, Undergrounds, 29.

183.   Phillips, "FARC," 21–22..

184.   ARIS, Undergrounds, 29.

185.   Roger V. Gould, "Patron-Client Ties, State Centralization, and the Whiskey Rebellion," American Journal of Sociology 102, no. 2 (September 1996): 400-429.

186.   ARIS, Undergrounds, 31 et seq.

187.   Michael J. Deane and Maegen Nix, "Liberation Tigers of Tamil Eelam (LTTE)," in Assessing Revolutionary and Insurgent Strategies, ed. Chuck Crossett (Laurel, MD: The Johns Hopkins University Applied Physics Laboratory, 2009), 49.

188.   Jerome Conley, interview with former rebel commanders, Asmara, Eritrea, June 1997

189.   Phillips, "FARC," 27.

190.   ARIS, Undergrounds, 31; ARIS, Human Factors, 25 et seq.

191.   Deane and Nix, "Liberation Tigers," 48.

192. Phillips, "FARC," 12–13; Catherine Bott, W. James Castan, Rosemary Lark, and George Thompson, Recruitment and Radicalization of School-Aged Youth by International Terrorist Groups, Final Report (Arlington, VA: Homeland Security Institute, 2009), 1.

193. Henrik Urdal, "A Clash of Generations? Youth Bulges and Political Violence," International Studies Quarterly 50, no. 3 (September 2006): 607-629.

194. Jack A. Goldstone, "Demography, Environment, and Security: An Overview," in Demography and National Security, eds. Myron Weiner and Sharon Stanton Russell (New York: Berghahn Books, 2001), 38-61.

195. Henrik Urdal, "A Clash of Generations? Youth Bulges and Political Violence," International Studies Quarterly 50, no. 3 (September 2006): 607-629.

196. Nils Petter Gleditsch, Petter Wallensteen, Mikael Eriksson, Margareta Sollenberg, and Håvard Strand, "Armed Conflict 1946–2001: A New Dataset," Journal of Peace Research 39, no. 5 (2002): 615-637.

197. Daniel C. Esty, Jack A. Goldstone, Ted Robert Gurr, Barbara Harff, Marc Levy, Geoffrey D. Dabelko, Pamela Surko, and Alan N. Unger, State Failure Task Force Report: Phase II Findings (McLean, VA: Science Applications International, 1998).

198. ARIS, Undergrounds, 37.

199. Robert O'Brien, Barbed Wire Battleground (Victoria, BC: Trafford Publishing, 2006); and T. R. Fehrenbach, This Kind of War (Washington, DC: Brassey's, 1963).

200. Mark S. Hamm, Terrorist Recruitment in American Correctional Institutions: An Exploratory Study of Non-Traditional Faith Groups (Washington, DC: National Institute of Justice, 2007), 4–6.

201. Deborah J. Yahsar, "Indigenous Movements and Democracy in Latin America," Comparative Politics 31, no. 1 (1998): 23-42.

202. Portions of this section are taken and adapted from Undergrounds in Insurgent, Revolutionary, and Resistance Warfare, as well as Conceptual Typology of Resistance. ARIS, Undergrounds, 58 et seq., 85 et seq.; Typology, 18-19.

203. Stephen M. Saideman, "Discrimination in International Relations: Analyzing External Support for Ethnic Groups," Journal of Peace Research 39, no. 1 (2002): 27-50.

204. Molnar, Undergrounds.

205. ARIS, Conceptual Typology, 18-19.

206. Thomas Hegghammer, "The Rise of Muslim Foreign Fighters: Islam and the Globalization of Jihad," International Security 35, no. 3 (Winter 2010/11): 53-94.

207. ARIS, Undergrounds, 85.

208. The following sections were taken and in some cases adapted from the ARIS volumes, Human Factors Considerations of Undergrounds in Insurgencies and Undergrounds in Insurgent, Revolutionary, and Resistance Warfare. Nathan ARIS, ed., Human Factors Considerations of Undergrounds in Insurgencies, (United States Army Special Operations Command, Fort Bragg, NC, January 25 2013); Robert ARIS, ed., Undergrounds in Insurgent, Revolutionary, and Resistance Warfare, (United States Army Special Operations Command, Fort Bragg, NC, January 25, 2013).

209. Ted Robert Gurr, Why Men Rebel (College Park, MD: University of Maryland Press, 1971).

210. Alan B. Krueger, What Makes a Terrorist? Economics and the Roots of Terrorism (Princeton, NJ: Princeton University Press, 2007).

211. James Fearon and David Laitin, "Ethnicity, Insurgency, and Civil War," American Political Science Review 97, no. 1 (2003): 75-90. See also Paul Collier and Anke Hoeffler, "Greed and Grievance in Civil War," Oxford Economic Papers 56, no. 4 (October 2004): 563-595.

212. Sidney Tarrow, Power in Movement: Social Movements and Contentious Politics (Cambridge, UK: Cambridge University Press, 1998).

213. Jeff Goodwin, No Other Way Out: States and Revolutionary Movements 1945-1991 (Cambridge, UK: Cambridge University Press, 2001).

214. Roger Petersen, Understanding Ethnic Violence: Fear, Hatred, and Resentment in Twentieth Century Eastern Europe (Cambridge, UK: Cambridge University Press, 2002).

215. Mark Juergensmeyer, Terror in the Mind of God: The Global Rise of Religious Violence, Fourth Edition (Berkeley: University of California Press, 2017), 14.

216. Fearon and Laitin, "Ethnicity, Insurgency, and Civil War." See also Collier and Hoeffler, "Greed and Grievance in Civil War."

217. Theda Skocpol, State and Social Revolutions: A Comparative Analysis of France, Russia, and China (Cambridge, UK: Cambridge University Press, 1979).

218. ARIS, Human Factors, 19.

219. ARIS, Human Factors, 15.

220. Ted Robert Gurr, Why Men Rebel (College Park, MD: University of Maryland Press, 1971).

221. Alan B. Krueger, What Makes a Terrorist? Economics and the Roots of Terrorism (Princeton, NJ: Princeton University Press, 2007).

222. ARIS, Human Factors, 17; ARIS, Undergrounds, 5.

223. Ibid., 123.

224. Georges Sorel, Reflections on Violence (Cambridge: Cambridge University Press, 1999), 14.

225. ARIS, Undergrounds, 4.

226. These case studies are taken from the ARIS volume, Undergrounds in Insurgent, Revolutionary, and Resistance Warfare. ARIS, Undergrounds, 5-6.

227. ARIS, Human Factors, 20.

228. Jack A. Goldstone, Robert H. Bates, David L. Epstein, Ted Robert Gurr, Michael B. Lustik, Monty G. Marshall, Jay Ulfelder, and Mark Woodward, "A Global Model for Forecasting Political Instability," American Journal of Political Science 54, no. 1 (January 2010): 190-208.

229. Lars-Erik Cederman and Luc Girardin, "Beyond Fractionalization: Mapping Ethnicity Onto Nationalist Insurgencies," American Political Science Review 101, no. 1

(February 2007); Paul Collier and Anke Hoeffler, "Greed and Grievance in Civil War," Oxford Economic Papers 56, no. 4 (June 2004).

230. Ted R. Gurr, "Why Minorities Rebel: A Global Analysis of Communal Mobilization and Conflict since 1945," International Political Science Review 14, no. 2 (January 1993): 161–201

231. ARIS, Human Factors, 22.

232. ARIS, Human Factors, 131.

233. Marc Sageman, Understanding Terror Networks (Philadelphia: University of Pennsylvania Press, 2004).

234. Ibid.

235. ARIS, Human Factors, 194.

236. John Horgan, Walking Away from Terrorism: Accounts of Disengagement from Radical and Extremist Movements (New York: Routledge, 2009).

237. Troy S. Thomas, Stephen D. Kiser, and William D. Casebeer, Warlords Rising: Confronting Violent Non-state Actors (New York: Lexington Books, 2005), 157.

238. ARIS, Human Factors, 194.

239. Lou Michel and Dan Herbeck, American Terrorist (New York: HarperCollins, 2001).

240. Clark R. McCauley and Sophia Moskalenko, "Mechanisms of Political Radicalization: Pathways Toward Terrorism," Terrorism and Political Violence 20, no. 3 (2008): 415–433.

241. ARIS, Human Factors, 197.

242. Ibid., 198.

243. Clark R. McCauley and Sophia Moskalenko, Friction: How Radicalization Happens to Them and Us (New York: Oxford University Press, 2011).

244. James Fearon and David Laitin, "Ethnicity, Insurgency, and Civil War," American Political Science Review 97, no. 1 (2003): 75-90. See also Paul Collier and Anke Hoeffler, "Greed and Grievance in Civil War," Oxford Economic Papers 56, no. 4 (October 2004): 563-595.

245. Fearon and Laitin, "Ethnicity, Insurgency, and Civil War."

246. Joerg Le Blanc, "The Urban Environment and its Influences on Insurgent Campaigns," Terrorism and Political Violence 25, no. 5 (2013): 798-819.

247. ARIS, Human Factors, 27.

248. Paul Collier and Anke Hoeffler, "Greed and Grievance in Civil War," Oxford Economic Papers 56, no. 4 (June 2004); James D. Fearon and David D. Laitin, "Ethnicity, Insurgency and Civil War," American Political Science Review 97, no. 1 (2003): 75-90.

249. James D. Fearon and David D. Laitin, "Weak States, Rough Terrain, and Large-Scale Ethnic Violence Since 1945" (paper presented at the annual meeting of the American Political Science Association, Atlanta, GA, September 2-5, 1999).

250. Bailey, M. D., Robert; Harris,Marc; Hendrex,Daniel; Melin,Nicholas; Russo,Richard. (2014). A Proposed Framework for Appreciating Megacities: A US Army Perspective. (Report number: HD-227318 Bethesda, MD:

251. Evans, M. (2016). Future war in cities: Urbanization's challenge to strategic studies in the 21st century. International Review of the Red Cross, 98(901), 37-51.

252. Anthony, R. M., & Robison, K. K. (2018). Forced urbanisation: A cross-national assessment of the effects of intranational political violence on a nation's largest cities. Urban Studies, 55(13), 2923-2945. See also Martin Ravallion, Shaohua Chen, and Prem Sangraula, "New Evidence on the Urbanization of Global Poverty," Population and Development Review 33, no. 4 (December 2007): 667-701.

253. Fox, S., & Bell, A. (2016). Urban geography and protest mobilization in Africa. Political Geography, 53, 54-64.

254. Glaeser, E. L., & Steinberg, B. M. (2017). Transforming cities: does urbanization promote democratic change? Regional Studies, 51(1), 58-68.

255. Muggah, R. (2014). Deconstructing the fragile city: exploring insecurity, violence and resilience. Environment and Urbanization, 26(2), 345-358.

256. Bailey, et al., A Proposed Framework for Appreciating Megacities.

257. McGinty, A. C. Urbanization and militant networks: An alternative futures analysis.

258. Hussain, N., & Shelley, L. (2016). Karachi: Organized Crime in a Key Megacity. Connections (18121098), 15(3), 5-15.

259. Schuberth, M. (2018). Hybrid security governance, post-election violence and the legitimacy of community-based armed groups in urban Kenya. Journal of Eastern African Studies, 12(2), 386-404.

260. Bailey, et al., A Proposed Framework for Appreciating Megacities.

261. Raleigh, C. (2015). Urban violence patterns across African states. International Studies Review, 17(1), 90-106.

262. Schuberth, "Hybrid security governance, post-election violence and the legitimacy of community-based armed groups in urban Kenya."

263. Fearon and Laitin, "Ethnicity, Insurgency, and Civil War."

264. Jacqueline L. Hazelton, "The 'Hearts and Minds' Fallacy: Violence, Coercion, and Success in Counterinsurgency Warfare," International Security 42, no. 1 (Summer 2017): 80-113.

265. For negotiations see Monica Duffy Toft, "Ending Civil Wars: A Case for Rebel Victory?," International Security 34, no. 4 (Spring 2010): 7-36. For concessions see Kathleen Gallagher Cunningham, "Divide and Conquer or Divide and Concede: How Do States Respond to Internally Divided Separatists" American Political Science Review 105, no. 2 (2011), 276.

266. ARIS, Conceptual Typology of Resistance, (United States Army Special Operations Command, Fort Bragg, NC), 28.

267. ARIS, Conceptual Typology of Resistance, (United States Army Special Operations Command, Fort Bragg, NC), 29.

268. Christoph Reuter, "The Terror Strategist: Secret Files Reveal the Structure of Islamic State," Spiegel Online, April 18, 2015, http://www.spiegel.de/international/world/islamic-state-files-show-structure-of-islamist-terror-group-a-1029274.html.

269. ARIS, Human Factors, 159.

270. Ibid., 160.

271. Nicole Winfield, "It's 'an Honor if the Americans Attack Me.' Pope Francis Acknolwedges Critics Within U.S. Catholic Church." Time (September 4, 2019), https://time.com/5668895/pope-francis-american-criticism/.

272. ARIS, Human Factors, 160.

273. Benn Eifert, Edward Miguel, and Daniel N. Posner, "Political Competition and Ethnic Identification in Africa," American Journal of Political Science 54, no. 2 (April 2010): 494–510.

274. ARIS, Human Factors, 161-163.

275. Henri Tajfel, M. G. Billig, R. P. Bundy, and Claude Flament, "Social Categorization and Intergroup Behaviour," European Journal of Social Psychology 1, no. 2 (1971): 149–178.

276. ARIS, Human Factors, 163.

277. For alliances and commitment between groups see Navin A. Bapat, and Kanisha D. Bond, "Alliances between Militant Groups," British Journal of Political Science 42, no. 4 (2012): 793-824. For power distributions between groups see Peter Krause, "The Structure of Success: How the Internal Distribution of Power Drives Armed Group Behavior and National Movement Effectiveness," International Security 38, no. 3 (Winter 2013/14): 72-116.

278. Paul Collier, Anke Hoeffler, and Mans Soderbom, "On the Duration of Civil War," Journal of Peace Research 41, no. 3 (2004): 253-273.

279. David E. Cunningham, "Veto Players and Civil War Duration," American Journal of Political Science 50, no. 4 (October 2006): 875-892.

280. Ibid., 26; ARIS, Undergrounds, 142.

281. Collier and Hoeffler, "Greed and Grievance in Civil War."

282. Paul Collier and Anke Hoeffler, "Greed and Grievance in Civil War," Oxford Economic Papers 56, no. 4 (June 2004).

283. Ibid.

284. Collier and Hoeffler, Greed and Grievance in Civil War, 1-2.

285. Paivi Lujala, "The Spoils of Nature: Armed Civil Conflict and Rebel Access to Natural Resources," Journal of Peace Research 47, no. 1 (2010): 15-28.

286. James D. Fearon and David D. Laitin, "Ethnicity, Insurgency, and Civil War," American Political Science Review 97, no. 1 (2003): 75-90.

287. Collier and Hoeffler, Greed and Grievance in Civil War.

288. Ibid.

289. Mary Kaldor, New & Old Wars: Organized Violence in a Global Era (Stanford, CA: Stanford University Press, 2007); Mark Duffield, "Globalization of War Economies: Promoting Order or the Return of History?" Fletcher Forum of World Affairs 23, no. 2 (1999): 27.

290. Steven Metz, Rethinking Insurgency (Fayetteville, AR: Juniper Grove, 2007), 30.

291.   ARIS, Human Factors, 220.

292.   "Arab Spring anniversary: When Egypt cut the internet," Al Jazeera, (January 25, 2016), https://www.aljazeera.com/indepth/features/2016/01/arab-spring-anniversary-egypt-cut-internet-160125042903747.html; See Ilhelm Allagui and Johanne Kuebler, "The Arab Spring and the Role of ICTs," International Journal of Communication 5, 1435-1442 (2011).

293.   ARIS, Human Factors, 220-228.

294.   ARIS, Human Factors, 220.

295.   ARIS, Human Factors, 223.

296.   Maura Conway, "Reality Bytes: Cyberterrorism and Terrorist 'Use' of the Internet," First Monday 7, no. 11 (2002).

297.   ARIS, Human Factors, 223.

298.   Gabriel Weimann, Terror on the Internet: The New Arena, the New Challenges (Washington, DC: United States Institute of Peace Press, 2006).

299.   Lorrain Bowman-Grieve, "Irish Republicanism and the Internet: Support for New Wave Dissidents," Perspectives on Terrorism 4, no. 2 (2010).

300.   ARIS, Human Factors, 225.

301.   Michael Moss and Souad Mekhennet, "An Internet Jihad Aims at U.S. Viewers," The New York Times, October 15, 2007.

302.   ARIS, Human Factors, 225.

303.   Gabriel Weimann, "WWW.AL-QAEDA: The Reliance of Al-Qaeda on the Internet," in Responses to Cyber Terrorism, ed. Centre of Excellence Defence Against Terrorism (Amsterdam, The Netherlands: IOS Press, 2008), 61.

304.   ARIS, Human Factors, 226.

305.   Myra Philip and Dennis Rice, "Omagh Killers Target William," Daily Express, October 14, 2000, http://www.mail-archive.com/kominform@lists.eunet.fi/msg03972.html.

306.   Weimann, Terror on the Internet.

307.   Lev Grossman, "Iran Protests: Twitter, the Medium of the Movement," Time Magazine, June 17, 2009, http://www.time.com/time/world/article/0,8599,1905125,00.html.

308.   Maximillian Forte, "America's Iranian Twitter Revolution," Open Anthropology (blog), June 17, 2009, http://openanthropology.wordpress.com/2009/06/17/americas-iranian-twitter-revolution/.

309.   Dusan Stojanovic and Jovana Gec, "Serbian Ousters of Milosevic make Mark in Egypt," Associated Press, February 22, 2011.

310.   ARIS, Human Factors, 228.

311.   This section is taken from ARIS, Undergrounds, 107-116.

312. John Arquilla, David Ronfeldt, and Michele Zanini, "Networks, Netwar, and Information-Age Terrorism," in Strategic Appraisal: The Changing Role of Information in Warfare, ed. Zalmay M. Khalilzad and John P. White (Santa Monica, CA: RAND, 1999).

313. Jacob N. Shapiro and Nils B. Weidmann, "Talking About Killing: Cell Phones, Collective Action, and Insurgent Violence in Iraq," September 6, 2011, https://bc.sas.upenn.edu/system/files/Shapiro_09.29.11.pdf..

314. Sean Kennedy, "New Media: A Boon for Insurgents or Counterinsurgents?" Small Wars Journal, September 4, 2011, http://smallwarsjournal.com/node/11414.

315. Evgeny Morozov, "Moldova's Twitter Revolution," Net Effect (blog), April 7, 2009, http://neteffect.foreignpolicy.com/posts/2009/04/07/moldovas_twitter_revolution.

316. Hunter, Samuel T., Neil D. Shortland, Matthew P. Crayne, and Gina S. Ligon. 2017. "Recruitment and Selection in Violent Extremist Organizations: Exploring What Industrial and Organizational Psychology Might Contribute." American Psychologist 72 (April): 242-254. http://psycnet.apa.org/journals/amp/72/3/242/

317. This section is taken from ARIS, Human Factors, 23 et seq.

318. Jack A. Goldstone, Robert H. Bates, David L. Epstein, Ted Robert Gurr, Michael B. Lustik, Monty G. Marshall, Jay Ulfelder, and Mark Woodward, "A Global Model for Forecasting Political Instability," American Journal of Political Science 54, no. 1 (January 2010): 190–208.

319. Paul Staniland, Networks of Rebellion: Explaining Insurgent Cohesion and Collapse (Ithaca: Cornell University Press, 2014).

320. Samuel P. Huntington, Political Order in Changing Societies (New Haven: Yale University Press, 1968). See also Staniland, Networks of Rebellion.

321. Bert Suykens, "Comparing Rebel Rule Through Revolution and Naturalization: Ideologies of Governance in Naxalite and Naga India," in Rebel Governance in Civil War, eds. Ana Arjona, Nelson Kasfir, and Zachariah Mampilly (New York: Cambridge University Press, 2015), 138-137. Suykens looks at the Maoist Naxalite rebel group which wanted to carry out a revolution in India and the Nagaland rebel group which was oriented around the Naga ethnic group.

322. Jurgen Willems and Marc Jegers, "Social Movement Structures in Relation to Goals and Forms of Action: An Exploratory Model," Canadian Journal of Nonprofit & Social Economy Research (ANSESRJ) 3, no. 2 (Autumn 2012): 67–81.

323. ARIS, Conceptual Typology of Resistance, 38.

324. Willems and Jegers, "Social Movement Structures," 71.

325. Ibid.

326. Ibid., 70.

327. Ibid.

328. Figure adapted from ARIS, Conceptual Typology of Resistance, 39. Luther P. Gerlach, "The Structure of Social Movements: Environmental Activism and Its Opponents," in Networks and Netwars: The Future of Terror, Crime, and Militancy, ed. John Arquilla and David Ronfeldt (Santa Monica, CA: RAND Corporation, 2001), 289–310.

329. Ibid., 289-290.

330. ARIS, Conceptual Typology of Resistance, 41.

331. Paul Staniland, Networks of Rebellion, 6-9.

332. Jeremy M. Weinstein, Inside Rebellion: The Politics of Insurgent Violence (Cambridge: Cambridge University Press, 2007), 6, 12-15. See also Jeremy M. Weinstein, "Resources and the Information Problem in Rebel Recruitment," Journal of Conflict Resolution 49, no. 4 (August 2005): 598-624. Weinstein approaches organizational theory through resource endowments and distinguishes between groups with economic endowments and social endowments.

333. David S. Alberts and Richard E. Hayes, Power to the Edge (CCRP Publication Series, 2003).

334. Geert Hofstede, "National Cultures in Four Dimensions: A Research-based Theory of Cultural Differences Among Nations," International Studies of Management & Organization 13, no. 2 (1983): 46–74.

335. This section is taken from ARIS, Undergrounds, 13.

336. This section is taken from ARIS, Undergrounds, 14.

337. This section is taken from ARIS, Human Factors, 43.

338. Frans P. B. Osinga, Science, Strategy, and War: The Strategic Theory of John Boyd (New York: Routledge, 2006).

339. See Chapter 1 of Undergrounds in Insurgent, Revolutionary, and Resistance Warfare for further discussion of the dilemma of inclusiveness.

340. This section adapted from ARIS, Narratives and Competing Messages (United States Army Special Operations Command, Fort Bragg, NC), 1-4.

341. Stefan Malthaner, "Spaces, Ties, and Agency: The Formation of Radical Networks," Perspectives on Terrorism 12, no. 2 (2018): 32-43. See also Daniel Byman, Understanding Proto-Insurgencies: RAND Counterinsurgency Study, Paper 3 (Santa Monica, CA: RAND Corporation, 2007).

342. Byman, Understanding Proto-Insurgencies. See also Aaron Y. Zelin, "Picture or It Didn't Happen: A Snapshot of the Islamic State's Official Media Output," Perspectives on Terrorism 9, no. 4 (August 2015): 85-97. James P. Farwell, "The Media Strategy of ISIS," Survival 56, no. 6 (2014): 49-55.

343. Mark A. Finlayson and Steven R. Corman, "The Military Case for Narrative," Sprache und Datenverarbeitung: International Journal for Language Data Processing 37, no. 1–2 (2013): 173–191.

344. Thomas Elkjer Nissen, "Narrative Led Operations." Militaert Tidsskrift 141, no. 4 (2013): 67-77.

345. Finlayson and Corman, "The Military Case for Narrative."

346. This section is taken from ARIS, Human Factors, 208 et seq.

347. ARIS, Conceptual Typology, 64.

348. This section is taken from the ARIS volume Haufler, Lauber, Agan, and Pinczuk, Narratives.

349. Shaul R. Shenhav, "Political Narratives and Political Reality," International Political Science Review 27, no. 3 (2006): 245-262.

350. Chuck Crosset, Summer Newton, and Jason Spitaletta, "The Role of Narrative in Insurgent and Revolutionary Warfare: Examples from 24 Case Studies Spanning 1962-2009," Journal of Cultural Intelligence (in press).

351. Table is taken from ARIS volume ARIS, Human Factors, 263.

352. This section is taken from ARIS, Human Factors, 209.

353. This section is taken from ARIS, Human Factors, 211.

354. Bruce Hoffman, Inside Terrorism (New York: Columbia University Press, 1998)

355. Ibid.

356. Ibid., 69.

357. ARIS, Human Factors, 218.

358. Christina Meyer, Underground Voices: Insurgent Propaganda in El Salvador, Nicaragua and Peru (Santa Monica, CA: RAND, 1991).

359. This section is taken from ARIS, Human Factors, 219 et seq.

360. This section is taken from ARIS Conceptual Typology of Resistance, 44.

361. Figure from ARIS, Conceptual Typology of Resistance, 45. ARIS, Undergrounds, 10–12.

362. This section is taken from ARIS, Undergrounds, 10.

363. Maegen Nix and Shana Marshall, "Liberation Tigers of Tamil Eelam (LTTE)," in ARIS, Casebook on Insurgency and Revolutionary Warfare, Volume II: 1962–2009.

364. This section is taken from ARIS, Undergrounds, 11.

365. This section is taken from ARIS, Undergrounds, 11.

366. This section is taken from ARIS, Conceptual Typology of Resistance, 45.

367. This section is taken from ARIS, Conceptual Typology of Resistance, 45.

368. Olivier Bangerter, Regulating Armed Groups from Within: A Typology, Research Note 13 (Geneva: Small Arms Survey, January 2012).

369. This section is taken from Cosgrove and Hahn, Conceptual Typology of Resistance, 46.

370. Figure from ARIS, Conceptual Typology of Resistance, 47. Czesław Sikorski, Kultura Organizacyjna (Warsaw: C. H. Beck, 2002), quoted in Sułkowski, "Typologies," 173–182.

371. Łukasz Sułkowski, "Typologies of Organisational Culture – Multi-dimensional Classifications," Przedsiębiorczość i Zarządzanie 14, no. 2 (2013): 181.

372. Ibid.

373. Ibid.

374. Ibid.

375. Max Abrahms and Philip B.K. Potter, "Explaining Terrorism: Leadership Deficits and Militant Group Tactics," International Organization 69, (Spring 2015): 311-342. See also Max Abrahms and Jochen Mierau, "Leadership Matters: The Effects of Targeted Killings on Militant Group Tactics," Terrorism and Political Violence 29, no. 5 (2017): 830-851.

376. Ted Robert Gurr, Why Men Rebel (College Park, MD: University of Maryland Press, 1971).

377. Edward N. Muller, "Income Inequality, Regime Repressiveness, and Political Violence," American Sociological Review 50, no. 1 (February 1985): 47-61.

378. Max Abrahms, "Why Terrorism Does Not Work," International Security 31, no. 2 (Fall 2006): 42-78.

379. Gene Sharp, Waging Nonviolent Struggle: 20th Century Practice and 21st Century Potential (Manchester, NH: Extending Horizons Books, 2005).

380. Erica Chenoweth and Maria J. Stephan, Why Civil Resistance Works: The Strategic Logic of Nonviolent Conflict (New York: Columbia University Press, 2011).

381. Herbert H. Haines, "Black Radicalization and the Funding of Civil Rights: 1957-1970," Social Problems 32, no. 1 (October 1984): 31-43.

382. Majken Jul Sorensen, "Humor as a Serious Strategy of Nonviolent Resistance to Oppression," Peace and Change 33, no. 2 (April 2008): 167-190.

383. Patricia Bauer and Bertold Schweitzer, "The Egyptian Revolution 2011: Mechanisms of Violence and Non-Violence," in Democracy in Crisis: The Dynamics of Civil Protest and Civil Resistance, eds. Bert Preiss and Claudia Brunner (Munster: LIT Verlag, 2012), 309-330.

384. Muller, "Income Inequality, Regime Repressiveness, and Political Violence."

385. Kristine Hoglund, "Electoral Violence in Conflict-Ridden Societies: Concepts, Causes, and Consequences," Terrorism and Political Violence 21, no. 3 (2009): 412-427.

386. James Raymond Vreeland, "The Effect of Political Regime on Civil War: Unpacking Anocracy," Journal of Conflict Resolution 52, no. 3 (June 2008): 401-425.

387. Roger Petersen, Understanding Ethnic Violence: Fear, Hatred, and Resentment in Twentieth Century Eastern Europe (Cambridge, UK: Cambridge University Press, 2002).

388. David B. Edwards, Caravan of Martyrs: Sacrifice and Suicide Bombing in Afghanistan (Berkeley: University of California Press, 2017).

389. Michael Freeman, "The Sources of Terrorist Financing: Theory and Typology," Studies in Conflict and Terrorism 34, no. 6 (2011): 461-475.

390. ARIS, Conceptual Typology of Resistance, 52.

391. This section is taken from ARIS, Conceptual Typology of Resistance, 53.

392. This section is taken from ARIS, Human Factors,

393. John R. Schafer and Joe Navarro, "The Seven-Stage Hate Model: The Psychopathology of Hate Groups," FBI Law Enforcement Bulletin 72, no. 3 (March 2003): 1–9.

394. John Horgan, Walking Away from Terrorism: Accounts of Disengagement from Radical and Extremist Movements (London and New York: Routledge, 2009).

395. This section is taken from ARIS, Thresholds of Violence.

396. Michael P. Atkinson and Moshe Kress, "On Popular Response to Violence during Insurgencies," Operations Research Letters 40, no 4 (2012): 223.

397. Eric P. Wendt, "Strategic Counterinsurgency Modeling," Special Warfare 18, no. 2 (2005): 4–5.

398. ARIS, Thresholds of Violence, 2019.

399. John Darby, "Legitimate Targets: A Control on Violence?," in New Perspectives on the Northern Ireland Conflict, ed. Adrian Guelke (Aldershot, England: Avebury, 1994), 63.

400. This section is taken from ARIS, Conceptual Typology of Resistance, 62.

401. ARIS, Conceptual Typology of Resistance, 63.

402. This section is taken from ARIS, Human Factors,

403. Gene Sharp, The Politics of Nonviolent Action (Boston: Portor Sargent, 1973), reproduced by The Albert Einstein Institution, accessed December 11, 2011, http://www.aeinstein.org/organizations103a.html.

404. Gene Sharp, Sharp's Dictionary of Power and Struggle: Language of Civil Resistance in Conflicts (New York: Oxford University Press, 2011).

405. Feliks Gross, The Seizure of Political Power in a Century of Revolutions (New York: Philosophical Library, 1958), 51.

406. This section is taken from ARIS, Human Factors, 283.

407. This section is taken from ARIS, Human Factors, 287.

408. John G. Williams, "Underground Military Organization and Warfare" (unpublished master's thesis [thesis 452], Georgetown University, Washington, DC, February 1950), 89–90.

409. David Martin, Ally Betrayed (New York: Prentice-Hall, 1946), 177–179.

410. This section is taken from ARIS, Human Factors, 288.

411. R. D. Wilson, Cordon and Search (Aldershot, England: Gale and Polden, Ltd., 1949), 33.

412. See Joan V. Bondurant, Conquest of Violence: The Gandhian Philosophy of Conflict (Princeton, NJ: Princeton University Press, 1958), 91ff.

413. Dorothy E. Denning, "Activism, Hacktivism, and Cyberterrorism: The Internet as a Tool for Influencing Foreign Policy," in Networks and Netwars: The Future of Terror, Crime, and Militancy, ed. John Arquilla and David Rondfelt (Santa Monica, CA: RAND Corporation, 2001).

414. This section is taken from ARIS, Human Factors, 293.

415. Mulford Q. Sibley, ed., The Quiet Battle (Garden City, NY: Anchor Books, 1963), 156-157.

416. This section is taken from ARIS, Human Factors, 295.

417. This section is taken from ARIS, Human Factors, 296.

418. This section is taken from ARIS, Undergrounds, 173.

419. Jerome Conley, "Revolutionary United Front (RUF), Sierra Leone" in ARIS, Casebook on Insurgency and Revolutionary Warfare, Volume II: 1962–2009.

420. This section is taken from ARIS, Undergrounds, 174.

421. This section is taken from ARIS, Undergrounds, 175.

422. This section is taken from ARIS, Undergrounds, 176.

423. This section is taken from ARIS, Undergrounds, 176.

424. This section is taken from ARIS, Undergrounds, 43 et seq.

425. Ron Buikema and Matt Burger, "New People's Army (NPA)," in ARIS, Casebook on Insurgency and Revolutionary Warfare, Volume II: 1962–2009.

426. Michael J. Deane and Maegen Nix, "Liberation Tigers of Tamil Eelam (LTTE)," in ARIS, Assessing Revolutionary and Insurgent Strategies, 56.

427. SORO, Undergrounds in Insurgent, Revolutionary, and Resistance Warfare (Washington, DC: Special Operations Research Office, The American University, 1963), 108.

428. Jerome Conley, "Orange Revolution (Ukraine): 2005–2005," in ARIS, Casebook on Insurgency and Revolutionary Warfare, Volume II: 1962–2009.

429. This section is taken ARIS, Undergrounds, 58 et seq.

430. SORO, Undergrounds in Insurgent, Revolutionary, and Resistance Warfare (Washington, DC: Special Operations Research Office, The American University, 1963), 62.

431. This section is taken from ARIS, Undergrounds, 62 et seq.

432. Rachel Ehrenfeld, "The Muslim Brotherhood New International Economic Order," The Terror Finance Blog (blog), October 13, 2007, http://www.terrorfinance.org/the_terror_finance_blog/2007/10/the-muslim-brot-1.html.

433. Ibid.

434. Ibid.

435. This section is taken from ARIS, Undergrounds, 65 et seq.

436. Jerome Conley, "The Revolutionary United Front (RUF)," in ARIS, Assessing Revolutionary and Insurgent Strategies, (Laurel, MD: The Johns Hopkins University Applied Physics Laboratory, 2009), 52–53.

437. Bryan Gervais, "Hutu-Tutsi Genocides," in ARIS, Casebook on Insurgency and Revolutionary Warfare, Volume II: 1962–2009.

438. "Philippines (Huk Rebellion), 1946-1956: Case Outcome: COIN Win," in Paths to Victory: Detailed Insurgency Case Studies, ed. Christopher Paul et al., 31–39 (Santa Monica, CA: RAND Corporation, 2013), 33.

439. Sanaz Miraz, "Taliban 1994-2009," in ARIS, Casebook on Insurgency and Revolutionary Warfare, Volume II: 1962–2009, 471–472.

440. Stephen Phillips, "Fuerzas Armadas Revolucionarias De Colombia—FARC," in ARIS, Assessing Revolutionary and Insurgent Strategies (Laurel, MD: The Johns Hopkins University Applied Physics Laboratory, 2009), 24.

441. This section is taken from ARIS, Undergrounds, 91 et seq., and ARIS, Human Factors, 299 et seq.

442. Ernest K. Bramstedt, Dictatorship and Political Police: The Technique of Control by Fear (New York: Oxford University Press, 1945), 210.

443. This section is taken from 94 et seq.

444. Magnus Ranstorp, "The Hizballah Training Camps of Lebanon," in The Making of a Terrorist: Recruitment, Training, and Root Causes, ed. James J. F. Forest, vol. 2 (Westport, CT: Praeger Security International, 2005), 243–262.

445. Ibid.

446. ARIS, Undergrounds, 95.

447. This section is taken from ARIS, Undergrounds, 99 et seq.

448. ARIS, Undergrounds, 100.

449. Gene Sharp, The Politics of Nonviolent Action (Boston: Portor Sargent, 1973), reproduced by The Albert Einstein Institution, accessed December 11, 2011, http://www.aeinstein.org/organizations103a.html.

Milton Keynes UK
Ingram Content Group UK Ltd.
UKHW051007010424
440216UK00002B/2

RED SEA

DIVING GUIDE

SWAN·HILL
PRESS

RED SEA
DIVING GUIDE

Texts
Andrea Ghisotti
Alessandro Carletti

Texts of the diving sites in Israel
Hanan Golombek

Biological information
Angelo Mojetta

Editorial production
Valeria Manferto De Fabianis
Laura Accomazzo

Graphic design
Patrizia Balocco Lovisetti

Illustrations of the dives
Arabella Lazzarin

Illustrations of the fish
Monica Falcone

Translation
Antony Shugaar

© 1994 Edizioni White Star
Via Candido Sassone, 24
13100 Vercelli, Italy

First Published in the UK in 1994 by Swan Hill Press
an imprint of Airlife Publishing Ltd.

British Library Cataloguing in Publication Data
A catalogue record for this book is available from the British Library.

ISBN 1 85310 553 8

All rights reserved. No part of this book may be reproduced or transmitted in any form or by any means, electronic or mechanical including photocopying, recording or by any information storage and retrieval system, without permission from the Publisher in writing.

Printed in Italy

SWAN HILL PRESS
an imprint of Airlife Publishing Ltd.
101 Longden Road, Shrewsbury SY3 9EB, England

Contents

1 A group of onespot snappers (Lutjanus monostigma) lights up the water with their silvery reflections. Photograph by Claudio Ziraldo.

2 The transparent water makes it possible to see the wall of the reef dropping away into the depths of the sea as if it were a reflection in a mirror. Photograph by Andrea Ghisotti.

3 In this satellite photograph, the long strip of the Red Sea wends its way from the Sinai Peninsula to the Gulf of Aden. Photograph by Worldsat International.

4-5 In this photograph, taken from the Space Shuttle, the triangular shape of the Sinai Peninsula stands out against the surface of the sea. Photograph by NASA.

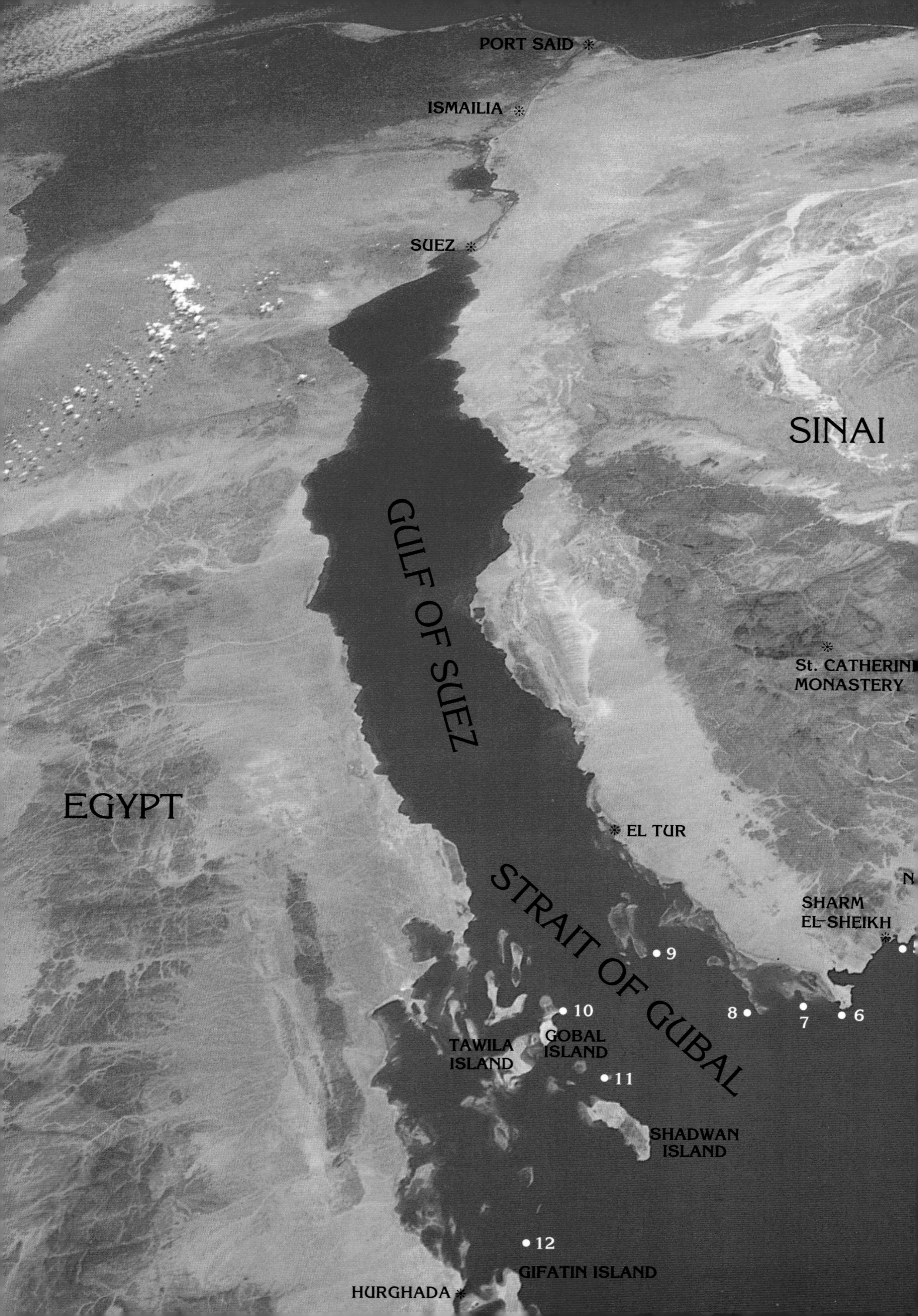
PORT SAID
ISMAILIA
SUEZ
SINAI
GULF OF SUEZ
St. CATHERINE
MONASTERY
EGYPT
EL TUR
STRAIT OF GUBAL
SHARM
EL-SHEIKH
9
10
8
7
6
TAWILA
ISLAND
GOBAL
ISLAND
11
SHADWAN
ISLAND
12
GIFATIN ISLAND
HURGHADA

ISRAEL
JORDAN
EILAT
AQABA
1
2
3
NUWEIBA
GULF OF AQABA
DAHAB
SAUDI ARABIA
SANAFIR ISLAND
RED SEA

INTRODUCTION

The Red Sea is the tropical sea closest to Europe, and it is therefore the ideal destination for Old World scuba divers; and in fact, ever since the first expedition by the pioneer Hans Hass to Sudan, long-ago in 1950, European divers have considered it as a choice diving area, both in winter months, when the waters of the Mediterranean become too cold, and in spring and summer months, despite the African heat that bears down upon the waves. After the first adventuresome expeditions, often organized with limited resources and an infinite spirit of adaptation, there has been a gradual development of tourism in certain areas, which have, in the course of time acquired lodging, diving centers, and charter boats specially equipped for underwater cruises. Over recent years, in particular, the phenomenon has literally exploded and the classic sites in the north, Hurghada and Sharm el-Sheikh, have been transformed into very sophisticated and well-equipped centers that are every bit the equal of better known spots around the world. The credit for all of this is chiefly due to the political stability of the region and the convenient charter flights that link all major European cities directly with these two sites, reducing the time-consuming and arduous travel of years gone by to a pleasant outing of just a few hours. This incredible proliferation of tourism has naturally brought about a perilous environmental impact with the reef and its inhabitants; there could be dramatic results from so great a number of visitors on a daily basis. Fortunately, parks have been set up - such as that of Ras Mohammad, at the far southern tip of the Sinai peninsula - with the specific aim of preserving and protecting from harm those areas of particular naturalistic importance. The effect of these parks has been noticeable and immediate, and even today Ras Mohammad and other sites for diving, such as the reefs in the Strait of Tiran, or CarelessReef, are among the finest dives, not only in the Red Sea, but in the whole world.

As one moves gradually south from the waters of the northern Red Sea, the tourist facilities begin to disappear, leaving a sea that - though it may be near Europe and visited regularly by divers - has an aura of mystery that makes it different from any other sea in the world, rich in contrasts and always unpredictable. A good example is the mythical islet of Zabargad, with its abandoned olivine mines, dating back to the sixteenth century B.C., or the small Rocky Island, with its noisy population of thousands of terns, or also the Brothers Islands, which are little

A

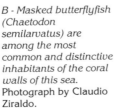

B

C

A - Great fans of gorgonians (Gorgonia ventalina) open along the walls of the reef, thus giving the seabed of the northern Red Sea its unmistakable appearance. Photograph by Claudio Ziraldo.

B - Masked butterflyfish (Chaetodon semilarvatus) are among the most common and distinctive inhabitants of the coral walls of this sea. Photograph by Claudio Ziraldo.

C- A group of blackspotted grunts (Plectorhynchus gaterinus) seems to gaze curiously in the direction of the scuba diver that is photographing them. Photograph by Vincenzo Paolillo.

more than crags breaking the surface some hundred miles south of the Sinai coast, or the unsettling waters of Dedalus Reef, which few scuba divers have had the good fortune to visit. Still further south one enters Sudanese waters, an underwater paradise that seems to close its doors to tourism, rather than to open them. This area requires a considerable spirit of adaptability, but it provides excitement and strong sensations. Last come the Dahlak Islands, a last earthly Eden that has been off limits for many years due to the war between Ethiopia and Eritrea. These 126 islands are close to the hearts of the Italians, who certainly recall the *Formica* expedition of 1953, the members of which bore names now legendary. Of all these places, so important to the history of scuba diving - oddly enough - there is no single book that serves as a guide to divers who wish to select an itinerary and have useful information during the trip. This guide was written in order to fill the gap, providing serious divers with an overview of the finest dives in the entire Red Sea, from the far north to the Dahlak Islands. The guide to each area includes an underwater route and a three-dimensional drawing documenting a complete dive.

THE RED SEA A MIRACLE TO BE PROTECTED

E

F

D - A tiny blenny (Helcogramma sp.) is poised on a slender branch of coral. Photograph by Paolo Fossati.

E - The remarkably transparent water makes it possible to enjoy a splendid dive to the wreck of a tugboat which sank in the waters off Southern Egypt. Photograph by Andrea Ghisotti.

F - In this picture, it is possible to admire the intricate structure of a branch of soft coral (Dendronephthya sp.). Photograph by Jeff Rotman.

The Red Sea possesses characteristics that make it unique, and which cannot be found anywhere else on earth. It is a basin closed to the north by the Strait of Suez and by the Gulf of Aqaba and to the south by the Strait of Bab el Mandeb, which is roughly 100 meters in depth, thus separating the Red Sea substantially from the system of currents of the Indian Ocean. Because of this "semi-continuity" with the ocean, the Red Sea is an ecosystem of the Indo-Pacific variety; it stands out, however, for the 20 percent of endemic fish species, and for the particularly varied coral makeup of its reefs (more than four hundred species of coral have thus far been recorded). With its 2,350 kilometers of length and its 350 kilometers of maximum breadth (off Ethiopia), its deep waters where the temperature can go as high as 30 degrees centigrade due to volcanic activity on the sea bed, its regular currents, driving northwards in winter and southwards in summer, its almost total lack of tides - with all these factors, the Red Sea constitutes a fantastic and unrivalled "biological niche."

Coral reefs, moreover, are almost the most stable among all the ecosystems that have been studied to date, because of their ability to regenerate and the sophisticated equilibrium between coral and inhabitants of the reef - all of these are conditions that might lead the casual observer to think that this is a treasure that we will never lose. As one might guess with a little thought, however, humanity must do its part in preserving the environment. Anyone who spends a day on the coasts of the Red Sea, especially near the Gulf of Suez, can hardly help but notice the endless line of huge freighters passing through. These ships, especially the oil tankers, constitute an ever-present threat of environmental disaster. It is therefore absolutely necessary for one and all to do their best, both government agencies and everyday people, to institute the strictest regulation of security and behavior on board these giant potential floating oil slicks in order to prevent the sort of events that might result in the destruction of huge breeding grounds and thousands of living creatures. Scuba-diving tourists,

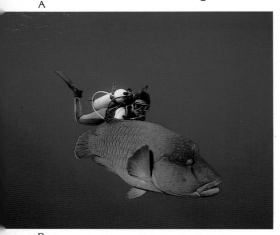

too, however, must do their part, shouldering the responsibilities that come with a love of the sea. Let us summarize a few of the most important rules, partly taken from Law n° 102 passed by the Parliament of Egypt in 1983, which apply to the regulations of the National Park of Ras Mohammad:
- Remove nothing that is alive, dead, or fossilized from the seabeds and from the beaches.
- Do not drive vehicles on the coral waterfront areas.
- Do not litter the beaches, and do not throw anything into the sea.
- Do not drop anchor on the reef if it is possible to make use of the special anchorages that have been prepared (always available

in Egypt's protected areas).
- Do not engage in underwater fishing or sports fishing in protected areas.
- Never engage in underwater fishing while using scuba diving equipment.
- Do not feed to the fish, as this will change their feeding habits.
- While diving, make sure that you do nothing to damage the sea bottom.
- If you are a beginner, or if you are taking diving lessons, limit your activities to those areas of the sea floor where you cannot do any damage to the environment (for instance, sandy seabeds with scattered coral formations). Lastly, we recommend that all our readers peruse some of the many books of popular science on undersea fauna: being able to recognize what you see when diving, and being familiar with its nature, at least in general terms, is often a required condition in order to keep from harming living species that are so distant from us. One can easily and thoughtlessly destroy that which one does not understand.

SCUBA DIVING EQUIPMENT

A - A splendid specimen of the humphead wrasse (Cheilinus undulatus) accompanies a diver through the deep seabeds of Ras Mohammad. Photograph by Itamar Grinberg.

B - Soft corals, with their limitless shades of color, are among the most spectacular features on the underwater scene of the Red Sea. Photograph by Vincenzo Paolillo.

C - Soft corals are present throughout the Red Sea in an infinite variety of shapes and colors, which is unrivalled in any other sea on earth. Photograph by Andrea and Antonella Ferrari.

A considerable factor in the success of a tropical diving expedition depends upon one's preparation and one's choice of equipment.
The Red Sea is no different, because, among other things, certain areas, such as southern Egypt, Sudan, and Eritrea, are completely lacking in stores in which it is possible to purchase diving equipment.
Therefore, the diver must bring everything with him or her from home, and must also be sure to test everything thoroughly, and it is wise to have everything "tuned up," unless you wish to run into a series of extremely annoying problems that can do much to endanger the success of your trip.

Let's take a look at the equipment. The choice of wetsuit is extremely important. One should not think for a moment that the entire Red Sea is always warm and "tropical." All through the northern part, Sinai and the Egyptian coasts, temperatures drop considerably during the winter months, and one could suffer greatly from the cold if one has not prepared adequately. Divers should use complete 5 mm. wetsuits, if possible, equipped with hoods, in short, the same wetsuits that one would use in summer in the Mediterranean, since the water is around the same temperature, roughly 24 degrees centigrade. Beginning in the month of April and running until the middle of November, light 3 mm. wetsuits are quite sufficient, although they also should cover the entire body, in order to prevent abrasions of one's skin on the reef. For the warmer waters of the central and southern Red Sea, light wetsuits can be used all year around.

The most practical fins are those with open heels, equipped with an adjustable strap, which can be worn over extremely comfortable boots with a sole. When wearing these, one can easily walk both on a sea floor dotted with sharp edges and out of the water, as comfortably as if one were wearing a pair of tennis shoes.

One definitely needs a buoyancy compensator, which is considered to be fundamental in a number of locations, and which also gives support to the tank. One should be particularly careful to ensure, before setting out, that the system for attaching the jacket to the tank is suitable for providing solid support to 12-liters tanks as well, as those are the ones normally used in diving centers here. Only on Italian charter boats does one find 15-liters tanks, which are larger in circumference. The tanks are generally equipped with single-outlet valves and have no backup supply, and therefore the diver must prepare an octopus with a pressure valve, attaching two second stages onto a single first stage. This makes it possible to rely upon an alternative air source underwater even though one may only have a single-outlet valve.

Aside from the mask and the snorkel, one definitely needs a good knife, a pair of leather or canvas gloves to protect one's hands from the blistering contact with certain animals, and from easy-to-obtain cuts from the corals.

One should also have an underwater flashlight for nighttime diving, or for looking into dark grottoes and caves. Extremely useful and nearly indispensable is the dive-computer, which automatically calculates the exact amount of nitrogen absorption going on, even though the diver may vary his or her depth continually, as is the case during exploratory dives or on photographic dives. Whether one has a computer or not, one should definitely not leave one's dive tables and watch at home, and one should always bring them along on a dive. A little box with tools and spare parts is of extreme importance: aside from a spare mask, one needs a spare mouthpiece with a strap for the regulator, a handful of O-rings for the tanks, an extra strap for one's fins and for the knife, and a tube of neoprene adhesive for repairing one's wetsuit.

By way of tools, one needs hex wrenches to unscrew the outlets of the first-stage regulator (with the spare stoppers), a pair of fixed wrenches (12/13 and 14/15 in size) and a screwdriver. A multifunction Swiss army knife is always useful, as are those special tool units that contain a great many wrenches, screwdrivers, and other things, which can be found in the best stores selling diving equipment.

D

E

F

D - A scuba diver lights up a school of masked butterflyfish (Chaetodon semilarvatus). For dives in the Red Sea, one is advised to make use of full wetsuits, in order to avoid the troublesome cuts and scratches that can result from contact with the reef. Photograph by Vincenzo Paolillo.

E - Protecting one's hands with gloves can prove to be a useful safeguard, as the coral reefs in the Red Sea abound in formations of fire coral, which tend to cause itching, blistering, and inflamation. In this photograph a moray eel (Gymnothorax javanicus) emerges from its den to take a closer look at a diver. Photograph by Andrea and Antonella Ferrari.

F - The buoyancy compensator is indispensable to the safety of the diver, and in many diving locations it has now become required equipment. Photograph by Marcello Bertinetti.

PHOTOGRAPHIC EQUIPMENT

Travelling to the Red Sea without bringing home some souvenir of those marvellous underwater gardens, etched into film, would be a true pity. Even with a modest amphibious camera, designed to withstand nothing more than the pressure encountered at 5 or 10 meters, one can obtain some decent images, especially if you make use of the new *Kodak Underwater Film*, especially designed for underwater use without artificial lighting. This film, in fact, makes it possible to capture a wider range of warm colors of the spectrum than it is possible with a traditional film, and it is therefore perfectly suited to these cameras, which are not generally equipped with strobes. Obviously, the best results are obtained with more complex equipment, first and foremost the famous *Nikonos* camera, the only underwater camera with interchangeable lenses available on the market. The wide-angle lenses ranging from 15 to 20 mm that come with this camera are of extremely high quality, and they are used successfully by the finest professional photographers.

For action shots, the *Nikonos* is unbeatable, due to its compactness, simplicity of the instrumentation, and the viewing and focusing system, which is empirical but works extremely well with wide-angle lenses. Less impressive, on the other hand, in the sector of light wideangle and normal and telephoto lenses, where a high minimum focus and a very limited depth of field make the user wish for a reflex viewfinder and focus system. For those who wish to take pictures of fish, using macrophotographic systems, the best choice available is that of a normal dry-land reflex camera with a waterproof housing, or else the new *Nikonos RS* reflex camera. With these cameras, focusing and framing can be extremely precise operations, while the vast range of lenses available allows one to choose freely between macro,

telephoto, and wide-angle. In terms of film, the most common types are the slides of mid- to low-range sensitivity (50-100 ISO), which are quite adequate in conditions of good lighting, found where the water is very clear and clean. In order to obtain colors, however, one must rely on artificial lighting, using one or two electronic strobes. This is true as well in the top few meters under the surface, where the eye may still succeed in distinguishing amongst the bright reds of soft corals and sponges, while the film is more demanding, and shows the same colors as more filtered, and tending to brown. For broader environmental scenes one should use the fill-in technique, which involves a careful mix of sunlight and artificial light, in such a way that one does not overshadow the other, and the pictures are uniformly lit: the foreground full of color thanks to the flash, and the background a perfect blue in the filtering sunlight.

One should make use of a light meter in order to calculate the amount of available light, which in the first few meters beneath the surface, especially near a sandy bottom, can be much more intense than one might expect. Of particular interest is photographic hunting. Every subject requires its own lens, with some consideration to the shooting distance at which one is as well. One should also remember that even the clearest water is full of particles in suspension, and that a telephoto lens cannot be used successfully to photograph fish at distances greater than 3-4 meters. For these shots taken at a considerable distance, the strobe is not only useless, but even harmful, because it lights up the particles in suspension, which appear on the final photograph as a series of large bright spots. For distant subjects, therefore, one should only take photographs using available light, and one should choose the right film.

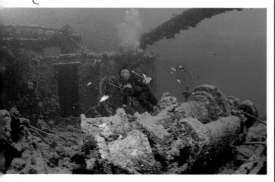

A - The *Nikonos* is currently the only amphibious camera with interchangeable lenses, and is reliable and easy to use. Photograph by Marcello Bertinetti.

B - The market offers a number of reliable waterproof cases for movie cameras. Photograph by Itamar Grinberg.

C - A scuba diver is photographing Thistlegorm *'s deck.* Photograph by Andrea and Antonella Ferrari.

DANGEROUS FISH AND CORALS

Underwater activity in a tropical sea involves a number of potential risks that are not so much linked to large predators, such as sharks, as much as to poisonous and venomous species. The *Scorpaenidae* are the main family of fish of which to beware - among the thirty-five species known to man, there are the lionfish (*Pterois volitans* and *Pterois radiata*), the scorpionfish (*Scorpaenopsis diabolus* and *Scorpaenopsis barbatus*), the notorious stonefish (*Synanceia verrucosa*).

While the former are equipped with spines that can provoke extremely painful punctures and states of fever which can be quite dangerous, the stonefish is lethal. All of these fish are capable of injecting neurotoxins, and the series of symptoms that ensue following a sting are quite characteristic: acute discomfort, local swelling which tends to spread, hypothermia, tachycardia, heavy sweating, and then fever.

It is important to know that neurotoxins are damaged by heat. It is therefore important to apply to the limb that has been stung extremely hot packs, in order to reduce the damage to the greatest possible degree. In the final analysis, however, all that is needed is a little attention to the way one steps on the reef, the use of a wetsuit, and protective footgear, and careful avoidance of strolls "upon" the coral reef. Among the venomous species, let us mention the fire coral (*Millepora dichotoma* or *Millepora complanata*) which is a hydrozoan and a distant relative of the jellyfish - one must never touch its ocher yellow fans, tipped with white, otherwise there is a good risk of being stung by its "nematocysts": these are organs found in coelenterates, consisting of a minute capsule containing a thread capable of being ejected and causing a sting, and they can cause extended and very

painful ustulation. It is therefore wise to make use of gloves, as these forms of coral are very common on the reef.

If you are stung, wash the area at great length with sea water, rubbing thoroughly, and then apply cortisone cream.

Nocturnal and far rarer are the venomous urchins (*Asthenosoma varium*), with long red spines tipped with white venom sacs, and the *Diadema*, with long black spines. The bluespotted stingrays (*Taeniura lymma*), which have a

tail sting connected to venomous tissues, and the moray eels (*Gymnothorax* sp.), whose ravaging bite can be easily infected, do not constitute a real danger because, if they are left alone, they will never attack human beings, and they are easily spotted and recognized.

D

E

F

G

H

D - Pterois volitans does not attack humans, except when it is threatened; but one must be keenly aware that its dorsal sting are poisonous. Photograph by Paolo Fossati.

E - Surgeonfish owe their name to the sharp spines, which protrude from the base of their tail. Photograph by Andrea Ghisotti.

F - Scorpaenopsis barbutus possesses excellent facilities for camouflage; combined with the poisonous dorsal shafts that are connected to poison sacs, they make this fish particularly

dangerous. Photograph by Andrea and Antonella Ferrari.

G - The bluespotted lagoon ray (Taeniura lymma) is usually quite timid; it should nonetheless be approached with care because it has two sharp poisonous spines at the tip of its tail. Photograph by Andrea and Antonella Ferrari.

H - The poison secreted from the dorsal sting of the stonefish (Synanceia verrucosa) is extremely toxic and can even kill humans. Photograph by Gianfranco d'Amato.

ISRAEL

A - The city of Eilat stands along the shore of the Gulf of Aqaba, in the southernmost point of the State of Israel, on the Jordanian and Egyptian border. Equipped with impressive tourist facilities, each year it receives some one million visitors, especially scuba divers and naturalists. Photograph by Marcello Bertinetti.

B - In the foreground, one can see the yellow submarine *Jacqueline* setting out on an excursion to the marvelous underwater world of Eilat. In the background stands the white tower of the Underwater Observatory, a building from which you can admire the world under the surface in all its glittering splendor. Photograph by Itamar Grinberg.

E ilat is the southernmost city in Israel, and is situated at the tip of the Gulf of Aqaba, at the intersection of Israel, Egypt, Jordan, and Saudi Arabia. Eilat lies within the global desert belt; climatic conditions are therefore typical of arid regions. The consequences can be clearly seen in the Arava valley, north of Eilat, and the surrounding hills, which have only a light covering of desert vegetation. If the heat discourages plant and animal life on land, it encourages the lush profusion of marine flora and fauna in the waters of the Gulf. Eilat is now a thriving city, prospering from international tourism. It was founded in the wake of the War of Independence, and its many fine hotels and the many flights available to the city from everywhere in Europe, make it a very popular vacation place. The chief attractions are the desert and the sea - an infinite universe with endless surprises in store. The shores of Eilat, stretching from Aqaba, at the Jordanian border in the north, to the Egyptian border (at Taba) in the south, and the offshore coral reefs, are all protected under the auspices of the Nature Reserve Authority. Most of the area is comprised of open beach, but a 1.2 kilometer stretch of the richest coral reef is enclosed in a private beach area, called Coral Beach, a nature reserve with paid admission. This is the northernmost coral reef in the world. All along the shores of the Gulf of Aqaba are numerous coral reefs creating a magical underwater world, dependent on the constant high temperatures of the waters of the gulf (between 20 and 28 degrees Centigrade) and the clarity of the water, which allows the sun's rays to penetrate into the depths. These coral reefs, called "strip reefs," typically grow in belts along the shore, at ten to fifteen meters from the line of high tide. Between the reef and the shore a shallow lagoon (rarely more than two meters deep) is formed.

- Jacqueline *offers the thrilling experience of venturing deep into the wonders of an underwater world teeming with life and with an unending array of surprises even to those who are not scuba divers. The submarine descends to depths up to as sixty meters.*
Photograph by
Itamar Grinberg.

- *A pier one hundred meters in length leads to the circular steel structure of the observatory, which rises twenty-three meters above the surface of the sea. From the top of the tower, it is possible to see the four nations that verge on the bay of Eilat: Israel, Jordan, Saudi Arabia, and Egypt.*
Photograph by
Marcello Bertinetti.

D

E

F

E - *The circular structure of the tower offers twenty-one windows allowing the visitor to look out upon the wonders of the seabed.*
Photograph by Cesare Gerolimetto.

F - *Inside the huge complex of Coral World, a great aquarium has been built to house all of the main species of fish found in the Red Sea.*
Photograph by
Cesare Gerolimetto.

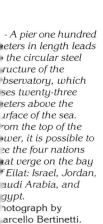

I

G - *At Dolphin Reef, it is also possible to swim in the company of large rays, which have become accustomed to the presence of humans, and therefore do not flee from divers, and can even be petted.*
Photograph by
Itamar Grinberg.

H - *Although fed by humans, the dolphins have not lost their natural instinct to hunt for food, living as they do in a habitat that is perfectly in tune with their customs and biological rhythms.*
Photograph by
Itamar Grinberg.

I - *In a fenced-in area covering over 10,000 square meters, in the south of Eilat, it is possible to approach the dolphins living in captivity here; the time spent with them is unforgettable. The seabed drops down to a depth of eighteen meters.*
Photograph by
Itamar Grinberg.

A - The seabeds of Eilat owe their remarkable wealth of fish, hard and soft corals to the unvarying temperature of water, never dropping below 20 degrees Celsius. Photograph by Itamar Grinberg.

B - A group of masked butterflyfish (Chaetodon semilarvatus) swims in close formation just off the wall of the reef. Photograph by Vincenzo Paolillo.

C - Two butterflyfish (Chaetodon fasciatus) swim just under the surface. Photograph by Andrea Ghisotti.

B

C

D - A twobar anemonefish (Amphiprion bicinctus) hides amidst the tentacles of a sea anemone, its customar refuge; these tentacles are toxic to all other species of fish. Photograph by Itamar Grinberg.

E - A coral grouper (Cephalopholis miniata) climbs up the wall of the reef. Photograph by Marcel Bertinetti.

F - The valves of a giar clam (Tridacna maxima) gape amidst the delicate formations of soft corals. Photograph by Itamar Grinberg.

Most of the Red Sea's coral reefs grow on a granite base, and many of them have a granite top. The reef wall plunges sheer into the depths of the sea. In order to allow all visitors - not just scuba divers - to enjoy the beauty of the depths, Coral World was built in March of 1975. The main attraction is the circular metal tower built directly above the reef, accessible from the beach along a walkway one hundred meters in length. The real surprise comes when one descends six meters below sea level, inside the tower. Here, a silent world made up of colors that verge on the surreal awaits the amazed visitors, who can look out from one of the twenty-one windows facing the seabeds of the Red Sea, and enjoy the natural rhythms and delicate grace with which tropical fish, coral, and many other lifeforms move. The view seen from the Observatory Tower, twenty-three meters above sea level, is unrivalled: the harsh deserts of Egypt, Israel, Jordan, and Saudi Arabia merge with the blue sea. Built with respect for the marine environment, nothing here is artificial.

The aquarium houses a number of species of fish, as well as corals, invertebrates, and other amazing lifeforms, which can usually only be seen by scuba divers at great depths.

In order to accommodate larger fishes, huge tanks were built: the shark tank allows one to admire the ocean predators at a safe distance, behind four large plate glass windows, while the turtle tank offers a more relaxing view of peaceful reptiles, living in harmony with rays. Coral World offers another breath-taking experience - an introductory dive sixty meters beneath the surface, even for mere amateurs. The Observatory also offers a submarine dive on the *Jacqueline*, which in the space of an hour explores the seabeds and other undersea wonders, for a safari to a usually forgotten world.

D

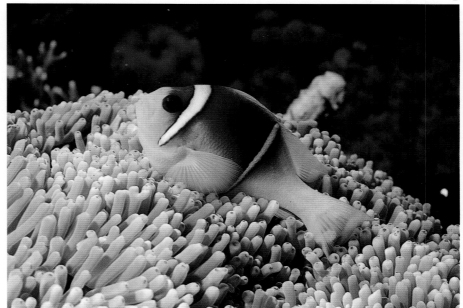

E

F

15

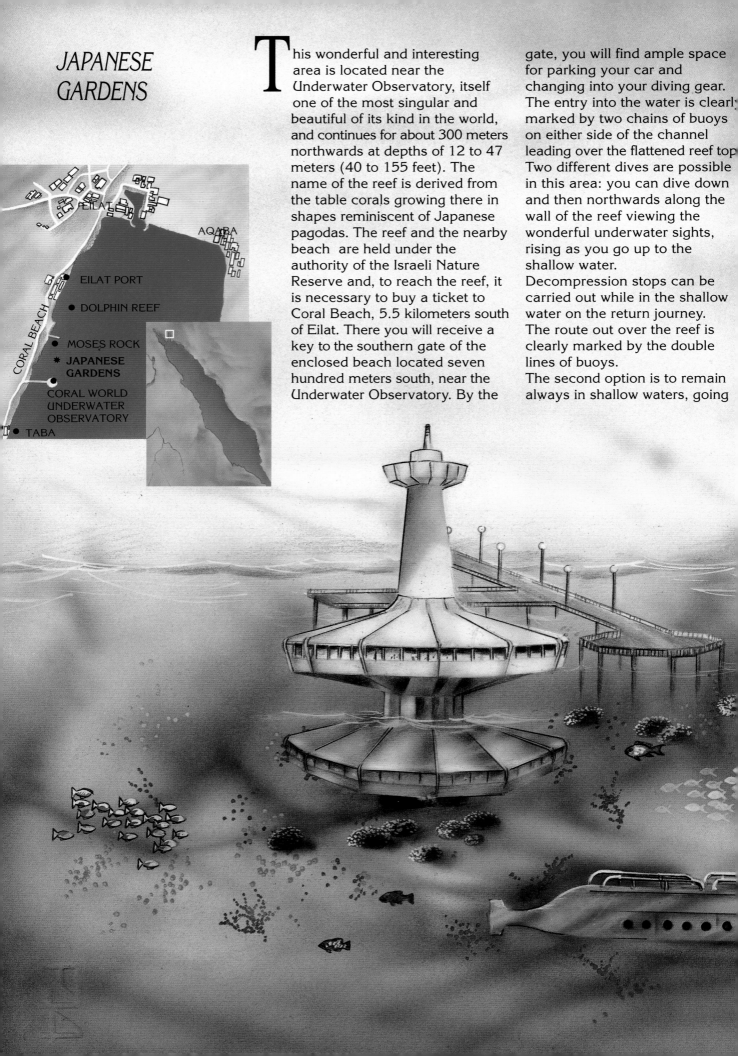

JAPANESE GARDENS

This wonderful and interesting area is located near the Underwater Observatory, itself one of the most singular and beautiful of its kind in the world, and continues for about 300 meters northwards at depths of 12 to 47 meters (40 to 155 feet). The name of the reef is derived from the table corals growing there in shapes reminiscent of Japanese pagodas. The reef and the nearby beach are held under the authority of the Israeli Nature Reserve and, to reach the reef, it is necessary to buy a ticket to Coral Beach, 5.5 kilometers south of Eilat. There you will receive a key to the southern gate of the enclosed beach located seven hundred meters south, near the Underwater Observatory. By the gate, you will find ample space for parking your car and changing into your diving gear. The entry into the water is clearly marked by two chains of buoys on either side of the channel leading over the flattened reef top. Two different dives are possible in this area: you can dive down and then northwards along the wall of the reef viewing the wonderful underwater sights, rising as you go up to the shallow water.

Decompression stops can be carried out while in the shallow water on the return journey. The route out over the reef is clearly marked by the double lines of buoys.

The second option is to remain always in shallow waters, going

EILAT

AQABA

EILAT PORT

DOLPHIN REEF

CORAL BEACH

MOSES ROCK

JAPANESE GARDENS

CORAL WORLD UNDERWATER OBSERVATORY

TABA

down to only 12 meters (forty feet), and to cruise along the sandy slope northwards and back again by the wall of the flattened 4-meter (thirteen-foot) reef. The Japanese Gardens, at depths of 25 to 45 meters (80 to 150 feet) is one of the routes taken by *Jacqueline,* the yellow submarine of the Underwater Observatory, and the lucky diver may catch sight of her, but be careful not to get too close! Special care must also be taken with regard to glass bottomed boats that cruise the area, especially in shallower places. It is advisable to telephone Coral Beach the day before you plan to dive and reserve dive time as the Japanese Gardens area is restricted to 20 divers per day.

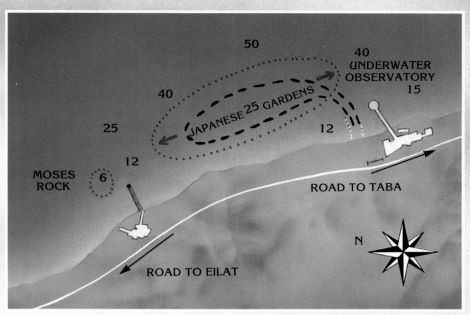

MOSES ROCK

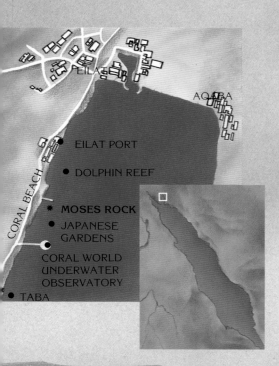

Just 5.5 kilometers south of the crossroad leading to the Eilat hotels, can be found the entrance to the Nature Reserve Coral Beach. From this point and continuing for 700 meters southwards towards the Underwater Observatory, lies the most beautiful and richest area in Eilat for corals and fish. An entrance ticket to Coral Beach pays for the use of many facilities, including showers, cloakrooms, shaded beach areas, drinking water, a souvenir shop, snorkeling gear for hire and a cafeteria.

There are two choices for enjoying the sea: you can swim over the rather narrow and flat top of the reef along a route marked out by two chains of buoys. Alternatively, you can cross over the reef via the 38-meter long bridge which leads to an area 5 meters south and 20 meters west of the Moses Rock. This beautiful column of coral, several meters in diameter, rises from its depths of 8 meters (26 feet) almost to the surface of the sea. The Moses Rock, home to many different species of fish who have no fear at all of divers, is richly hued in corals showing all the colors of the rainbow. The area around the rock is mainly sandy with many small colonies of corals. Here the sandy seabed gradually slopes downwards to a depth of 47 meters (155 feet).

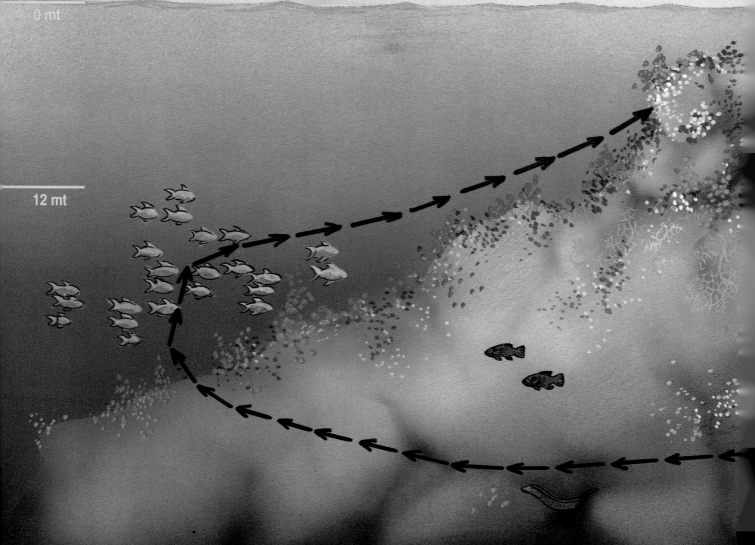

0 mt

12 mt

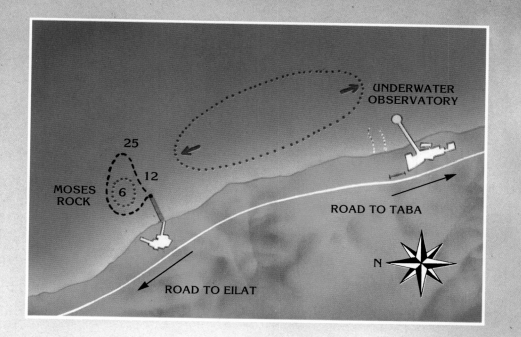

MOSES ROCK

25

12

6

UNDERWATER OBSERVATORY

ROAD TO TABA

ROAD TO EILAT

N

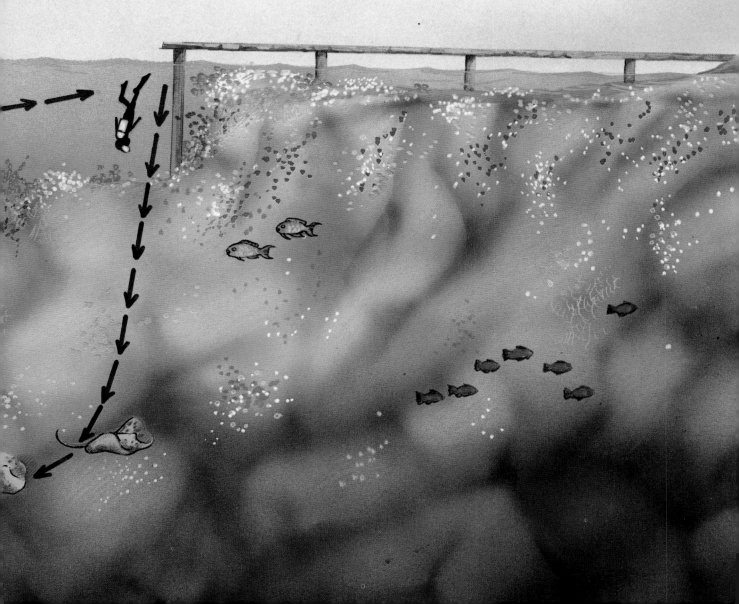

DOLPHIN REEF EILAT

EILAT

AQABA

EILAT
PORT

* **DOLPHIN REEF**

● MOSES ROCK

● JAPANESE
GARDENS

CORAL BEACH

CORAL WORLD
UNDERWATER
OBSERVATORY

● TABA

0 mt

3 mt

8 mt

15 mt

After receiving the equipment required for diving, and after receiving thorough instruction on what is permitted and what is forbidden, the guide takes one to the beach, where a unique experience awaits: diving with dolphins in their natural habitat. As soon as one enters the water, there is the sensation of being in a special place.
In just a few moments, the first dolphins draw close to play with the guide, who is an old friend of theirs. Everyone who dives or swims off Dolphin Reef must be accompanied by an instructor

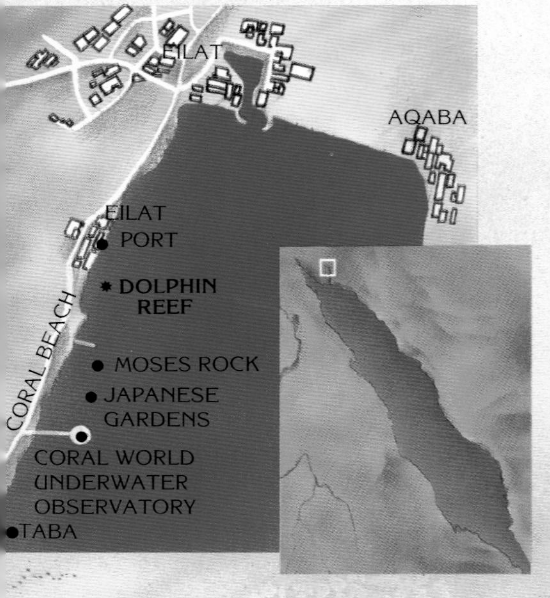

who has taken special courses on interacting with dolphins.

The skin of these cetaceans is soft and pleasing to the touch; nonetheless, even though the dolphins may behave in a friendly manner with humans, and love to swim rapidly in amongst scuba divers in search of contact, it is absolutely forbidden to grab hold of them, nor should one seize their fins. One should always keep in mind that at the Dolphin Reef of Eilat, the dolphin is the unrivalled king of the environment, and the scuba diver is only a guest.

Therefore, divers must behave correctly, so that they can come back again, and enjoy the marvelous company of these remarkable creatures.

The area of the Dolphinarium, which extends over ten thousand square meters, reaches a depth of 18 meters (sixty feet). Besides diving with dolphins, one can get close to large rays which normally lie dormant on the sea bottom. One can also explore the small wreck of a wooden boat called *DAN*, located at a depth of between 6 and 10 meters (ninteen to thirty feet).

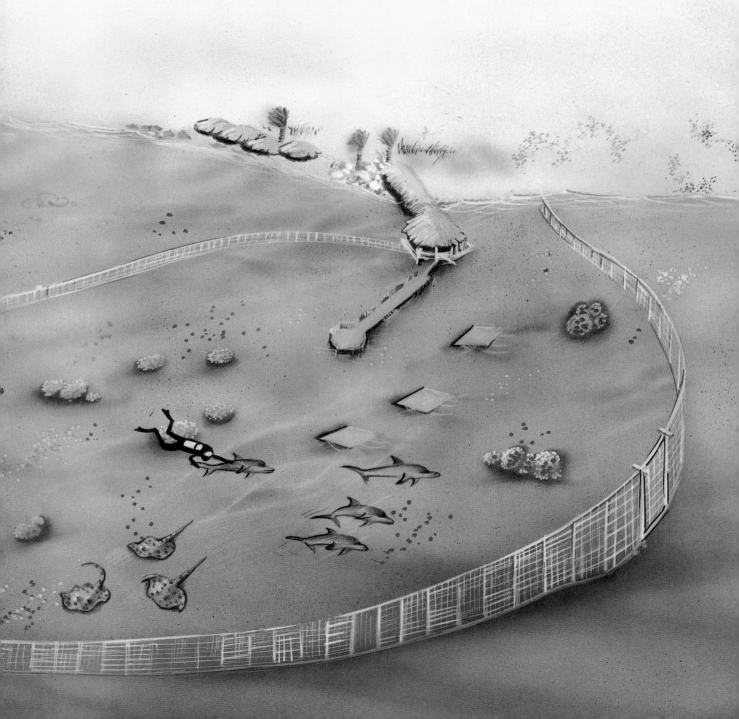

NORTHERN EGYPT
SHARM EL-SHEIKH

Sharm el-Sheikh is today a major tourist facility standing where there was once nothing but a small fishing village. Surveying the eastern coast of the Sinai desert, roughly midway between the Strait of Tiran and the southernmost tip of Ras Mohammad, both of which are locations famed for their beauty, Sharm boasts an enviably strategic situation from the point of view of vacationers.

Since the entire area is nestled in the lee of desert highlands, it is protected from the powerful north wind that so often troubles the waters of the Red Sea, chasing scuba divers back onto dry land. The climate is cool in the winter months (20 degrees centigrade) and muggy and hot in summer (40 degrees centigrade): the water is unfailingly warm, and it is possible to dive with 5 mm wetsuits in winter and with 3 mm suits or lycra suits in summer. Sharm is the first basin to be protected by environmental laws in the entire Red Sea: in 1989, the National Park of Ras Mohammad was established, with a permanent staff of scientists and rangers working to enforce compliance with environmentally sound rules of behavior; these rangers also perform research into the wildlife and geology of the entire area. In this manner, despite the powerful impact of tourism over the past few years, all of the coast has been preserved virtually intact, in terms of both surface and underwater features.

A - The Gulf of Sharm el-Sheikh opens out onto the Red Sea, where the Sinai comes to an end; in a remarkable contrast of colors, the rocky and uniform expanse of the desert verges on the varied colors of the coral reef.
Photograph by Itamar Grinberg.

B - The bay of Na'ama near Sharm el-Sheikh has witnessed a remarkable development of its hotel facilities, which has made the place one of the favorite destinations for European tourists, and not just scuba divers.
Photograph by Itamar Grinberg.

C - Along the coast, in the area around Na'ama, the desert extends all the way down to the edge of the sea.
Photograph by Marcello Bertinetti.

D - The cape of Ras Mohammad, the southernmost point of Sinai, doubtless one of the most famous locations for diving in the entire Red Sea.
Photograph by Marcello Bertinetti.

The true heart of the structures and facilities at Sharm el-Sheikh has developed at Na'ama Bay, five kilometers north of the bay of Sharm el-Moya, the site of the original village. The tourist facilities at Na'ama Bay date back to Israeli occupation of the Sinai: along the coral beach, stand the Hilton Fayrouz, the Möwenpick, the Ghazala, the Aquamarine, and many other hotels that maintain international standards. Over the past few years, hotels were built at Sharm el-Moya too, such as the Hilton Residence. A few kilometers north of Na'ama Bay, a new resort facility called Sheikh Coast is under construction; there will be a new hotel and a village of individual cottages and beachside apartments.

You can get anything you want at Sharm: there are banks, post offices, car rental facilities, desert motorcycle rentals, horses, tourist outings into the Sinai Desert and to the Monastery of Saint Catherine. It is clear that hotel owners are hoping to expand the attractions of the area beyond the narrow focus of scuba divers. At any rate, each hotel possesses its own efficient diving center, which runs daily boat excursions with two guided dives, the possibility of going on nighttime dives, courses for international diving licenses, and equipment rentals.

Air travel to Sharm el-Sheikh involves direct flights from Milan, Rome, and Frankfurt: you should make sure that your visa for Egypt applies to the entire country,

E - Diving at Ras Mohammad inevitably provides mighty excitement, because of both the lushness of the reef and the phenomenal depths to which the Red Sea drops in this area.
Photograph by Andrea and Antonella Ferrari.

F - The great fans of the gorgonians extending their branches towards the open sea are one of the most distinctive features of the coral reef of Ras Mohammad.
Photograph by Vincenzo Paolillo.

G - The walls of the reef are here literally covered with a dense mantle of manicolored soft corals.
Photograph by Vincenzo Paolillo.

H - Among these fish it is possible to recognize a number of the most common species found in the seabeds of the North of Egypt: sweetlips, parrotfish, onespot snappers, squirrelfish.
Photograph by Gianfranco d'Amato.

and not solely to the coast of Sharm. If it is so limited, in fact, this will keep you from traveling freely should you want to make excursions or cruises beyond the cape of Ras Mohammad. Underwater cruises leaving Sharm go to all of the finest diving locations along the west coast of the Sinai Peninsula, on the Gobal Strait. The cruises may cross the latter strait only with a specific permission by the port authorities.

HURGHADA

Connected, as it is, by direct flights to Rome, Milan, and Frankfurt, Hurghada is about halfway down the Egyptian coast of the Red Sea, 600 kilometers south of Cairo. This small fishing village, originally named Ghardaga, was the base of operations in the Fifties for the American biologist Eugenie Clark, whose studies were major contributions to scientific research into the sea, and to a

A - Hurghada, once called Ghardaga, was founded by the English in 1909. Between 1952 and 1953 it became a base of operations for the American biologist Eugenie Clark and the Egyptian scientist Yohar, who devoted themselves to in-depth studies of the fish in the Red Sea. Their studies led to the preparation and publication of a large and important volume. Today, Hurghada is a major

better understanding of the Red Sea in particular. It was not until the Seventies and Eighties, at the decision of the late President Anwar Sadat, that the Egyptian government began to promote the development of mass tourism in the area, with the construction of tourist villages and hotels, alongside the already existing Sheraton.

The coastline to the south of the village was thus transformed into a long series of settlements such as the Giftun Village, Sonesta, Princess Village, Jasmine Village, and many more. Almost every hotel possesses a perfectly equipped diving center, offering daily excursions to the archipelago of Hurghada, which includes the two islands of Gifatin, the island of Abu Ramada, Magawish, Umm Gamar, Abu Mingar, Abu Hashish, and a number of reefs just breaking the surface. Despite the massive impact of tourism, the seabeds of

and well-equipped tourist center, and the starting point for many splendid diving expeditions. Photograph by Vincenzo Paolillo.

B - On the beach of the island of Safaga, it is easy to see a number of holes dug by crabs. Safaga is the most important Egyptian seaport on the Red Sea. Photograph by Marcello Bertinetti.

C - Scalefin anthias (Anthias squamipinnis), with their lively orange color, are among the most common inhabitants of the lush coral walls. Photograph by Marcello Bertinetti.

E

Hurghada, though not protected like those of Sharm el-Sheikh, maintain an incredible plenitude of life. The variety of the coral and the quantity of tiny fish that live permanently in the area are among the greatest to be found along the Egyptian coastline, while along deep walls it is always possible to observe passing pelagic fish.
The ideal location along the coastline also makes it possible

D - Shadwan, the largest island in the Red Sea off the Egyptian coast, is distinguished in particular by the presence of a lighthouse showing the beginning of the Strait of Gobal channel, leading toward Suez. Photograph by Marcello Bertinetti.

G

to reach, with a boat trip of just a few hours, both the Gobal Islands and such well known reefs as Sha'ab Abu Nuhâs and the Brothers Islands.
It is possible to organize brief cruises which can be alternated with time spent on the coast. The village of Hurghada has developed into a small town providing all necessary facilities: banks, post offices, restaurants, stores, and taxis. It is possible to organize outings by bus to Luxor, or by plane to Aswan.
The climate is rather cool and airy in winter months (in December and January, one should wear a windbreaker while sailing, and a 5 mm wetsuit) and extremely hot in summer (40 degrees centigrade) although there is almost always a breeze: in these months, a 3 mm suit or a lycra suit are more than adequate.

E - Behind a curtain of large gorgonian fans, a school of surgeonfish (Naso hexacanthus) parades past, a constant presence on the seabeds off the Brothers Islands. Photograph by Itamar Grinberg.

F - A splendid branch of soft coral stands out clearly against the dark blue background of the sea. Photograph by Vincenzo Paolillo.

G - A number of shortnose blacktail sharks (Carcharhinus wheeleri) swim in the waters around the reef. This particular species can be recognized chiefly by the black coloring on the rear portion of the tailfin, and attains a length of up to two meters. Photograph by Jack Jackson.

THE STRAIT
OF TIRAN

The Strait of Tiran closes off the Gulf of Eilat some twelve miles to the northeast of the port of Sharm el-Sheikh.
It was named after the island of Tiran, whose highlands tower above sea level, with yellow-orange cliffs that testify to the island's volcanic origins.
We are on the line of the gigantic eastern African trench, the tectonic fault that begins under the Dead Sea and, continuing along the Valley of the Jordan River and along a great part of the Red Sea, terminates in the region of the great African lakes. That is the reason why the Gulf of Eilat, which is barely nine kilometers across at its very widest point, is over one thousand meters deep at its center, while the Strait

SINAI

TIRAN
ISLAND

STRAIT
OF GOBAL

TIRAN
REEF

SHARM
EL-SHEIKH

RAS
MOHAMMAD

SHADWAN
ISLAND

HURGHADA   GIFATIN
ISLAND

0 mt

12 mt

20 mt

of Tiran is over two hundred and fifty meters deep.

The four reefs that stretch lengthwise along the Strait, and are set in its center, are actually the pinnacles of a single underwater ridge just breaking the surface; all year long powerful currents sweep across it southwestwardly, toward the open sea.

The walls of the reefs - which drop pretty much straight down to the depth of some 60 meters (two hundred feet), and then plunge down into the midnight blue - therefore contain an exceptional soft coral population, whose growth is favored by the continual passage of water rich in microscopic nutrients. Sightings of very large ocean fish occur

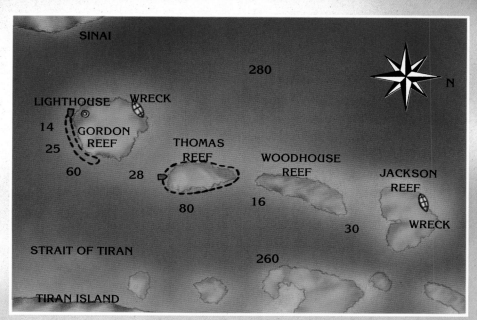

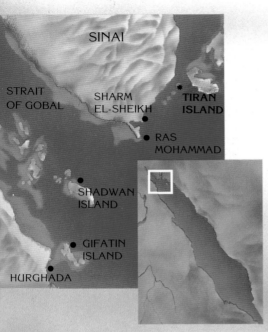

frequently; they are forced to pass through this Strait in order to enter or leave the Gulf.

The first reef from the north is Jackson Reef, made evident to shipping by a freighter that grounded on its northern side. The fixed anchorages for the boats of divers (it is forbidden to drop anchor anywhere in the maritime domain of Sharm el-Sheikh) are on the southeast side, protected from the rage of the ocean on windy days, and caressed by gentle currents. When diving, one heads north, reaching depths between twenty-five and thirty meters. At regular intervals, on the rocks jutting from the walls, one encounters splendid compositions of gorgonian fans, upon which

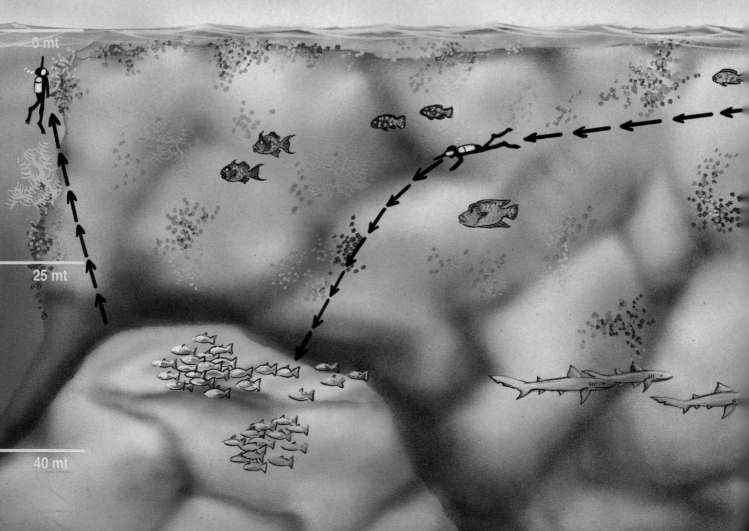

multicolored soft corals have lodged. There is a remarkable proliferation of black coral with its flimsier green "fronds" dancing in the current.

Along the reef the very quick orangespotted jack (*Carangoides bajad*) are constantly hunting, striking panic into the numerous species of smaller fish that populate the coral.

As we return to the boat, in the first few meters under the surface, we glide through a garden of fire coral, *Acropora* umbrellas, and round formations of *Favites* and *Gonioporae*.

There are a number of surface inlets upon the reef, with a sand bottom that offers a peaceful haven to angelfish and tropical grunts.

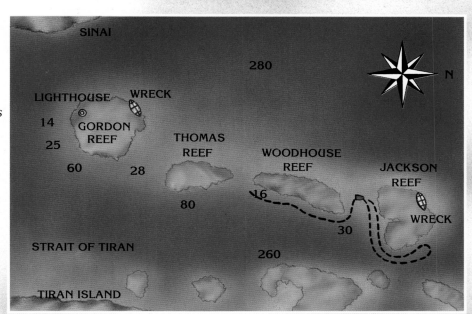

Another species often sighted on or near the surface are sea turtles, while deeper down, on the slope that separates Jackson Reef from Woodhouse Reef, grey sharks often pass, as do white tip reef sharks, eagle rays, and, during winter, manta rays.

Woodhouse is a narrow and long reef, the walls of which have a less colorful appearance, and are sedimentary for the most part. There is less variety of coral, and in extensive parts the reef is "dying" due to its

A

E - Large gorgonian decidedly common the Gordon Reef. T tend to proliferate a depth of less than twenty meters, in particularly clear waters.
Photograph by And and Antonella Fer

F - Soft corals tend grow on a rocky o coral base, on sha seabeds where the sunlight still reach
Photograph by Vincenzo Paolillo.

B

A - This aerial shot shows, in order, the four reefs that lie before the strait of Tiran: in the foreground is Gordon Reef, then comes Thomas Reef, Woodhouse Reef, and Jackson Reef.
Photograph by Itamar Grinberg.

B - Up to a depth of twenty meters, Thomas Reef presents a remarkable concentration of soft corals, with a vast range of colors.
Photograph by Pierfranco Dilenge.

C - Along the walls of the reef, great gorgonian fans extend; they grow particularly well in this stretch of sea due to the powerful currents.
Photograph by Gianfranco d'Amato.

D - Great schools of barracuda (Sphyraena qenie) swim with the current.
Photograph by Pierfranco Dilenge.

disadvantageous angle in terms of currents. Even today it is impossible to anchor, as there is a lack of mooring structures, but one would be well advised to dive from north to south from a moving boat. About midway down the eastern wall, around 40 meters (one hundred and twenty feet) in depth, there has developed a narrow canyon with a sandy bottom and a small "satellite" reef: about eighteen meters long and dotted with underwater grottoes and nooks, it is the most intriguing part of the dive.

At Woodhouse as well, which is not heavily frequented by divers, there are surprises galore: on the shelf at 30 meters (a hundred feet) depth that runs almost the entire length of the reef, there are often nurse sharks, which are easy to approach and to photograph.

Thomas Reef is the smallest of the four, and due to its round shape and exposure, it has always been a mystery for underwater guides,

as it is extremely difficult to guess which way the current is flowing without first making a test dive. In terms of colors and excitement, however, it is probably the finest point in the Strait.

The northern extremity is a true phantasmagoria of white, pink, orange, and purple soft corals over which you can swoop, pulled along by the current which determines, on one day or the other, whether your underwater tour will be in a clockwise or counterclockwise direction. It is nearly always possible during a dive to cover three-quarters of the circumference of the reef, with the boat following the divers. This is an experience to be left to more expert divers due to the violent currents, and it is certainly less than wonderful when things are calm because all of the soft corals close the tentacles of their coral polyps, and appear to wither in the absence of current-borne nutrients.

Gordon Reef, with its lantern, is the easternmost point of the actual Strait of Tiran: Cape Ras Nusrani, with its lighthouse, on the Sinai coast, is only a little farther than a mile away.

Not far from the lantern is the fixed anchorage, just fifty meters away from the point where the reef breaks the surface, on a seabed constituted by a broad coral clearing some ten meters down. Extensive formations of *Favites* and *Porites* look like giant coral "brains." A great variety of small coral-dwelling fish swim back and forth in search for food. If one dives northwards, one encounters dozens of old drums, which have been turned into dens for groupers, transformed by underwater creatures. These are the remains of the cargo of a freighter that grounded on the reef, in a position that, by chance, was parallel to that of the wreck on Jackson Reef.

A rare and intriguing encounter is also possible on the sandy seabed some four or five meters deep: here reside a number of

colonies of "garden eels," small, slim, grey *Heterocongridae* that tend to emerge from the sand in which they have dug their dens, like many blades of grass, swaying gently in the current. Even the slightest vibration causes them to rapidly retreat into their dens. White tip reef shark are more frequent, and a few of these are permanent residents of the reef, while eagle rays swim not far from the eastern rim of the sea bed, at about sixty meters' depth.

Returning to Sharm el-Sheikh, during a trip which requires about ninety minutes, one often encounters large schools of bottlenose dolphins and, with some good luck, a few large pilot whales.

G - A pair of butterflyfish (Chaetodon fasciatus) swim in the clear waters found on the seabeds of Tiran. Photograph by Vincenzo Paolillo.

H - A group of goggle-eyes (Priacanthus hamrur) displays daytime coloration; by night, in fact, these fish change their color and shift from bright red to a silvery color. Photograph by Vincenzo Paolillo.

RAS UMM SID

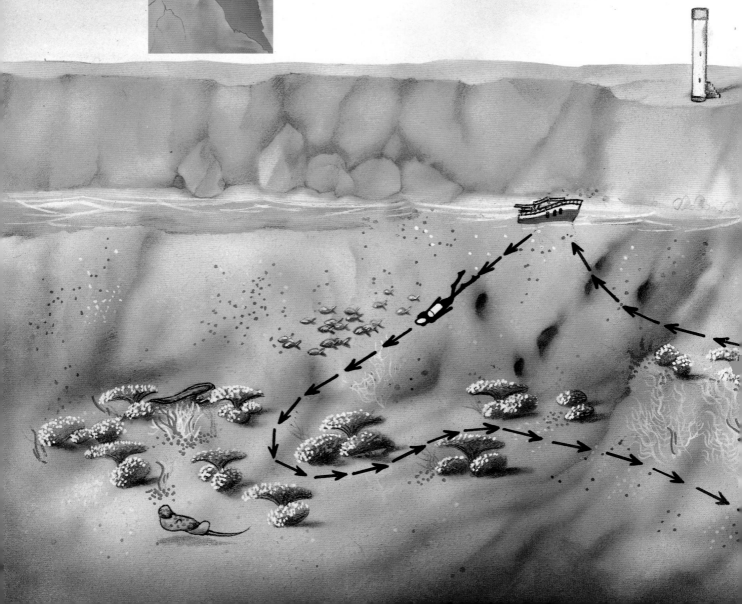

At a distance roughly equivalent to a fifteen minutes' trip by boat, east of the bay of Sharm el-Moya (the harbor of Sharm el-Sheikh), one reaches the cape of Ras Umm Sid, with its lighthouse. The promontory, which is distinguished by a relatively high shoal and by a coastal reef that breaks the surface, at about thirty meters (one hundred feet) away from the shore, became famous because of the "forest" of giant gorgonians which adorn its underwater walls. At this point, in fact, the almost incessant presence of a northern current has led to the creation of an ideal habitat for these *octocoral*, which extend their fans that serve as excellent "nets" in which to capture plankton. Normally, boats moor at the buoys which have been prepared in the bay of Temple Reef, just outside the cape - from here the divers reach the gorgonians area, by swimming at a depth of about 15 meters (50 feet). The seafloor is, at first, distinguished by a shelf area dense with coral and small coral fish, a number of groupers and the occasional moray eel. If one continues toward the point, the reef wall tends to steepen, and the floor drops away sharply, as does the presence of life forms. Great clumps of soft corals gather on the rocks that are most exposed to the sweeping currents, creating huge blooms of color that alternate with the darkness of the grottoes. The area of the gorgonians, which covers about fifty square meters

SINAI

TIRAN ISLAND

STRAIT OF GOBAL

SHARM EL-SHEIKH

*RAS UMM SID

RAS MOHAMMAD

SHADWAN ISLAND

GIFATIN ISLAND

HURGHADA

of sea floor, ranges from 15 to 35 meters (fifty to one hundred and fifteen feet) in depth. Amidst the gorgonians swim vast schools of glass fish, small transparent fish with golden highlights, while small groupers, angelfish, and red anthias find an undisturbed haven here. On days when the seas are rough and the current is strong, one is advised to sail about one hundred meters past the cape, and then to dive without anchoring. And so, you will be diving at an easy angle onto a vast shelf, at a depth of about 15 meters (fifty feet), distinguished by a dense coral "vegetation," and then you will reach the "upper" corals. The boat, after following you for a while, will wait for you at the permanent anchorage.

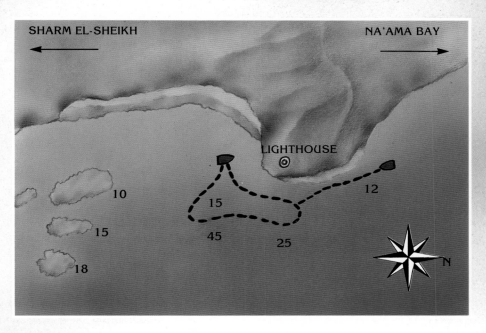

SHARM EL-SHEIKH   NA'AMA BAY

LIGHTHOUSE

10
15
15
45   25
18
N

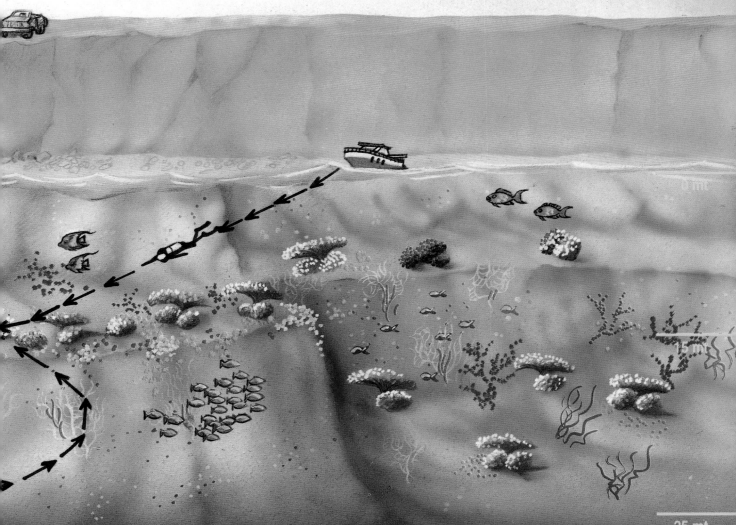

25 mt

RAS MOHAMMAD

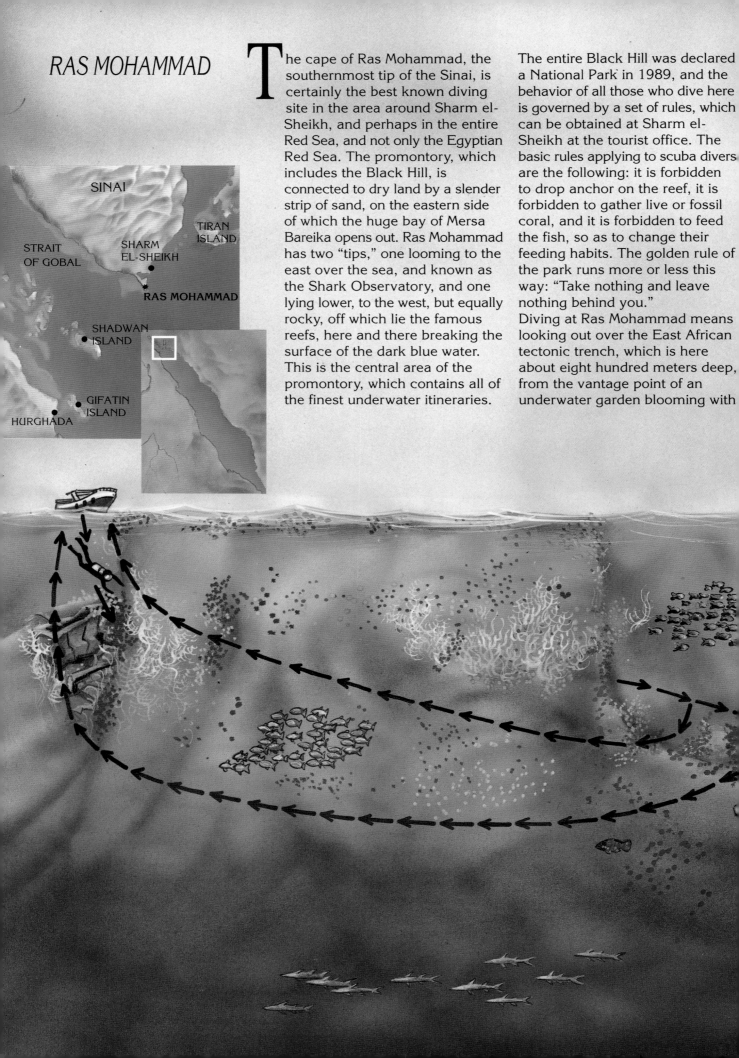

The cape of Ras Mohammad, the southernmost tip of the Sinai, is certainly the best known diving site in the area around Sharm el-Sheikh, and perhaps in the entire Red Sea, and not only the Egyptian Red Sea. The promontory, which includes the Black Hill, is connected to dry land by a slender strip of sand, on the eastern side of which the huge bay of Mersa Bareika opens out. Ras Mohammad has two "tips," one looming to the east over the sea, and known as the Shark Observatory, and one lying lower, to the west, but equally rocky, off which lie the famous reefs, here and there breaking the surface of the dark blue water. This is the central area of the promontory, which contains all of the finest underwater itineraries.

The entire Black Hill was declared a National Park in 1989, and the behavior of all those who dive here is governed by a set of rules, which can be obtained at Sharm el-Sheikh at the tourist office. The basic rules applying to scuba divers are the following: it is forbidden to drop anchor on the reef, it is forbidden to gather live or fossil coral, and it is forbidden to feed the fish, so as to change their feeding habits. The golden rule of the park runs more or less this way: "Take nothing and leave nothing behind you."
Diving at Ras Mohammad means looking out over the East African tectonic trench, which is here about eight hundred meters deep, from the vantage point of an underwater garden blooming with

multicolored soft corals and giant gorgonians, in the midst of a great variety of marine fauna: ranging from grey sharks to barracuda and snappers, jacks, tuna, humphead wrasses, moray eels, and coral fish.

Because of the currents that sweep out from the Gulf of Eilat, the underwater population of the promontory is particularly exceptional, and a great many pelagic species gather there from the open sea in search of food and shelter.

As one can see from our graphic reconstructions of the sea floor, the central area is distinguished by an extensive coastal reef, which encloses a vast lagoon along the beach and then drops in a gentle saddle ranging from 5 to

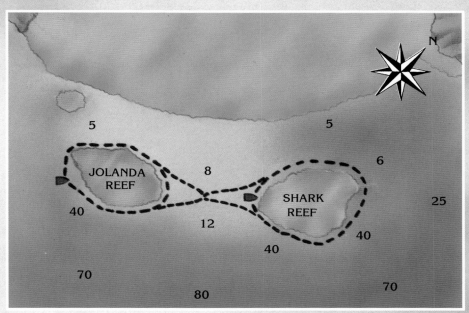

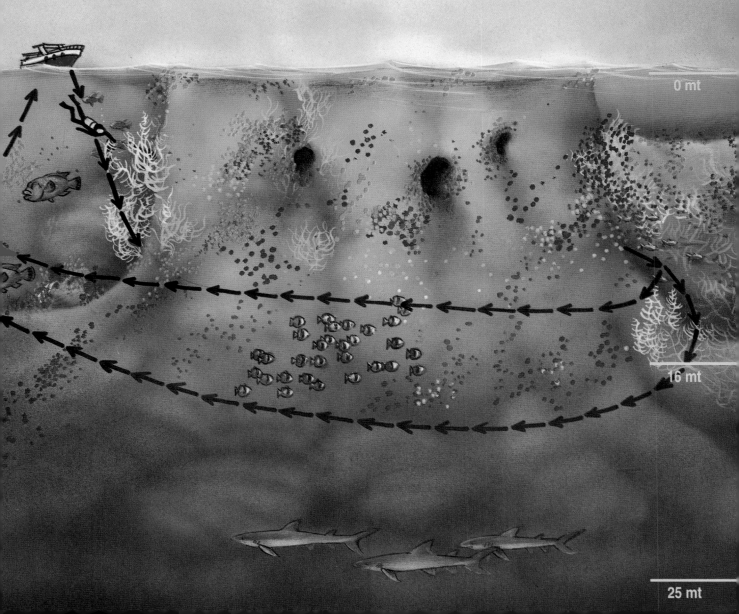

A - The splendid reef of Ras Mohammad, which has nearly become legendary in the world of scuba divers, was recently made a National Park, protected by extremely strict regulations. In this picture, it is possible to recognize the tip of Shark Reef, which owes its name to the considerable number of sharks that, until recently, swam beneath the waves.
Photograph by Itamar Grinberg.

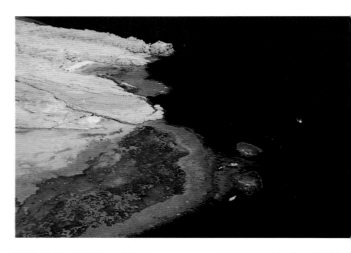

15 meters (fifteen to eighty feet) in depth. From this slope emerge the two huge coral towers of Jolanda Reef, to the west, and Shark Reef, to the east, some 40 meters (one hundred and thirty feet) each side.

The outer wall of Shark Reef rises practically sheer over the abyss, and is almost constantly pounded by heavy currents. Around Shark Reef, one continues along the diving itinerary in a counter-clockwise direction - setting out from the saddle between the two reefs, where large humphead wrasses (*Cheilinus undulatus*, of the family of the *Labridae*) and giant moray eels *(Gymnothorax javanicus)* reside permanently, and then one swims against the current, making one's way along cables that are arranged on the seafloor, until one reaches the thrilling drop into the deep. Here, on the lefthand wall of the coastal reef, there are gorgonians with fans of astonishing size (some twenty-five meters in depth), and in the center of the channel that

C

separates this area from Shark Reef, a large school of huge snappers often gathers - this is one of the best known spectacles of Ras Mohammad.

Once one has reached the outer slope, the northern current that was hindering one's progress will now help the diver along his or her circular route. Thus, one swims past the wall, covered with handsome soft corals, amidst which swarm thousands of tiny red *Anthias squamipinnis*. In the blue depths it is possible to observe, as we were saying, every imaginable pelagic species, and quite often there are grey sharks or white tip reef sharks and barracudas.

The dive ends where it started, between the two towers in the area protected from the current. The absence of a northern current, which is a rather infrequent event, allows one to enjoy a more relaxing dive,

B - The walls of the reef of Ras Mohammad drop away to as deep as eight hundred meters. Photograph by Marcello Bertinetti.

C - Great schools of silver batfish (Platax orbicularis) populate the waters of Ras Mohammad. Photograph by Marcello Bertinetti.

D - Nature seems to have run riot on the coral reef, creating the most sensational combinations of shape and color. Photograph by Paolo Fossati.

D

E

F

G

H

A grey reef shark (Carcharhinus amblyrhynchos) menacingly swims towards the photographer. Though sharks have considerably diminished their number, it is possible to encounter a few of them in these waters, especially in the winter months, when there are relatively few tourists. Photograph by Franco Banfi.

Humphead wrasses (Cheilinus undulatus) are now considered one of the distinctive features when diving at Ras Mohammad. Adult specimens may be longer than two meters. Photograph by Gianfranco d'Amato.

Impenetrable schools of bigeye trevallies (Caranx sexfasciatus) illuminate the depths of the sea with flashes of light. Photograph by Marcello Martinetti.

The usual description of soft corals, which tend to cover the reef entirely, is "living upholstery." This photograph offers the most significant confirmation of the simile. Photograph by Gianfranco d'Amato.

though there is less to see, as the presence of creatures in this area is closely related to a constant stream of plankton and microscopic animals of all sorts, swept here from the open sea. The route around Jolanda Reef is less deep - the outer wall, in fact, is less steep for a considerable stretch, though it then drops off into the abyss as well.

The name of the reef is taken from the presence of a wrecked freighter named *Jolanda*, which sank here after a violent storm in 1981. Remains of the hull are nowadays at more than two hundred meters (six hundred and fifty feet) below the surface, while on the reef one can still find a number of different materials, including cables, poles, masts, and two shattered containers which once held bathroom sinks, tubs, and toilets - it is interesting to observe the way they have been "enveloped" by undersea creatures, transforming themselves into dens and havens for angelfish, grunts, or bluespotted stingrays.

The eastern side of Jolanda Reef, too, is dotted with many colorful soft corals and a great variety of corals, while gorgonians are almost entirely absent.

One should also dive in a counter-clockwise direction here. A third point to explore is "Anemone City," which lies about one hundred meters (three hundred and thirty feet) to the northeast of Shark Reef, just under the tip of the cape. Here, on a shelf ranging from sixteen to twenty meters (fifty to sixty-five feet) in depth, is an absolutely unbelievable quantity of enormous anemones, surrounded by dozens of twobar anemonefish (*Amphiprion bicinctus*) and dominoes (*Dascyllus trimaculatus*).

Such a gathering of these alluring *Actiniaria*, just under one hundred square meters in expanse, is without a doubt unparalleled on the planet, and constitutes a biological mystery.

BEACON ROCK: WRECK OF DUNRAVEN

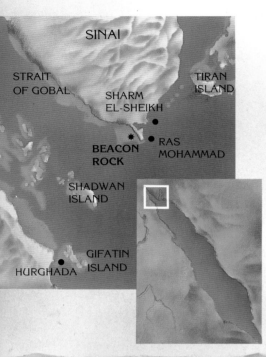

SINAI

STRAIT OF GOBAL

TIRAN ISLAND

SHARM EL-SHEIKH

BEACON ROCK

RAS MOHAMMAD

SHADWAN ISLAND

GIFATIN ISLAND

HURGHADA

I f you sail westward from Ras Mohammad for about an hour, you will sight the great surface-breaking reef of Beacon Rock, which is marked by a sea lantern. Beacon Rock is the farthest tip of Sha'ab Mahmud, the large coral reef that extends for six miles to the northwest, almost touching the coast of western Sinai. The general appearance of the reefs in this area is affected by the sedimentary nature of the sea bottoms of the Gulf of Suez, attaining a maximum depth of just over 60 meters (two hundred feet), and by the frequent

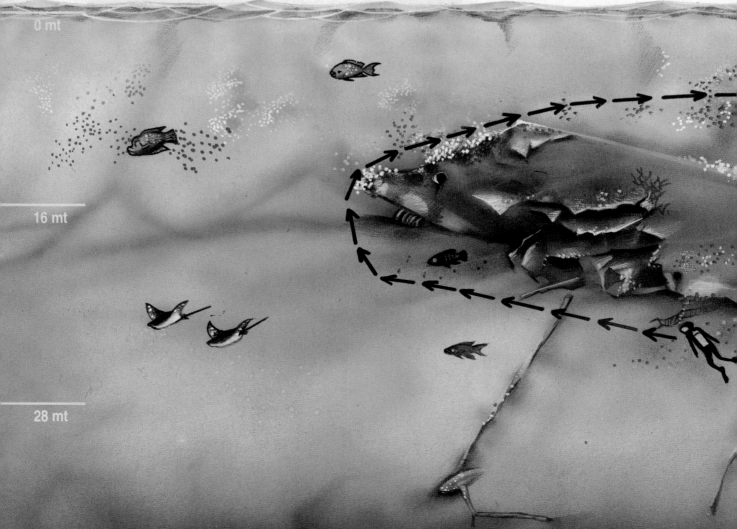

0 mt

16 mt

28 mt

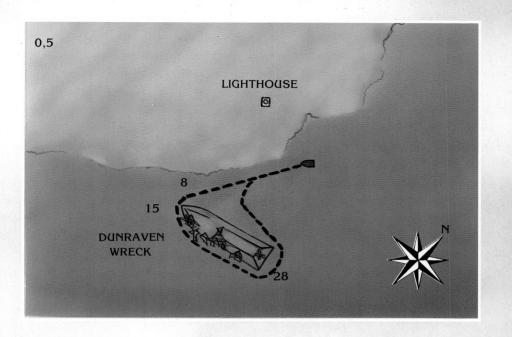

A

A - The Dunraven, *an English steamer that was sailing for the East Indies, met a tragic fate on Beacon Rock in April, 1876. The wreck was discovered by the Israelis in 1978, just over one hundred years after it sank. In this picture, it is possible to distinguish the rudder and the huge propeller.* Photograph by Andrea Ghisotti.

B - Lying flat on the seabed is one of Dunraven's *masts, now encrusted with coral. It is possible to distinguish the crow's nest and part of the rigging.* Photograph by Andrea Ghisotti.

C - The impact against the reef and the continuous pressure by currents have scattered the remains of the wreck across the seabed. Photograph by Andrea Ghisotti.

D - Silvery clouds of glass fish (Parapriacanthus guentheri) cast light on the contorted beams of the hold. Photograph by Andrea Ghisotti.

murkiness of the waters, which are tossed by the mistral wind. Great formations of *Goniopora* alternate with *Porites* and *Favites* corals - all of these factors contribute to give the reef a compact and rounded appearance, but leave it fairly devoid of color. There are humphead wrasses, less sociable than those found at Ras Mohammad, a great many burrfish (*Tetraodon hispidus*), pufferfish, and tropical groupers. Moreover, it is not uncommon to sight sea turtles close to the surface, and the occasional eagle ray, which may be permanent residents of the area.
The only sharks ever sighted at Beacon Rock are white tip reef sharks (*Triaenodon obesus*),

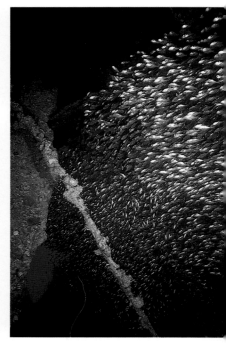

B

C

which swim along peacefully and scoot off timidly if they are disturbed.
At the tip of Beacon Rock, there is a solid and permanent anchorage - from here one can swim easily toward the wreck of the *Dunraven,* which sank a good 60 meters (two hundred and thirty feet) away, along the outer wall of the reef. The *Dunraven* was an English steamer, built at Newcastle around 1870; it sank here in April, 1876. Steamers were fast ships with steam

engines that had supplanted, after the inauguration of the Suez Canal, the great clipper ships that were so well suited to sailing around Africa. They were driven by two sailing masts and by a central coal-driven boiler. The *Dunraven* sank at Beacon Rock while on its way back from the Indies with a cargo of cotton and wool. It hit the reef on the starboard flank, ripping open at three spots, and it sank after a fire broke out on board, overturning on the sea bottom. A hundred years later, in 1978, it was discovered by Israeli scuba divers. Today, a scuba diver bent on exploring the wreck will first encounter the ship's stern, at a depth of 28 meters (ninety feet), with the huge screw and the rudder pointing toward the surface, decked with soft corals. The ship's entire keel is pratically intact and is thoroughly covered with coral.

It is possible to enter the hull through one of the gashes that

drove the ship to the sea bottom; the interior is quite dark, and the bottom is covered with sand, mud, and detritus. In the central area of the holds, one can see the great coal boiler around which tiny glass fish provide a remarkable show, swimming amidst the shafts of light that filter through the hull. A few large Malabar groupers have chosen the wreck as their home.

As one swims along the ship, one reaches the prow, about 16 meters (fifty-two feet) below the surface, where one can see the rings that once held the bowsprit, long since lost. From the chain holes, the great chain still dangles, while the anchor is far off, on the reef. On the sea bed, stretching out toward the open sea, are the various components of the deck structure, as well as the two masts of the *Dunraven*, upon one of which the crow's nest can still be seen.

One ends the dive by swimming up the wall of the reef and setting off once again for the anchorage.

E - The screw of the Dunraven *appears totally transfigured by abundant coral encrustations and colorful soft corals that adorn it.*
Photograph by Andrea Ghisotti.

F - Many groupers live in the structures of the wreck. In this picture, one can see a coral grouper (Cephalopholis miniata)
Photograph by Paolo Fossati.

G - Near the wreck, it is fairly common to encounter sea turtles (Eretmochelys imbricata).
Photograph by Andrea Ghisotti.

ALTERNATIVE REEF

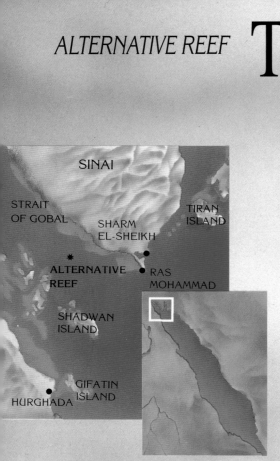

Three miles to the west of Ras Mohammad, there extends a system of coral towers called "Alternative": these reefs are nothing more than the southernmost tip of the reef of Sha'ab el Utaf, which stretches here all the way from the western coast of the Sinai. Although all the coral towers constitute very interesting territory in which to dive, certainly the second-to-last one on the east is the richest and the most colorful, teeming as it is with varieties of coral and tropical fish. On its northern edge, at about 50 meters (one hundred and sixty-five feet) from the peak, that just breaks the surface of the water, a solid anchorage is provided - from here one can dive and travel around the reef, exploring its southern ridge, which is definitely richer in life forms. You will be able to observe a complete array of gorgonians, red and green sea whip corals, hard and soft corals around which swim sabre squirrelfish (*Adioryx spinifer*), glass fish, angelfish (*Pomacanthidae*), and butterflyfish (*Chaetodontidae*), all hard at work searching for food on the reef. We should also point out the moray eels and the ever-present humphead wrasses. A nocturnal dive is definitely advisable because, considering

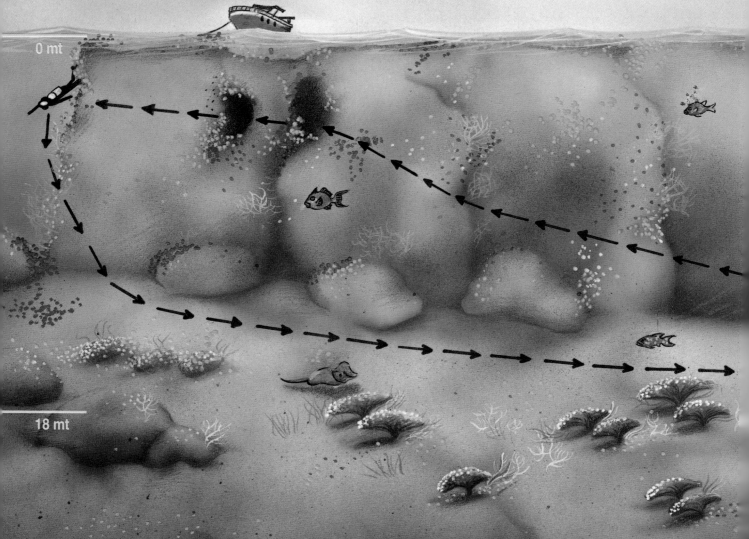

how easy the itinerary is and how calm the waters are almost without exception, you can well re-explore the entire reef in the dark. Moreover, by night, the "coral-eaters" crown of Thorns starfish (*Acanthaster planci*), the splendid crinoids, or sea lilies, and the lavish pencil urchins make their appearance, while many pufferfish (*Tetraodontidae*) sleep on the soft corals as if they were in their nests.

The maximum depth for diving is about 18 meters (sixty feet), and it is moreover possible to explore a small "satellite" reef, as you can see from the drawing.

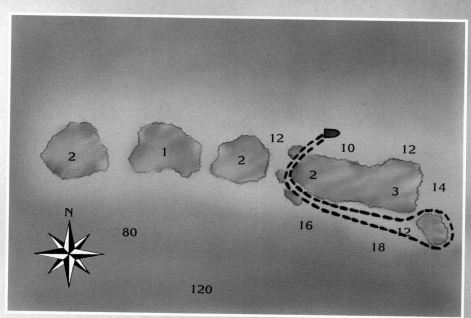

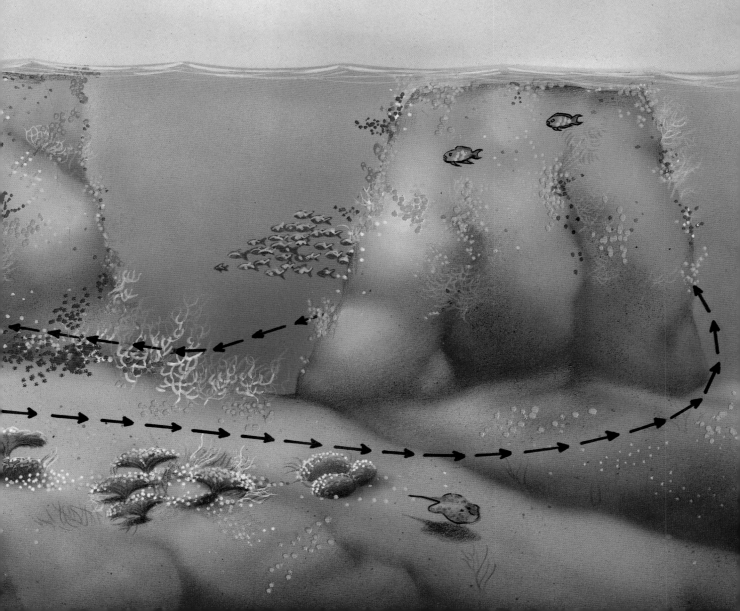

SHA'AB ALI: WRECK OF THISTLEGORM

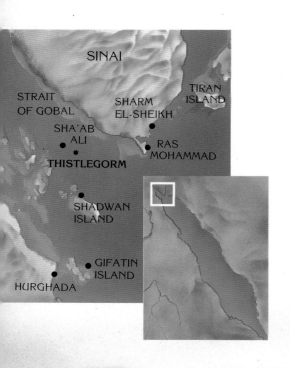

A few miles to the northeast of Shag Rock, the southern tip of the great reef of Sha'ab Ali in the Gulf of Suez, the wreck of the armed English freighter *Thistlegorm* lies abandoned on a sandy seabed at a depth of 28 meters (ninety feet). Discovered during one of Jacques-Yves Cousteau's first expeditions aboard the *Calypso* in the early months of 1956, the *S.S. Thistlegorm* was bombed by the Germans on October 6, 1941 while waiting for the Suez Canal - which had been temporarily rendered inoperative through attack - to be reopened.
Built in England, in the shipyards of Joseph Thompson and Sons at Sunderland, at the end of 1940, this freighter, intended for the transport of war material, was probably part of "Operation

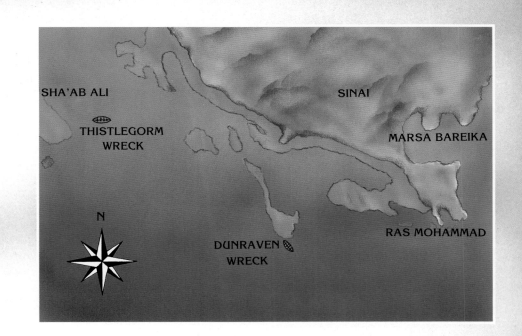

SHA'AB ALI

THISTLEGORM
WRECK

SINAI

MARSA BAREIKA

N

DUNRAVEN
WRECK

RAS MOHAMMAD

A

Crusade" - a major allied offensive supplying men and material in an effort to relaunch the Eighth Army against Rommel. The *Thistlegorm* had circumnavigated Africa and, after putting in briefly at Aden, had sailed up the Red Sea toward her destiny. After the bombing, only nine men died out of the crew of forty-nine. The ship sank after the stern section was ripped out by the explosion of the ammunitions stowed below. Today this impressive, nine-thousand-ton hull lies in sailing position, on a sedimentary sea floor, at a depth of 28 meters (ninety feet). The ship's superstructure rises to a depth of 12 meters (forty feet), assisting scuba divers who wish

A - This big anti-aircra[ft] gun reaches out futile[ly] toward the bottom of the sea. The Thistlegorm *sunk in 1941, and was then discovered by Jacque[s] Yves Cousteau in 195[6]* Photograph by Itamar Grinberg.

B

to climb back to the surface after their dive. The water in this area becomes clouded very easily, and there is often a strong current from the north. The *Thistlegorm* carried four railroad cars on the main deck, along with two large torpedoes, and three of her holds were loaded with material that is still intact and can be made out clearly despite silt and corrosion. There are a number of automobiles, and trucks with their loading platforms crowded with *BSA* and *Norton* motorcycles, jeeps, tires, tracks for tanks, uniforms, and boots for the troops - an array of material of considerable variety, making

B - Still lined up perfectly, a number of BSA *motorcycles are stowed in the hold of the freighter.* Photograph by Andrea and Antonella Ferrari.

C - One of the twenty trucks carried by the English freighter seems nowadays almost intact, though covered by the sedimentary si[lt] of the Gulf of Suez. Photograph by Itamar Grinberg.

this wreck an unforgettable voyage to the past for adventuresome scuba-divers. The section of stern lies on its side to port of the hull, surrounded by all sorts of material from the hold: towing equipment, two tanks, boxed ammunitions and weapons. On the stern deck there is a large four-inch anti-aircraft gun, now pointing uselessly toward the seabed, while inside the ship one can see the crew's quarters. The central deck is not particularly interesting, because much of the equipment has been removed.

This is a wreck to which at least two dives should be made, starting from the bow and proceeding toward the stern.

D - The inevitable glass fish (Parapriacanthus guentheri) sail along amidst the structures of the wreck, bedecked with luxuriant soft corals. Photograph by Itamar Grinberg.

E - The most common encounters close to or inside wrecks are with groupers. The Thistlegorm *is no exception to this rule, and enormous Malabar groupers (Epinephelus malabaricus) can be found there. Photograph by Paolo Fossati.*

F - Diving onto a wreck is always an exciting experience; diving onto the Thistlegorm *is particularly thrilling because the cargo is still virtually intact. Photograph by Itamar Grinberg.*

G - The entire English freighter and a considerable portion of its cargo are covered with thick undersea growth. This picture shows a number of motorcycles in the ship's hold. Photograph by Andrea and Antonella Ferrari.

H - The cargo of warfare materials of the Thistlegorm, *stowed in the ship's three holds, includes bombs, torpedoes, ammunition, twenty trucks, motorcycles, two tanks, two locomotives, uniforms for the troops, and a great deal more. Photograph by Itamar Grinberg.*

BLUFF POINT

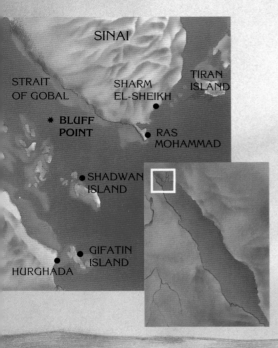

A narrow spit of coral sand, incessantly covered and uncovered by the tides, separates the two islands of Gobal, the Big one, Kebira, and the Little one, or Seghira. This is the western side of the strait named after them - the Strait of Gobal - at the mouth of the Gulf of Suez. The automatic lighthouse with solar panels at Bluff Point, on Little Gobal, marks the exit and entrance to the Gulf. Once one has anchored in the great bay looking southward, which is protected from the mistral winds, the scuba divers enter the water and follow the coastal reef on the right, out to the point. The maximum depth is reached under the lighthouse, around 35 meters (one hundred and fifteen feet). In the first few meters under the surface, one can observe a remarkable proliferation of hard and soft corals - in small grottoes, one can find glass fishes, and all sorts of coral fishes, while sea turtles are common (*Chelonia mydas*) and come to hunt the small crustaceans and mollusks on the reef. During the spring, sea turtles lay their eggs on the island. When diving, it is possible to observe bottlenose dolphins, which belong to a large permanently residing school that normally stays just off the Gobal Islands. And, on the underwater wall of Bluff Point, around 25 meters (eighty feet) in depth, there grow a great many black corals *Antipatharia*. Nearly at the center of the bay, on the other hand, it is possible to engage in a very pleasant nighttime dive upon the wreck of a hull some 20 meters (sixty-five feet) under - this is probably an Egyptian gunboat that went down during the War of

Independence. Here, at a depth of no more than 13-14 meters (forty or forty-five feet), at nightfall, there are moray eels, scorpionfish, lionfish *(Pterois volitans* and *Pterois radiata)*, *Asthenosoma varium*, which is the most venomous echinoid occurring in the Red Sea, nudibranches and crinoids, while red and orange soft corals hang from the ship's structures. Lastly, we should point out the presence of the wreck of a freighter that was carrying electrical material, and which sank on the north side of the island, 300 meters (nine hundred and eighty feet) beyond the lighthouse along the coastal reef. The wreck is covered with corals and is badly damaged; nonetheless it is home to a great variety of fauna, given that the entire reef teems with life, exposed as it is to the currents.

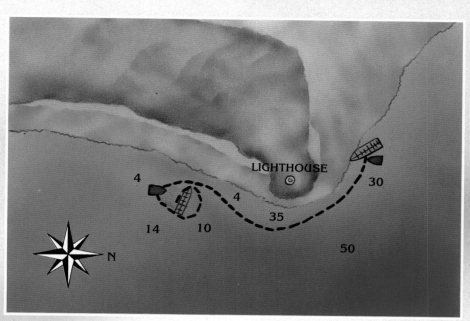

SHA'AB ABU NUHÂS: WRECKS OF CARNATIC AND OF GHIANNIS D.

The great reef of Sha'ab Abu Nuhâs emerges two miles to the north of the Shadwan Island at the mouth of the Strait of Gobal. Its location, so much a menace to navigation, has made it famous to all the sailors of the area and, therefore, in more recent times, to all scuba divers. On the seabeds of the surrounding area there lie no fewer than seven sunken ships from different eras. Among these hulks, the most intriguing are certainly the *Carnatic* and the *Ghiannis D.*

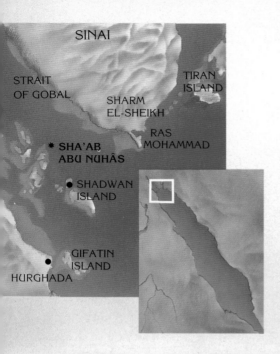

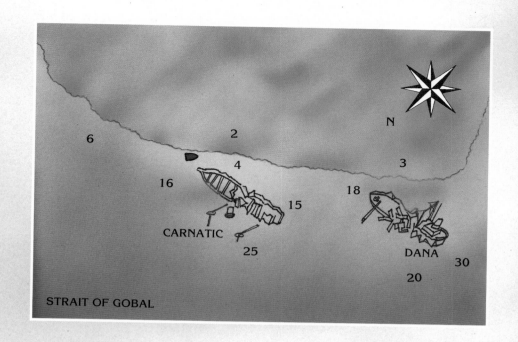

6

2

N

3

16   4

18

15

CARNATIC

DANA   30

25   20

STRAIT OF GOBAL

A - On the flattened poop of the *Carnatic*, it is still possible to see the great windows that provided light for the covered deck. It is also fairly easy to make out the large rudder and the three-bladed screw. Photograph by Andrea Ghisotti.

B - A scuba diver swims through remains of the first-class deck. Photograph by Andrea Ghisotti.

C - The prow of the *Carnatic* appears to be completely covered with coral formations and stupendous soft corals. Photograph by Andrea Ghisotti.

The *Carnatic* was a splendid sail-and-engine steamer launched in 1862 by the Peninsular and Oriental Steam Navigation Company. It was sailing the Indies route with a destination of Bombay and continuation for Calcutta - it had left Suez on September 12, 1869. The cargo consisted of wine and "London soda water," contained in distinctive oval bottles made of transparent opaline glass. The ship was ninety meters in length, it had two masts on which to set sail, and a central coal-fire boiler. It collided against the reef on the night of September 13 and, after remaining aground for a number of hours, sank at 11 o'clock in the morning, settling on one side with the bow at 16 meters (fifty feet) and the stern at 24 meters (eighty feet). The deck is facing the open sea, and one can clearly see the blackened support structures - the wooden

B

components are long gone as is much of the navigating equipment, while the keel is virtually intact. Tremendously impressive are the stern, with its windowed quarter-deck and the large screw, and the prow with its giant ring and the supports of the long-vanished bowsprit.
In the forward hold, one can still see numerous bottles of wine, still sealed with corks, and with a large No. 2 engraved in the glass. The wreck is rather dark because, aside from being blackened, it

has a northern exposure and is shaded by the walls of the reef for many hours of each day: it is advisable to do your diving in the morning. There are frequently strong currents and a less-than-excellent visibility.
On the sand seabottom before the wreck one can see the remains of the smokestack, the masts, and numerous other bits of detritus.
At some 60 meters (two hundred feet) from the *Carnatic*, just slightly to the south, lies the wreck of a large and modern freighter: the *Ghiannis D.*, displacing 3,500 metric tons. Now on the enormous bow one can read the word *Markos*, which was probably the original name of the ship, brought to light by encroaching corrosion. In the area, the wreck is referred to as *DANA*, after the huge D still visible on the smokestack (after the *Danae* shipping company). After hitting the reef, by the bow, the ship remained grounded on the reef for six weeks, and nothing could be done during that time to keep it from slowly sinking. The hull was shattered at three points by the violence of the waves: the bow and stern sections remain intact, while the central holds have been destroyed, and there remains only a weltering mass of rusted sheet metal, cables, and pipes. The latter objects were actually the ship's cargo.
One should swim first toward the prow, where the great anchor chain lies draped on the reef, and then swim back toward the stern, which can be entered: the command bridge, residential quarters, and engine-room offer a series of impressive tours. The deepest point on the seabed is 28 meters (ninety feet). Of particular interest are the resident groupers in the central section of the boat, while it is possible to observe all sorts of fish swimming by: snappers, jacks, eagle rays, and sharks.

E

D

F

D - The large "D" that appears on the smoke stack refers to the name of the shipping company: Danae. Photograph by Andrea Ghisotti.

E - In this photograph, we can gather some of the tragedy of the shipwreck: the stern section of the Ghiannis D. lies intact on the sand at a depth of twenty-five meters, while the holds appear to have been completely destroyed. Photograph by Andrea Ghisotti.

F - Metal structures in the area of the quarterdeck on the freighter Dana stand out clearly against the transparent water. Photograph by Andrea Ghisotti.

G - A great barracuda (Sphyraena qenie) swims majestically across the deck of the Ghiannis D. Photograph by Vincenzo Paolillo.

G

CARLESS REEF

This is the most famous coral shoal in the coastal area of Hurghada. It can be reached from the various diving centers in little longer than an hour by boat. Carless Reef is made up of a coral ridge extending from east to west, the peak of the ridge lying at a depth that varies from 12 to 20 meters (forty to sixty-five feet). The anchorage point lies in the area of two coral towers that just pierce the surface, with an approximate diameter of 30 meters (one hundred feet). The sea bed between the towers is at no point deeper than 15-16 meters (fifty or fifty-five feet), while just slightly further to the east, it plunges suddenly to a depth of 60 meters (two hundred and thirty feet), with a wall dotted with caverns populated by glass fish and lionfish.

The make-up of the coral is extremely varied but, of all the corals, the acropora umbrellas are the most common, and they offer shelter and haven to small anthias, grunts, angel fish, and a great many other species.

Along the walls of the towers, there are numerous colored soft corals and, in the surface layers, a great deal of fire coral with its distinctive reddish-ochre color (*Millepora dichotoma*). Even though grey sharks can often be seen swimming not far from the deep cliff, as well as white tip ree

sharks and other pelagic fish do, the particular attraction of Carless Reef is constituted by the many giant moray eels (*Gymnothorax javanicus*). It is quite common to find them out of their dens, and to observe them in their full extension as they swim amongst the coral formations. Underwater guides know how to approach them safely, and when they are at rest in their dens, if one takes the proper precautions, it is even possible to pet them. The menacing appearance of the moray eel is in fact a result of its perennially open mouth - in reality this is not meant as a way of frightening its enemies, but is simply its way of breathing!

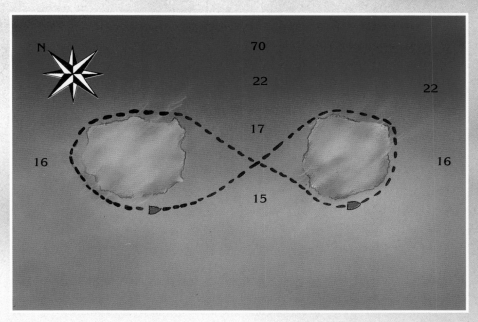

GIFTUN SEGHIR ISLAND

SINAI

STRAIT OF GOBAL

TIRAN ISLAND

SHARM EL-SHEIKH

RAS MOHAMMAD

SHADWAN ISLAND

GIFATIN ISLAND

HURGHADA

GIFTUN SEGHIR

This is the smallest of the two Gifatin Islands, set at the center of the archipelago of Hurghada, at about a half-hour's sail from the coast facing the town. The most intriguing and demanding dive on the island is along its eastern wall, incessantly thrashed by the northern current. Boats cannot anchor, and divers must enter the water just off a small rocky inlet, some 50 meters (one hundred and sixty feet) to the north of a military installation. The underwater wall drops away sheer into the dark blue and alternates sedimentary rocks with jutting crags, literally blanketed with the slowly undulating fans of giant gorgonians (*Subergorgia hicksoni*), black coral, and yellow and red sea whip corals. All of these species of coral develop quite rapidly in situations of exposure to a constant current. After drifting in the current for about five hundred meters, at a depth of 30 meters (one hundred feet), one can swim along another promontory where, at a depth of 46 meters (one hundred and fifty feet), there is a grotto reaching clear through, with double arches, one set atop the other, and there is a great deal of black coral and a bed of white sand. Once one has swum through the grotto, one heads straight up and reaches the coral bed at some 15 meters (fifty feet) in depth - continuing westward, one reaches the underwater wall of the very island, and a lagoon where the boat will await the divers. Just off the deep underwater wall one can see tuna, jacks, and all sorts of common pelagic fish, while in the lagoon live a great many humphead wrasses, coral fish, and moray eels. This is a demanding dive: an underwater computer, excellent training, and a great deal of experience are needed.

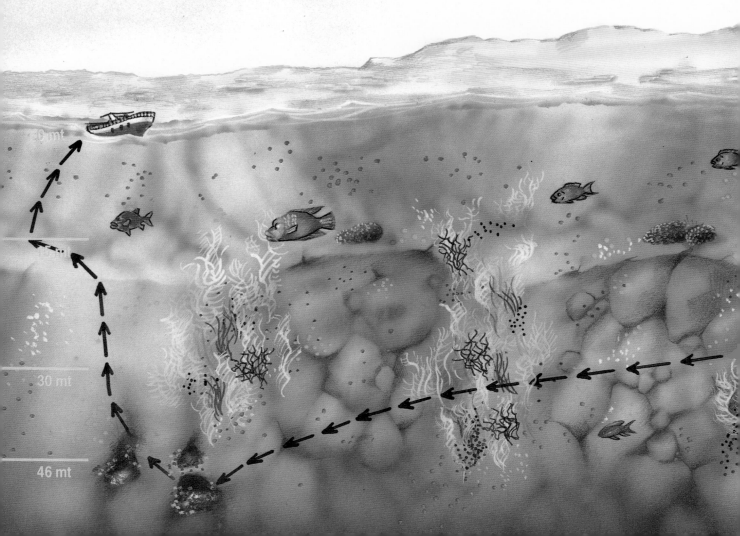

9 mt

30 mt

46 mt

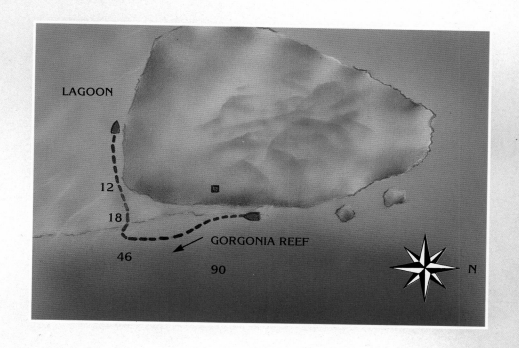

LAGOON

12

18

46

GORGONIA REEF

90

N

ERG ABU RAMADA

This small group of reefs breaks the surface just 50 meters (one hundred and sixty feet) off the southeastern coast of the Abu Ramada Island, some forty-five minutes' by boat from Hurghada. "Erg" in this context means small reef, while "sha'ab" is the word for coral shallows or coral barrier reef. Four small coral towers, only two of which break the surface, are set on a bed of rock and coral that lies 17 meters (fifty-six feet) beneath the surface. The boat anchors at a mooring point attached to the largest reef.

This point is also frequently exposed to the current and rage of the open sea, so that coral life, particularly soft corals, is extremely plentiful and abounding due to the powerful thrust of water bringing food in considerable volume. Atop the reefs are swarms of red anthias and silvery

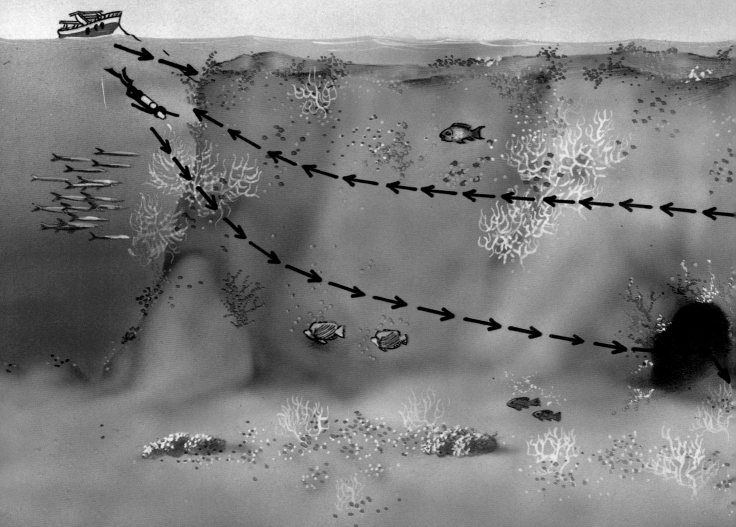

lunar fusiliers (*Caesio lunaris*), while the seabed abounds with tropical groupers.

When diving, the current is not a major problem, as the route involves moving among the towers over an area of approximately 100 meters (three hundred feet).

Small orangespotted jacks often hunt in this area, swimming by at great speed amongst the narrow canyons which separate the three formations. It is common to sight barracudas here, in small schools.

Erg Abu Ramada is a classical example of the way underwater life in the Red Sea can surprisingly concentrate in a narrow point, that is however exposed to the best conditions for food exchange and light for the coral micropolyps. The extensive lifeforms of the coral reef attracts small and large fish.

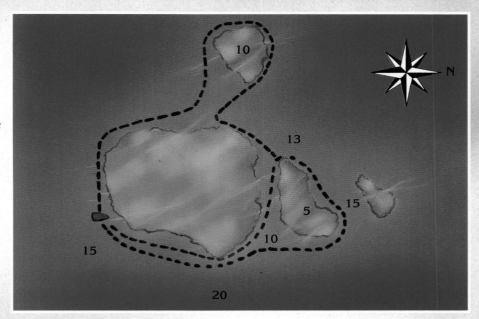

BROTHERS ISLANDS

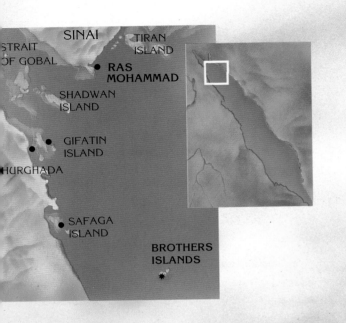

El Akhawein, the two Brothers, are the small islands that just break the surface in the center of the Red Sea, just opposite Al Quseir. The larger island, about one hundred meters across, and no more than four hundred meters in length, with two extremities to the east and the west, is easily identified by an automatic lighthouse which is tended by a few Egyptian soldiers on rotating duty. The lighthouse was built by the English in 1880, and just a few years ago it still had a really

0 mt

30 mt

60 mt

marvellous petroleum searchlight with Fresnel lenses. The pivoting of the search light derives from a counterweight mechanism made by the Change Brothers of Birmingham. The smaller island, which lies about 800 meters (two thousand six hundred feet) east of the larger one, is round and several dozen meters across. The islands are the peaks of two pillars surrounded by a narrow coastal reef, which rises up from an abyss 300 meters (one thousand feet) deep.

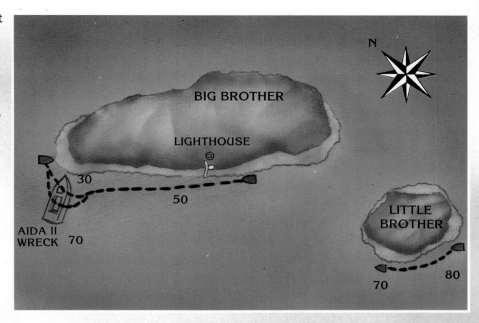

A - El Akhawein - The Brothers Islands - stand virtually at the center of the Red Sea, far away from the usual tourist attractions. The larger of the two islands (The Big Brother) can be easily recognized by the military lighthouse, built by the English in 1880.
Photograph by Marcello Bertinetti.

B - From the deep seabeds, which drop down to depths of three hundred meters, at times menacing oceanic white tip sharks (Carcharhinus longimanus) will rise. Distinguished by the rounded dorsal fin with a white tip, it grows up to four meters in length. It is considered dangerous to humans.
Photograph by Andrea and Antonella Ferrari.

They therefore constitute the only preserve breaking the surface for dozens of square miles around, and this is why a great number of pelagic fish regularly converge on this spot in search of food.
Moreover, the exposure of the two islands to the currents from the open sea has promoted the proliferation of coral, and giant gorgonians and soft corals above all, which, especially around the

C

D - During dives off the Brothers Islands, it is not uncommon to encounter sea turtles (Eretmochelys imbricata). This specimen shows no fear of humans, and allows the diver to approach quite closely.
Photograph by Carlo De Fabianis.

C - The smaller of the two islands (Little Brother) lies eight hundred meters from the larger one, and is little more than a sohal; the reefs here abound in gorgonian fans and splendid soft corals.
Photographs by Marcello Bertinetti.

Little Brother, constitute a spectacular show and setting in the top 30 meters (one hundred feet) or so of water.
The Brothers Islands can be reached only by short cruises that set out from, say, Hurghada or Port Safaga - it is necessary to select the time of the year in order to have excellent conditions of water. The islands are, in fact, too small to constitute a safe haven for an anchored vessel,

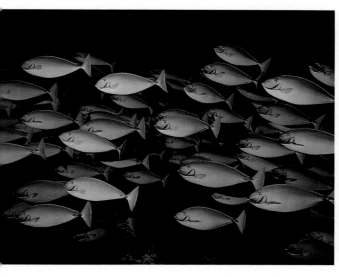

The entire wall to the south of the island offers an excellent location in which to dive: schools of barracuda, jacks, ambere jacks, snappers, and then sharks (*Carcharhinus plumbeus, wheeleri, longimanus*) can be sighted in the deep blue waters. Tiger sharks (Galeocerdo cuvieri) can also be met from time to time. Along the wall, as we were saying, there is a great deal of coral life, even though the more colorful of the islands is the Little Brother, which is worth exploring around its entire perimeter.

E - Large schools of surgeonfish (Naso hexacanthus) swim along the reef in the dark nighttime waters, in search of food. Photograph by Camar Grinberg.

F - Along the sheer walls, one finds all on the life forms typical of the coral reef, in their most spectacular versions. Photograph by Andrea and Antonella Ferrari.

and the steep underwater walls plunging down into the blue make anchoring quite difficult. The best months are May, June, and July.
On the western tip of the Big Brother, the *Aida II* went down in 1957. The *Aida* was a military craft, which had sailed from Alexandria and was transporting troops.
During the changing of the tide, due to an erroneous mooring procedure, it hit the reef and the crew had barely time to reach the island before the ship began to sink.
Today, the *Aida* lies in sailing position, with the prow 30 meters (one hundred feet) under the surface, and the stern 70 meters (two hundred and thirty feet) under.
The hulk is heavily overgrown with coral and almost always exposed to heavy currents - if one takes the proper precautions, one can dive into the interior of the wreck.

F

G

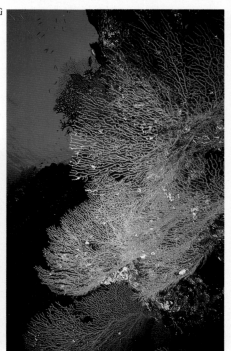

G - A forest of giant gorgonians reaches seaward from the wall of the Little Brother. Photograph by Pierfranco Dilenge.

H - An orangestriped triggerfish (Balistapus undulatus) shows off its brilliant coloring, with yellowish orange stripes on a dark background. Endowed with extremely tough sharp teeth and powerful jaws, it can feed on any type of creatures, including sea urchins and crustaceans. At times, especially when defending its grotto or its eggs, the orange striped triggerfish will take on a rather aggressive stance. Photograph by Andrea and Antonella Ferrari.

SOUTHERN EGYPT

A

B

The southern coasts of Egypt are the latest development in recent years in the general field of scuba-diving along the Red Sea coastline. Areas of particular interest are, starting from the north: the small and solitary Dedalus Reef, forty miles off the coast, the extensive coral system of Fury Shoal, which includes dozens of reefs of all sizes, the area around Ras Banas, which is one of the most imposing promontories facing the Red Sea, south of which stands Port Berenice, and lastly the Island of Zabargad, with the small Rocky Island.

Here tourism has been permitted to flourish again after a long period of prohibition: in fact, relations with Sudan are still strained, and the entire area is heavily fortified and garrisoned by Egyptian troops, and specific permits are required to sail and moor cruise boats.

The latter constitute the only conveyance available to scuba divers, given the total lack of facilities of any kind along the coast. The point of embarkation for cruise ships is invariably off the small military dock of Ras Qulan, near the village of Hamata, just a few kilometers north of Ras Banas.

One arrives by bus, from Hurghada and along some four hundred kilometers of coastal

C

D

road through the cities of - in order - Port Safaga, Al Quseir, Mersa Alam, and a numerous series of checkpoints.

Land travel makes it possible to avoid a voyage which, considering the round trip, would involve three days of sailing quite far from any interesting diving sites.

The cruise boats that work in this area are all fairly large (carrying a minimum of eight passengers) and comfortable, and are equipped with navigational gear granting great autonomy, an important issue given the distance from any tourist facility. Accommodations on board, then, are quite comfortable despite the climate, which can feature temperatures of higher than 40 degrees in summer.

Throughout the year, the humidity level is considerable. The north wind generates massive seas, and only the larger reefs or the islands provide shelter.

Opportunities to dive are numerous, given the almost totally unspoiled nature of the seabeds, and the no-limit approach to diving is commonly in effect. The water temperature remains almost always above 25 degrees, and in summer it often attains 30 degrees, triggering an abundant proliferation of plankton, which often cuts visibility greatly.

The makeup of the coral is far less varied than in the northern regions, while permanent coral fish species are found less extensively on the reefs closer in to the coast and more commonly in an ample area of shallow seabed where the circulation of water is certainly less rapid.

Around all of the outer reefs and the islands, life is plentiful, and numerous large pelagic fish can be observed.

Just a few miles to the south is the Tropic of Capricorn, cutting through the Red Sea.

E - Elegant and majestic, giant mantas (Manta birostris) ply the seas off Southern Egypt. Photograph by Vincenzo Paolillo.

F - Great assemblies of hammerhead sharks (Sphyrna lewini) surely constitute one of the most exciting and moving sights that the sea can offer. Photograph by Bob Cranston/Jeff Rotman Photography.

G - Little bottlenose dolphins (Tursiops truncatus) swim in Dolphin Reef. Photograph by Andrea Ghisotti.

H - A gorgonian sea fan, illuminated by the scuba diver's spotlight, reveals the delicate fabric of its branches. Photograph by Vincenzo Paolillo.

DOLPHIN REEF

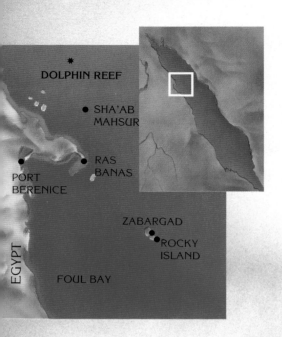

Sataya Reef, widely known as Dolphin Reef, is the largest surface on the coral ridge in the system of Fury Shoal, a few miles to the north of the great promontory of Ras Banas. Approximately three kilometers in length and at its very widest sixty meters across, this reef girds, along its southeastern side, an enormous sand-bed lagoon, no more than 10 meters (thirty feet) in depth.

The bed is a sort of raised area that, just a few meters further in the general direction of the Egyptian coast, plunges back into the blue waves with a coral wall.

In the shallow seabeds, one often encounters a permanent local school of bottlenose dolphins (*Tursiops truncatus*), which tend to repose in the greatest tranquility, though they are generally reluctant to be approached very closely. The school numbers more than a hundred of individuals, including a few particularly sizeable males and a great many females accompanied by their young. The northeastern wall of the reef, surveying the open sea, plunges briskly to a depth of 80 meters (two hundred and sixty feet), and after a narrow step, drops off into the blue.

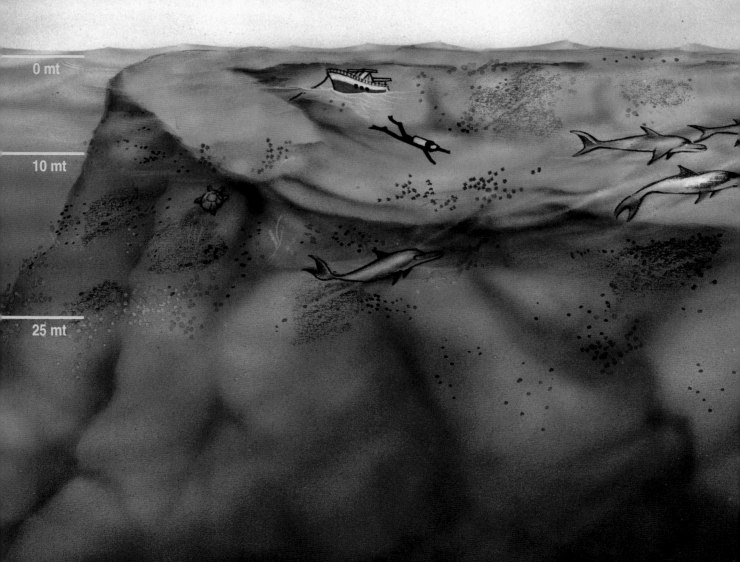

Its appearance, after the first meters below the surface, where hard and soft corals proliferate, tends toward the sedimentary, and it is often possible to observe spectacular underwater slides of coral sand.

Sightings of large predators, such as hammerhead sharks or grey sharks, are possible (one should be aware that the sharks in this area are rather touchy and show a powerful territorial instinct), while jacks are very frequent, as are ambere jacks and small tuna fish.

Sea turtles often swim on the surface.

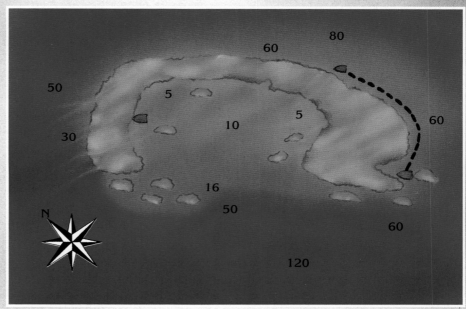

SHA'AB MAHSUR

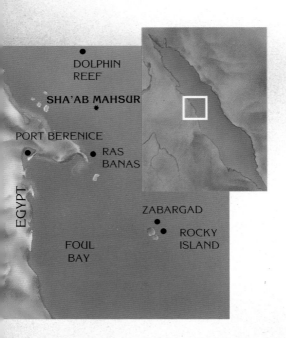

S etting off from the northwestern
tip of Dolphin Reef and sailing
north for about half an hour, one
reaches the reef of Sha'ab
Mahsur. It too is elongated in
shape, although much smaller
than Dolphin Reef, and it
presents the two largest walls
exposed to the north and the
south. On the southern side, the
wall is very steep, and generally
tends to teem with life, dotted
with commodious rifts inhabited
by coral fish and red and violet
soft corals. The red coral, as it
has in the rest of the region, has
built ochre colored "candelabra"
with extremely fine white tips,
which reach toward the surface in
a most spectacular manner.
The two tips of the reef compete

for the greatest abundance of life: there sightings of sea turtles and blacktail sharks can also occur. At the tip pointing out to sea, there are a few small satellite reefs, of which one displays an intriguing little grotto that extends clear through to the other side. This is a perfect spot to end one's dive after covering the outer reef in its entire length, in a forty-five-minute dive.

If one wishes to organize a really deep dive, one should concentrate on one of the two points, which offer greater chances of interesting sightings, rather than moving along the decidedly less interesting walls, relatively devoid of life below 30 meters (one hundred feet).

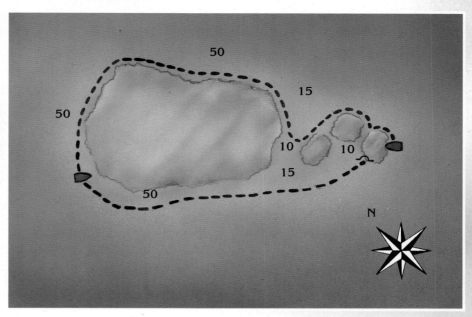

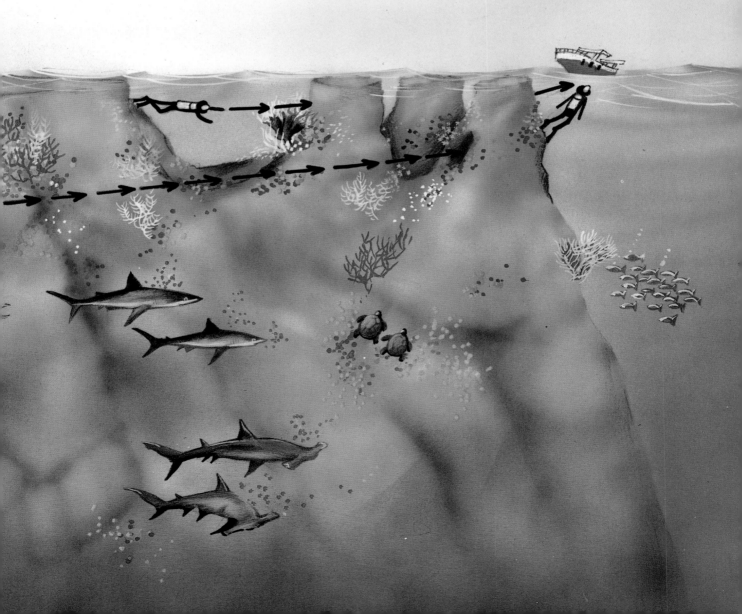

ZABARGAD ISLAND

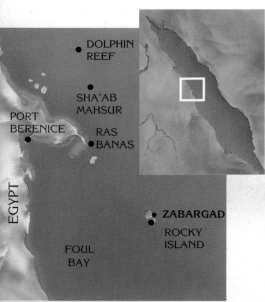

Just forty miles to the southeast of the city of Port Berenice, Zabargad is considered by some to be the ancient *Topazos* referred to in the Annales by Pliny the Elder. From this legendary island of mineral resources, the Pharaohs, the Romans, and even the Egyptians at the turn of the twentieth century extracted the green gems of "olivine," a common magnesium iron silicate which attains a certain value only if found in a pure state and in large-sized chunks. The only pieces of olivine of any particular renown in the mineralogical history of the world appear to have been found on Zabargad and, after disappearing for centuries from the markets of precious stones, they reappeared at the turn of the century when, for a brief period, mining resumed here.

The geological importance of this reddish volcanic island extends well beyond the potential value of the olivine - many scientists are interested in performing studies here to plumb its unique features. Today, however, the island is uninhabited and under close control by the Egyptian army, with regular gunboat patrols, due to the strained relations with the nearby Sudan.

Across from the old dock, on the great eastern beach, the seabed drops rapidly to a depth of 15-20 meters (fifty to sixty-five feet). Here it is possible to observe

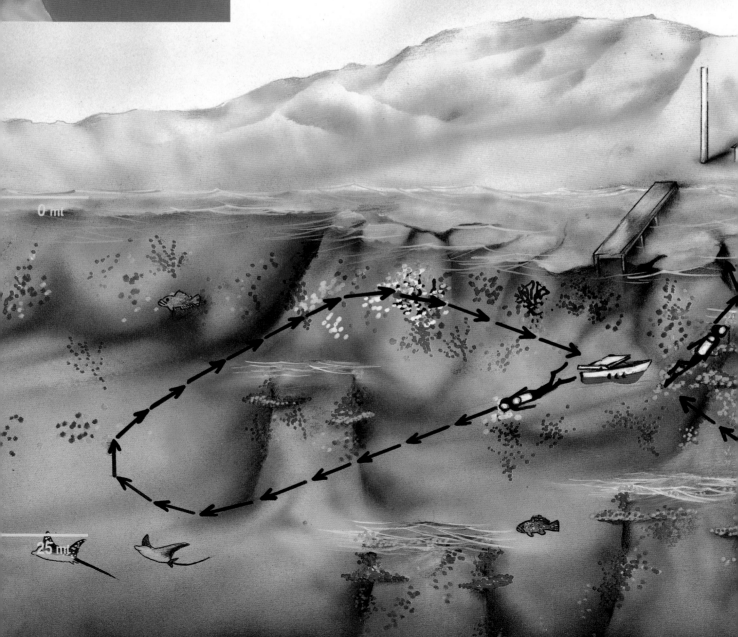

dozens of slender coral towers which make the bay look like an underwater city - great coral umbrellas of *Acropora* open out like terraces or balconies on the towers, while the *Favites* and the *Goniopora* have built innumerable cupolas.
And around the dock the tips of the pillars have joined, just under the surface, only allowing few penetrating shafts to light the long underwater corridors.
Here live a great many tropical groupers, which are easily approached and photographed during a dive without equals in its category, to be made by night as well, when octopus, crustaceans, crinoids, and nudibranches emerge to crowd through the coral grottoes.

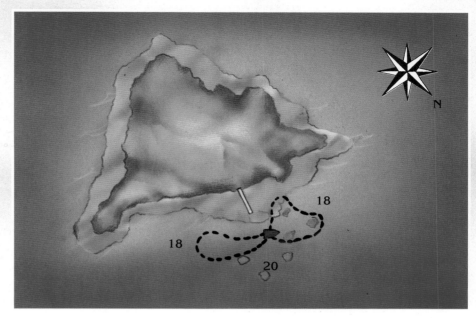

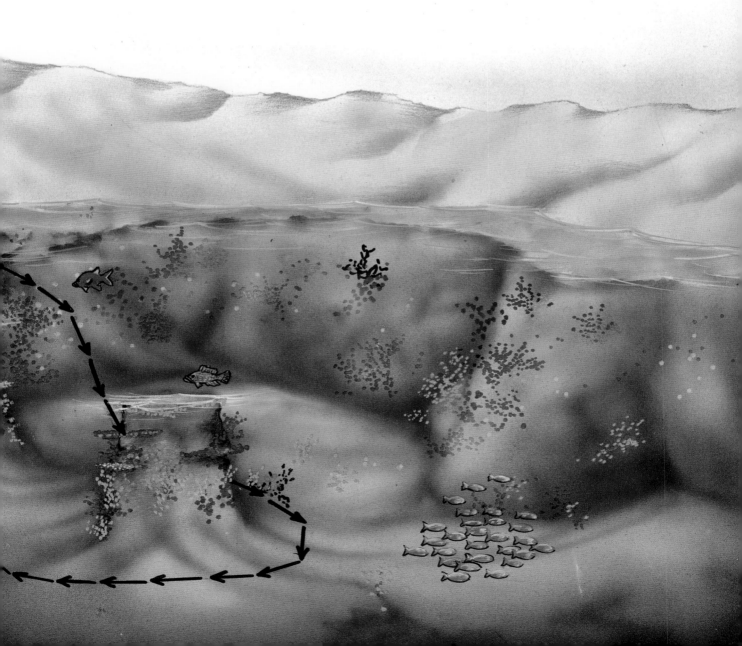

ROCKY ISLAND

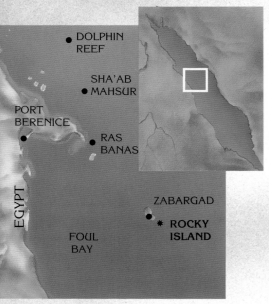

This small fossil-coral island emerges from the surface at about a twenty-minute sail from Zabargad in a southeasterly direction. Elliptical in shape, surrounded by a surface-level reef for a few dozen meters around, the island sinks its walls down into more than 1,000 meters (three thousand two hundred feet) of water. Deep canyons cut into the coral rock while huge gorgonians, branches of black coral, and soft corals float and wave in the current. Practically the entire perimeter of the island offers significant sightings of pelagic fish, and a

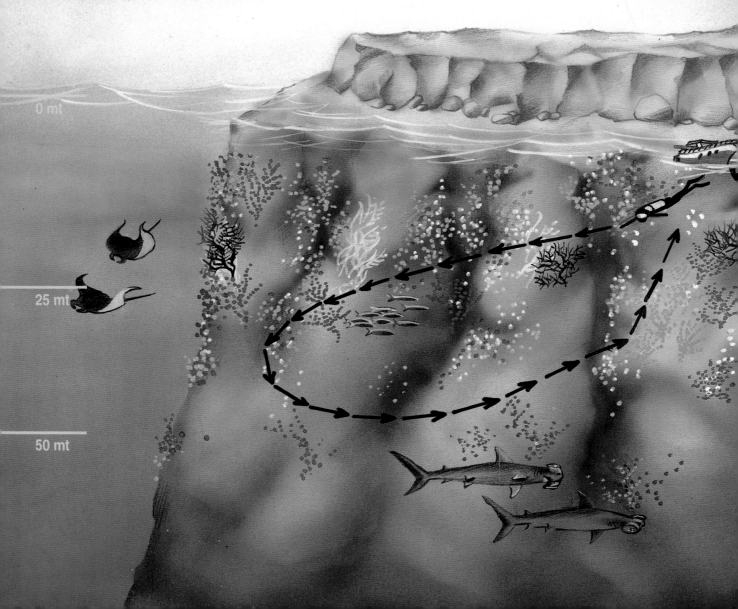

few days of partial diving are really advisable.

With some luck, it ought to be possible to sight many species of shark; blacktail sharks (*Carcharhinus wheeleri*) are always present, as are eagle rays, jacks, barracuda, manta rays, and tuna fish. It is vital for the support ship to keep moving constantly due to the difficulties in anchoring, depending on frequent high seas and strong currents. Rocky Island offers dives that can be compared, in the Egyptian Red Sea, only to Brothers Island, Dedalus Reef, and Ras Mohammad.

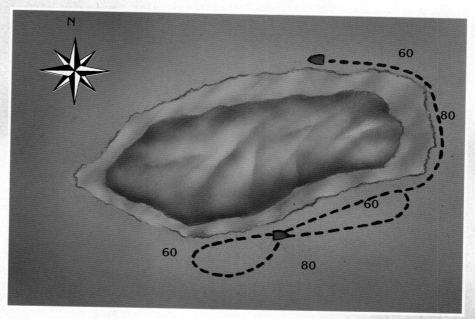

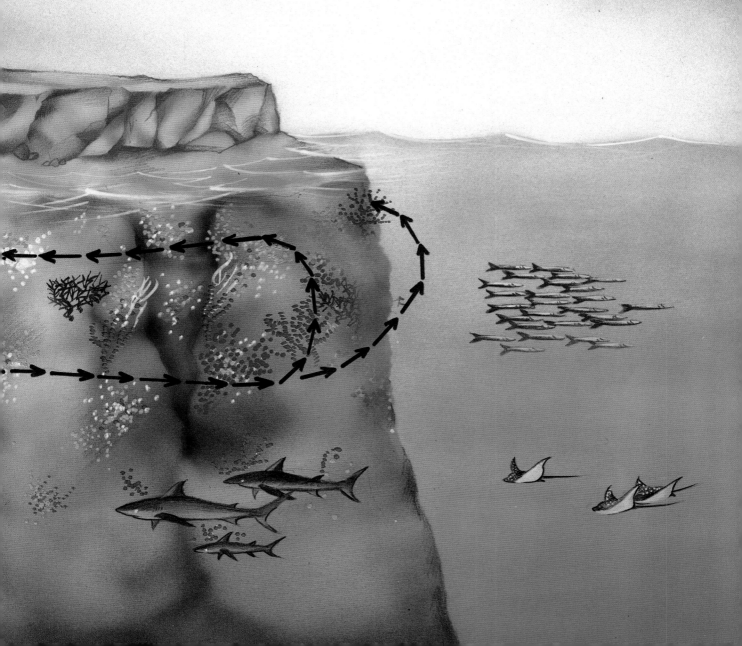

SUDAN

A

A - A blacktail shark (Carcharhinus wheeleri) calmly plies the waters off Sudan, close to the sandy bottom. Accompanying the shark is the inevitable sharksucker (Echeneis naucrates), swimming alongside. Photograph by Jack Jackson.

B - The reefs of the Sudanese Red Sea are also spangled with gorgonian fans, which attain remarkable dimensions, and form an intricate and delicate forest. Photograph by Gianfranco d'Amato.

Sudan, of all the Red Sea which can be toured, is probably the part offering the greatest sensations of adventure. It may be the first part that was explored underwater by the expedition of Hans Hass in 1950, and then by Cousteau, and yet it still conceals most of its secrets. Aside from the occasional cruise aboard charter boats that come directly from the north, practically all the trips in this area set out from Port Sudan, which must be reached by air with flights once arriving from Khartoum and now coming from Cairo. These flights are pretty much the worst part of travelling in this area, as the scheduling is extremely unreliable, and it may happen, especially on return trips, to remain stuck for dozens of hours

B

C

E

C - The red tones of the sea whip corals create a pleasant contrast with the darker hues of the depths. These corals, which belong to the order of the Gorgonacea, undulate sinuously in the current. Photograph by Andrea Ghisotti.

in Port Sudan while waiting for an airplane to Cairo, because there are also connections for Jedda, and precedence is automatically given to pilgrims on their way to Mecca. In any case, the fact remains that a flight which from Europe might be a simple matter of six hours can here turn into an extenuating exodus lasting all of two days. This is too bad because the beauty of a cruise in these waters would attract a great many more tourists if this annoying problem could be solved

Those who decide to go to Sudan for scuba diving must definitely prepare an arsenal of patience and a considerable spirit of adaptability, in the area of cruises as well, as it is difficult for charter boats (which are almost all Italian) to offer any comfort that can be compared to the standards found on board boats operating in the Caribbean. The climate is extremely warm, the port facilities leave much to be desired, supplies are difficult to obtain, and spare parts are almost non-existent. Each piece of equipment must be brought all the way from Europe, and this makes the skipper's job particularly difficult. Let us say, at any rate, that the overall standard of living on board is reasonably acceptable and anyway sufficient to allow full enjoyment of the beauties of the seascape, a seascape which is unquestionably one of the most beautiful and complete in the world. The classic itineraries are two, one toward the north, the other toward the southeast. In both cases, one generally begins with a first dive onto the wreck of the *Umbria*, just slightly out of the port, and then one continues, in the first case, toward Sanganeb and Sha'ab Rumi. If so desired, one may further move northwards, all the way to Sha'ab Sua'di or Angarosh, but the sea must be very calm in this case, and one must be ready to spend a considerable part of the time sailing. The itinerary toward the south, instead, involves exploring reefs and islets in the Suakin group, spending the night at Sha'ab Anber, and making daily excursions toward the varied nearby diving spots. In this case, it is possible to take a little side trip to Suakin, the ancient Venice of the Red Sea, long fallen into total ruin, but one must make sure to obtain the correct permits first. This second itinerary, however, requires calm sea and wind, conditions that can be found only rarely (most likely in March). The climate is warm all the year round, and it becomes sweltering during the summer months. Perhaps the best time for a visit are the spring and autumn months, when the temperature is a little less extreme, but during summer the visibility of the water can be exceptional, and one can spot some remarkable creatures. But don't expect to sleep in your cabin! Water temperature remains around 26-28 degrees centigrade in the spring months, drops a few degrees in winter, and becomes still hotter in summer. Charter boats are generally equipped with Italian 15-liters tanks, generally featuring double valves and weights. One is advised to bring the rest of the needed equipment. There is absolutely no chance of obtaining films, accessories, or

F

batteries locally, so bring it all with you. For recharging strobes and lights, each boat has a generator and an inverter, which works at least six hours each day. Although no particular vaccinations are required, do not forget to bring certain medicines, because local health facilities are not always well stocked, and naturally one is advised to dive with great caution, so as to cut your risks of bends or embolism to a minimum, as help would definitely not be forthcoming.

D - A graceful soft coral grows on the sheer reef wall, a further confirmation of the Red Sea's reputation as an undersea garden. Photograph by Andrea Ghisotti.

E - A grouper (Plectropomus p. marisrubri) rivals the lavish and varied colors of the reef with its garish coloring. Photograph by Claudio Ziraldo.

G

H

F - Forty miles to the north of Port Sudan, on the seabeds of Sha'ab Suadi, lies the wreck of the Blue Bell, a large freighter, loaded with Toyota trucks, that sank in the second half of the Seventies after hitting the reef for unknown reasons. Photograph by Andrea Ghisotti.

G - Sha'ab Rumi, located some twenty-five miles from Port Sudan, represents one of the most complete and exciting dives in the entire southern Red Sea. Photograph by Andrea Ghisotti.

H - The long wooden pier that leads to the lighthouse of Sanganeb extends out over the reef. Photograph by Andrea Ghisotti.

SHA'AB SU'ADI : WRECK OF BLUE BELL

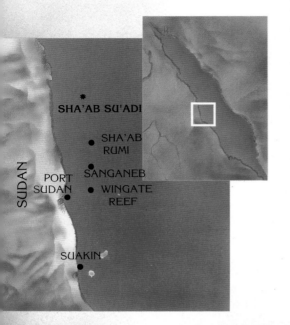

About forty miles north of Port Sudan, Mersa Arakiyai opens out onto the coast, one of the many "Mersas," or sheltered bays, with shallow and sometimes marshy waters, where one can occasionally spot a dugong, approaching the coast at night in search for algae and aquatic plants. Here is a small military installation, four wooden shacks with a lookout tower and a radio station, apparently intended to keep an eye on local smugglers. Just off the coast, on the other hand, is the reef of Sha'ab Su'adi, which can be easily recognized even by an inexpert sailor, as the reef is covered by masses of metallic wreckage, the remains of a few automobiles tossed onto the reef during the wreck of the *Blue Bell*. The tour of this imposing hulk is the destination of our visit. This was a large cargo ship that sank in the second half of the Seventies after inexplicably striking the reef, which opened a huge tear in its keel and then drove it to the bottom. The ship's cargo was a hold of *Toyota* vehicles of all sorts: from four-doors to pickups, from large trucks to panel vans, which all lie on the seabed or are wedged amidst the sheet metal of the ship itself. This ship is overturned on the scarp, the prow pointing landward and the stern resting on the sea bottom, some 80 meters (two hundred and sixty feet) beneath the surface. This dive is truly exciting, both because of the clarity of the water, and because of the amazing setting provided

by the huge hulk and scattered land-vehicles, and because pelagic fish are present too. About midway along the ship, the scarp drops off sharply to 50-55 meters (one hundred and sixty or one hundred and eighty feet), leaving a gap between the bottom and the hull of the ship, where the current nourishes some amazing soft corals of unusual size to grow. Further down, one could also explore the bridge, the screw, and the rudder, all of which are intact and intriguing, but far too deep - no less than 70 meters (two hundred and thirty feet)! By night large sharks emerge from the depths, including the dangerous mako sharks and tiger sharks, which should discourage night-time dives to the wreck.

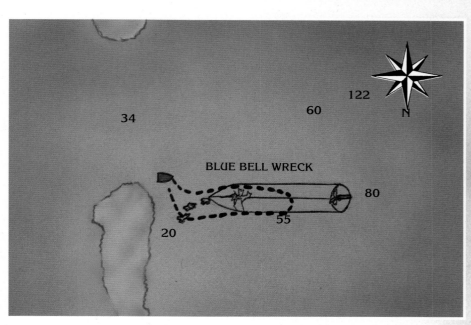

SHA'AB RUMI: SOUTH POINT

If I were asked to select just one place in which to dive in Sudan, I would probably choose the South Point of Sha'ab Rumi, which is one of the most complete diving spots in this sea. The reef lies at a distance of twenty-five miles from Port Sudan, and it is fairly well protected from rough seas if one takes shelter on the interior of the lagoon, accessible through a pass on the western side. The South Point can be reached from here with a short row in a dinghy, and one can leave one's boat anchored in the calm waters of the lagoon (just right for a night-time dive,

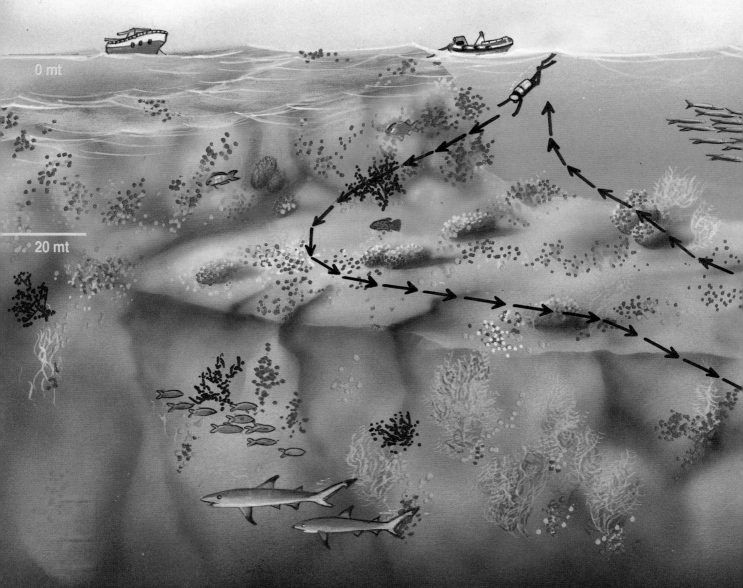

given that the bottom is mainly sandy). The South Point, as the name suggests, is the southernmost tip of Sha'ab Rumi, the reef of Cousteau, who organized the huge experiment in underwater living, *Precontinent II*, in 1963. Like all points, this one is often subject to strong currents, which can sweep in a number of different directions, but which are generally directed in a southwesterly direction. The dive begins just off the coast, where it is possible to nose around the corals in just a few centimeters of water - this is a huge underwater pool, inaccessible to scuba divers

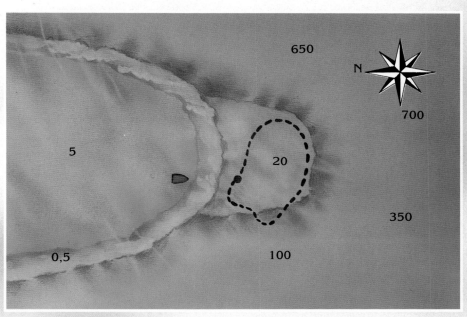

A

other hand, it drops away sharply toward inaccessible depths. This shelf is one of the underwater wonders of the world, and is a must in the list of dives for those who want to see the finest that the underwater world has to offer, literally upholstered with soft corals and small gorgonians. Here it is possible to find nearly all of the reef fish of the Red Sea, but that is true of many places, and so all that seems to set it apart is the beautiful clean water and the unquestionable wealth of fish.

due to the very low water, and where surgeonfish live in peace, along with young individuals of a number of other varieties of fish, which have selected the area as their nursery. Toward the open sea, the underwater wall immediately drops to a depth of 15-20 meters (fifty to eighty feet), and then continues along descending none too sharply for another one hundred meters or so toward the south, gradually dropping away. On the sides, on the

B

C

D

The true distinctive feature of the South Point lies in the platform that extends out toward the open sea, like some diving board that plunges down on three sides towards inconceivable depths, on the order of 700 meters (two thousand three hundred feet). During the entire dive therefore one witnesses an endless procession of pelagic fish, which tend to approach scuba divers quite readily, making for some excellent photographs. Among the most exciting encounters are certainly those with dense schools of barracuda, which tend to congregate along the eastern ridge, but which of course move about as they please, and then of course there are the run-ins with sharks. The sharks are in general represented by small reef sharks, such as the white tip reef shark (*Triaenodon obesus*) and the grey shark (*Carcharhinus wheeleri*), but also (and this is the true specialty of the place) by hammerhead sharks (*Sphyrna*

A - A school of tropical goatfish (Mulloides vanicolensis) swims in close formation along the rocks. This diurnal fish lives in groups of two hundred, often moving along the sandy seabeds or at the base of the reef. With the long barbles set just beneath their mouth, they monitor "their territory" during their search for food: mollusks and small prey. Photograph by Vincenzo Paolillo.

B - Hammerhead sharks (Sphyrna lewini) are easily encountered in the waters off the South Point of Sha'ab Rumi. These much feared predators move in schools of twenty to thirty individuals, but they are actually quite shy, and when followed by divers they head out toward deeper waters. Photograph by Andrea Ghisotti.

C - A parrotfish (Scarus ferrugineus) is accompanied on its rounds on the rocky seabed by a single butterflyfish (Chaetodon fasciatus). Photograph by Andrea and Antonella Ferrari.

D - The South Point extends toward the open sea, reaching great depths of as much as seven hundred meters. An exciting and frequent presence in these waters are silvery walls of barracudas (Sphyraena qenie). Photograph by DUBA.

E - A coral grouper (Cephalopholis miniata) moves freely along the intricate forms of the reef. This typical coral fish is about forty centimeters in length, and lives at depths ranging from two to one hundred meters. Photograph by Andrea and Antonella Ferrari.

lewini). These tend to go out on patrol together, in the deeper waters alongside the platform, and they can be seen by heading out to sea (only when there is no current!), and dropping down to at least 30 meters (one hundred feet). At times, one has to descend even further, but in any case, one has to float motionless in the water, given that the much feared predators tend to display a timid nature, and they move off if they are followed. At times, one may see imposing formations of hammerhead sharks, groups as big as 20-30 individuals, some of them of considerable size. A typical dive at South Point involves a circumnavigation of the shelf, with brief excursions into deeper water, reaching the deepest areas during the first part of the dive, then drawing back toward the end of the dive onto the shelf that rises from a depth of 20 meters (sixty-five feet) all the way back up to the surface, where one can spend a considerable time in an aquarium that is truly rich in life and color.

F - The squirrelfish (Adioryx spinifer) is easily recognized by its large curious eyes and garish red coloring. This is a typically nocturnal fish, and during the day it remains hidden in cavities of the reef. It is only after nightfall that the fish emerges in search for food, chiefly coelenterates. Photograph by Vincenzo Paolillo.

H

One should not rule out in this final stage, encounters with the occasional grey shark, risen from the deep, and crisscrossing the shelf nervously, as if it wanted to reclaim its territory.

G - A group of scuba divers swims around a giant coral umbrella. Photograph by Andrea Ghisotti.

H - In shallow Sudanese waters it is possible as well to admire the structure of the reef, lavishly adorned with colorful soft corals. Photograph by Vincenzo Paolillo.

SHA'AB RUMI: REMAINS OF PRECONTINENT II

On the interior of the huge reef of Sha'ab Rumi a handsome lagoon opens out, which can be reached through a narrow pass, and just offshore of this pass, one is almost certain to encounter dolphins, which dance cheerful attendance on the boats that come close to shore. Just outside of the pass are the remains of one of Cousteau's most famous expeditions, that of *Precontinent II* in 1963, in which for the first times, divers attempted to make, truly longterm underwater stays, of divers, and for which a special "village" was set up. A dive to the remains of *Precontinent II* has all the flavor

of nostalgia mixed with amazement at what was done thirty years ago in open Red Sea, and which would be no mean feat to reproduce today.

The structures were designed and constructed on the Côte d'Azur and transported aboard the Italian support ship, *Rosaldo*. The main structure was constituted by the lodgings of the oceanauts, a star-shaped structure that was, unfortunately, recovered at the end of the mission. The circular garage of the *Soucoupe plongeante*, the disk-shaped research submarine used for deep explorations, is somewhat similar to the exoskeleton of a

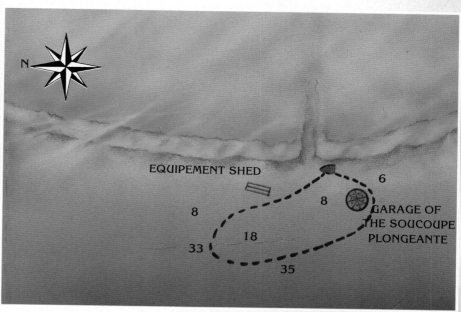

EQUIPEMENT SHED

GARAGE OF THE SOUCOUPE PLONGEANTE

6

8

8

18

33

35

0 mt

6 mt

30 mt

A

A - The project of an underwater village, to be built under the direction of Jacques-Yves Cousteau, dates back to 1963; the plan was to have a group of men live there for an entire month. In this picture, it is possible to see the underwater garage of the Soucoupe Plongéante, small, disk-shaped submarine that was used for deep-sea exploration. Photograph by Andrea Ghisotti.

B

C

B - The shape of the underwater garage for the Soucoupe Plongéante is clearly inspired by the shape of a sea urchin skeleton without its spines. The sheet metal, which was once painted yellow, is now covered with coral encrustations, some of which are quite large. Photograph by Andrea Ghisotti.

D

sea urchin. The garage has remained on the seabed and is the largest and most impressive surviving structure among those that were abandoned when the expedition was over. This is a sort of huge bowl, overturned and anchored to the bottom, and equipped with a series of circular portholes. The lively yellow color has long since faded, and it is interesting to note on the metal, aside from a number of small madrepores of various species, the presence of a giant coral umbrella, which serves as a shade for the garage, and where it is not uncommon to find a handsome grouper. It is easy to make one's way into the underwater garage and explore the interior. Here lives a numerous colony of glass fish, typical inhabitants of the shadiest and darkest parts of every wreck. The high part of the garage has no portholes, and is still hermetically sealed; in fact, the numerous dives by scuba divers left a huge air bubble inside. It therefore becomes possible for divers to emerge, remove their masks and regulator, and talk briefly, with an unusual and bizarre echo. On the right side of the garage, the tool shed is still

C - Multicolored encrustations of hard and soft coral cover the abandoned constructions of Precontinent II. Photograph by Andrea Ghisotti.

D - A scuba diver observes the few remains of the equipment shed. The underwater village was the set upon which Cousteau's film, Le Monde sans Soleil (World without Sun), was shot. Photograph by Andrea Ghisotti.

E - A lunartail grouper (Variola louti) swims just above the seabed, made nervous by the presence of scuba divers.
Photograph by DUBA.

F - The zebra shark (Stegostoma fasciatum) can grow to as long as three meters, but is not considered to be dangerous to humans; it lives chiefly near coral reefs and sandy areas, at moderate depths.
Photograph by Andrea and Antonella Ferrari.

G - The coloring of the emperor angelfish (Pomacanthus imperator) is without a doubt one of the most spectacular, alternating different shades and hues, ranging from dark blue to bright yellow, and from white to purple.
Photograph by Marcello Bertinetti.

F

G

H

H - A bluespotted ray (Taeniura lymma) lies flat on the sea floor, partially covered with sand.
Photograph by Andrea Ghisotti.

I - Around the remains of Cousteau's village, life continues at the usual pace. In this photograph, a giant moray (Gymnothorax javanicus) curiously emerges from its grotto.
Photograph by DUBA.

I

there, and a little further on one can glimpse the remains of what was once the fish corral, where fish were penned in for certain experiments, as can be seen in the unforgettable documentary *Le Monde Sans Soleil* (The World Without Sunlight). These remains are perhaps the most striking and intriguing, because they are covered with such a rich coat of life and color as to strike one dumb. In particular, the sponges and the soft corals have transformed the cold metal into a lovely structure, in the midst of which it is not rare to spot the graceful lionfish and the occasional bluespotted stingray which roots in the sea bottom searching for prey. Still further down, one can see the shark cages, again covered with splendid sponges and incrustations. What is missing, however, compared with the film, is the enormous quantity of fish

present in the early 1960s. There is an explanation for this, however: before beginning *Precontinent II*, after Albert Falco had chosen the area suitable for the placement of the village, the pass and the surrounding reef were grazed continually for over a month, creating a sort of oasis in the Red Sea. Even today, however, there is no lack of fish, even though there is no guarantee of sighting sharks on every dive, and the wall of jacks is a little more threadbare...

SANGANEB

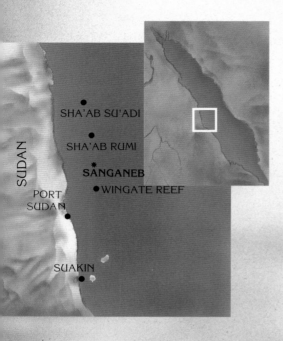

SUDAN

SHA'AB SU'ADI

SHA'AB RUMI

SANGANEB

PORT SUDAN

WINGATE REEF

SUAKIN

Sanganeb is the first true reef that one sees when heading northeast from Port Sudan, save for the Wingate Reef, famous for the wreck of the *Umbria*. With respect to this latter reef, however, Sanganeb is a reef in the open sea, separated from the coast by seabeds that reach depths of 800 meters (two thousand six hundred feet), and it can therefore be considered, in all propriety, to be a full-fledged fortress in the midst of the sea.

0 mt

20 mt

40 mt

Among other things, it also constitutes the means of access to the canal that leads to Port Sudan, and it is therefore surmounted by a tall lighthouse, constructed upon a cement platform that, in turn, stands directly upon the corals of the southern area of the reef. The lighthouse is inhabited by three watchmen who remain on the island for many days at a time, and who will be just delighted to exchange a few words with

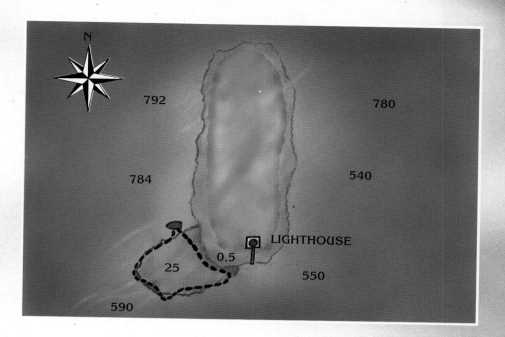

tourists; they will also allow anyone who is interested in slogging their way up quite a few steep steps to climb all the way up to the lantern, whence one can enjoy an exceptional view of the lagoon and the reef of Sanganeb. The lighthouse is linked to the water by a long catwalk, which rests directly upon the partially submerged reef, where surgeonfish live undisturbed, crowded only by the occasional moray eel and a fish-hawk or two. This remarkable range of shallows, only a few inches deep, ends suddenly toward the south, with a sharp plunge. The outer wall drops away completely sheer toward great depths, covered with one of the densest and most colorful forests of soft corals in the Red Sea. It is such an ideal photographic gymnasium that some charter boats spend their entire cruise here, since it is unlikely that one can find a more colorful and lively place to dive anywhere in the Red Sea. The wall is also split and fissured with grottoes and cuts swarming with fish, groupers and grunts for the most part, and those fish move around in families of fifty to a hundred individuals. Moving westward, one reaches a saddle that joins the vertical wall to a sandy shelf at about 20 meters (sixty-five feet) in depth. This is one of the finest dives in Sudan and in the entire Red Sea. The coral sand on the bottom in fact makes the setting very bright and perfect for underwater photography. There is a great abundance of creatures, and perhaps the creatures have become somewhat tamed by the continual arrival of scuba divers (not as many as in other places, of course!) who often feed the fish in order to get photographs. In fact, there is always a large school of barracuda that float in the water and which can be approached without any particular difficulty, while large parrotfish shuttle between the

A - The platform before the lighthouse of Sanganeb seems to be set in the splendid, emerald-green reef. Photograph by Andrea Ghisotti.

B - From the top of the lighthouse, which is linked to the water by a very long catwalk, one enjoys a remarkable panoramic view of the coral reef, here dropping away sheer to enormous depths. Photograph by Andrea Ghisotti.

C - The walls of the reef of Sanganeb are extremely rich in life, and the fish, by now quite accustomed to the presence of scuba divers, allow them to approach without fear. In this picture, a burrfish (Chilomycterus spilostylus) takes on the typical defensive position, with its spines erected all over the body, and does not flee from direct contact with humans. Photograph by Andrea Ghisotti.

D - A scuba diver observes the sinuous branches of sea whip corals rising from the bottom to be rocked by the flow of currents. Photograph by Andrea Ghisotti.

surface and the sea bottom. Here are a few coral pinnacles that stand in all their glory, and they are a true concentrate of fauna: gorgonians, soft corals, sponges, black coral, mollusks, and bryozoans provide shelter to a multitude of crustaceans and small coral fish. In the midst of this aquarium, there is an almost constant procession of grey sharks, which cruise not only on the outer sides of the shelf, but also come quite close to the scuba divers without the slightest hesitation. In deeper waters, to the south or southwest, there are hammerhead sharks that cruise in groups of considerable numbers, and at times they come close enough to photograph. Almost always, it is possible to see large schools of silvery jacks and numerous bluespotted stingrays (*Taeniura lymma*) which root around on the sandy bottom, in search for small crustaceans and fish; from time to time, it is possible to spot a manta ray or a sea turtle. One should also keep an eye out for the splendid sea whips, at first sight a dark brownish color, but in reality a bright reddish-brown, which enliven photographs with a splash of color, if shot with an electronic strobe.

E

E - A blacktail shark (Carcharhinus wheeleri) allows a glimpse of its white belly as it turns. In these waters, the constant passage of sharks makes diving particularly exciting. Photograph by Pierfranco Dilenge.

F

F - The imposing silhouette of a hammerhead shark (Sphyrna lewini) stands out sharply against the blue of the water. Photograph by Andrea Ghisotti.

G

G - The formations of soft corals here attain remarkable concentrations, often as far as to cover the sheer walls. Photograph by Andrea Ghisotti.

H

H - A great many fish take shelter in the endless labyrinth: in this picture, a coral grouper (Cephalopholis miniata) in its safe cranny looks out curiously at the diver. Photograph by Vincenzo Paolillo.

I - A titan triggerfish (Balistoides viridiscens) moves warily across the reef, guarding and keeping an eye on its territory. Photograph by Gianni Luparia.

I

WINGATE REEF: WRECK OF UMBRIA

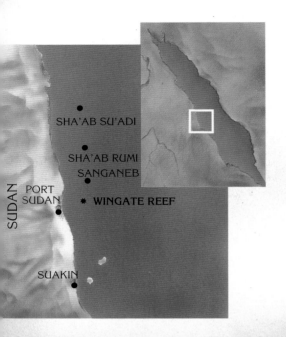

E ver since the first exploration by the Austrian pioneer Hans Hass back in 1950, the wreck of the *Umbria* has become one of the obligatory destinations for all of the scuba divers who come to Sudan, and in absolute terms one of the most famous sunken ships in the world. Her story is bloodless, even though she was sunk during wartime, and to be precise just a few hours before the fatal hour of midnight on June 9, 1940 when Italy would officially enter the war.
The *Umbria* was a freighter built in Hamburg in 1912 and christened the *Bahia Blanca*; she was later purchased by the *Compagnia Italia* which rechristened her with her more

famous name, and then sold her to *Lloyd's Triestino* in 1937. The ship was 150 meters (five hundred feet) in length, had a displacement of 10,000 tons, and was driven at a cruising velocity of twelve knots by two engines with an overall horsepower of 4,600. The ship's last trip saw her loaded chiefly with war material destined to the Italian troops in East Africa: 360,000 bombs, as well as sacks of cement, automobiles, and all of the material which constitutes the usual cargo of a ship. Bureaucratic delays by the British, who were fully aware of the cargo of the ship, and were doing everything they could to get their hands on it as soon as

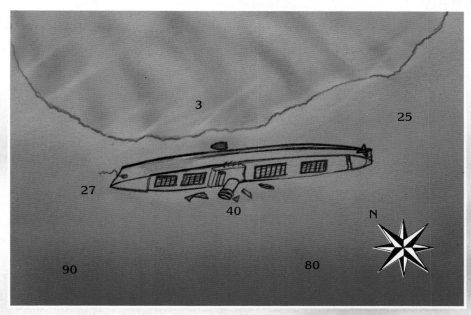

A - The Umbria, one of the most famous wrecks in the world, sank off Port Sudan, near Wingate Reef, on June 10, 1940. Since then she has lain on her port side, with her lifeboat gantries breaking the surface. In this picture, the large stern is shown. Photograph by Andrea Ghisotti.

Italy entered the war, saw to it that the ship was still at Wingate Reef on June 9, just a little way off from Port Sudan, where it was subjected to close examination by the British. Captain Muiesan, however, managed to discover through a radio news report, that hostilities would begin at midnight on that date, and he secretly gave the order to the engine room to scuttle the ship. Then he brought the entire crew onto the deck, with the excuse of staging a rescue drill. When the English realized just what was

D - The Umbria was a freighter displacing 10,000 tons, and could carry as much cargo. This photograph shows the center of the ship, with the starboard lifeboat gantries breaking the surface. Photograph by Andrea Ghisotti.

B - The narrow prow sprawls upon the seabed. The Umbria was 150 meters long, and was equipped with two engines allowing her to reach a cruising speed of twelve knots. Photograph by Andrea Ghisotti.

C - Abundant coral encrustations have taken over the great starboard screw as well as the rest of the ship, which is covered with hard and soft corals. Photograph by Andrea Ghisotti.

going on, it was too late, and nothing could be done but to abandon the ship to her destiny. The Umbria settled with her port flank on the seabottom, so that the starboard gantries of the lifeboats emerged from the water. No one has ever tried to handle her dangerous cargo of explosives, which is still nicely stacked in the hold, and which makes the exploration of the wreck still more exciting. Given the relatively shallow waters, ranging from a few meters to a maximum of 35-40 meters (one hundred and fifteen or one hundred and thirty feet), it is possible to tour the wreck in a single dive, even though a more thorough

E

E - In one of her side holds, the Umbria was carrying three Fiat 1100-long- wheelbase automobiles, designed specifically for the colonies in East Africa. Photograph by Andrea Ghisotti.

exploration certainly demands a longer stay. Divers generally start with the ship's midsection, where the starboard gantries of the lifeboats emerge from the water. Without tanks, one can dive down to the area of the central quarter-deck, which is spectacular, with the remains of the huge smokestack prone on the quarter-deck. In order to explore the various decks, one needs airtanks, which also make it possible to hover amidst the metal flanks, offering some tasty morsels to the large triggerfish, which can be approached much more easily than is the case on other Sudanese reefs. If one allows oneself to drop onto the sea floor, which in this area attains a depth of some 40 meters (one hundred and thirty feet), one can see one of the lifeboats, which is still in excellent state, a giant wind-sleeve, and the smokestack. As one swims toward the stern, one sees the holds where the bombs are stacked up, with the fuses, along with other material. The exploration of the holds is easy and does not create any particular sensations of claustrophobia. One should not miss a trip to the extreme stern, which is very impressive, with its huge rudder and, on the starboard side, the enormous starboard screw, intact, with its four well-encrusted blades. After returning to the midsection, one can explore the bow holds, in the first of which, in front of the quarter-deck, are hidden three *Fiat 1100 Lunga* automobiles in the colonial version, with distinctive treads and three rows of seats, one of the most exciting sights imaginable underwater. The forward holds contain an enormous quantity of material, ranging from cement sacks and bottles of wine to zippers, light bulbs, airplane tires, and perfumed essences. Lastly, one can examine the gigantic bow, with the anchor chain that disappears into the blue water beneath.

F - A considerable portion of the cargo consisted of warfare materials sent to the Italian troops in East Africa. More than 360,000 bombs still lie in the ship, neatly stacked in the holds along with 60 crates of fuses and incendiary devices. Photograph by Andrea Ghisotti.

G - The Umbria has become a permanent home for many fish. This picture shows an angelfish (Pomacanthus maculosus) with its unmistakable coloration. Photograph by Andrea and Antonella Ferrari.

H - A parrotfish (Scarus ferrugineus) swims through the twisted girders of the wreck. Photograph by DUBA.

ERITREA
DAHLAK ISLANDS

A - Angelfish (Pomacanthus afur) tend to lead a solitary life, moving throughout protected lagoons or in the shelter of coral reefs. Photograph by Andrea Ghisotti.

B - Bluestriped snappers (Lutjanus kasmira) usually move in dense schools consisting of more than a thousand fish; the schools tend to break up into smaller groups during the night, when the fish hunt crustaceans on the reef. Photograph by Claudio Ziraldo.

A

It was only after the shooting stopped and after the popular referendum of 1993 that Eritrea reopened its doors to tourism, albeit with many organizational problems linked to the precarious state of the nation after so many years of war. For the time being, there are no structures suited to scuba diving, though a few diving centers are cautiously beginning to be organized. Anyone who wishes to visit the Dahlak Islands, then, must plan on making his own way and having plenty of time on hand, taking advantage of the availability of the local sailing craft, extremely seaworthy vessels that are however rather spartan for a Western tourist accustomed to a minimum of comfort. The situation is changing rapidly, and in the space of a few years, well-equipped charter cruises will certainly be organized for scuba-diving excursions. The point of departure for trips to the Dahlak

C - Manta rays (Manta birostris) live around the Dahlak Islands in great numbers, often coming close to the shore. In these waters, it is sometimes possible to see enormous specimens, with wingspans as wide as six meters. Photograph by Vincenzo Paolillo.

B

C

Islands is the port of Massaua, connected with Asmara through a road one hundred and thirty kilometers long, which can be driven in about 2-3 hours. In Massaua, there are a number of hotels, all damaged by the war, but undergoing reconstruction. In order to be able to dive, one must ask for a fishing permit, which is issued at Massaua (ID-format photographs are needed) and which should be renewed each time

D - A large member of the Haemulidae family has allowed the photographer to come very close, and displays no fear whatsoever. These fish, quite numerous off the Dahlak Islands, are distinguished by their protruding lips. Photograph by Andrea Ghisotti.

one returns to the port, while every group of scuba-divers must be accompanied by a local guide. The archipelago is made up of 126 islands with a coral base (save for the two islands of Dissei and Seil, rather rocky) which rise from a sandy seabed that varies in depth from 50 to 100 meters (one hundred and sixty to three hundred and thirty feet). And it is this fairly shallow shelf that conditions the underwater environment, which is not always the greatest in terms of setting and visuals. The sheer underwater cliffs and the fissures are rare, and are at the highest only a few meters, while the seabed is sandy everywhere. Major coral constructions are absent therefore, and so there are none of the classic reefs near the surface; instead there are only agglomerations and small rises on the scarps. The water is rather murky due to the exceptional richness of plankton, and due to the relatively shallow bottom. Therefore, the sea bottoms off the islands are not among the Red Sea's finest, and in some cases they may somewhat disappoint those who have already made dives in Sudan or in the Egyptian Red Sea. In terms of fish there is a remarkable wealth of species, assisted moreover by the forced protection that these islands enjoyed during wartime. It is not uncommon to find very large fish (groupers, grunts, snappers), which have never seen humans and allow divers to approach freely. Mantas and eagle rays come close to the shore, and may be seen in large groups in certain periods of the year. Sea turtles are very common, and they emerge from the water at night to lay their eggs in the sand. Sharks can be found in these waters in relative plenty, and this stretch of sea was once considered to be the most shark-infested in the Red Sea. If you dive without fishing, then you see no more sharks than you might expect in Sudan, and even the dangerous tiger sharks, which live in these waters, are encountered rarely. If one is travelling to the Dahlak Islands, one should make sure that one carefully chooses the time of the year, in an attempt to take advantage of the period with the best water conditions. Leaving aside winter, which is characterized by cloudy skies and considerable rain, it is best to travel here during the months of April and May, or in October and early November. Summer, which is characterized by a calm sea, is the least appropriate time to come here because the high temperatures make Massaua one of the hottest cities on the planet.

DIFNEIN ISLAND

Difnein is the northernmost of the Dahlak Islands, and it is certainly the island most beloved of those who visited the archipelago before the outbreak of the war between Eritrea and Ethiopia blocked off access for many years. In the Seventies, in fact, one tended to come to the Dahlak Islands chiefly to engage in underwater hunting, and Difnein was a particularly lush reserve given its isolation. It is in fact some seventy miles from Massaua, and it is uninhabited. It is now once again possible to visit the seabeds of the island, but one cannot go on land, because the coasts are mined, and apparently at least one fisherman has lost a foot by stepping on a mine. This is unfortunate, because the white beaches of the island are alluring and inviting and the lavish varieties of birds and animals deserve a closer examination. The water of Difnein is the cleanest of any of the Dahlak Islands, by virtue of its location far to the north, at the far limit of the sandy bottom from which the archipelago rises. The sea floors around the island are about 60-70 meters (two hundred or two hundred and thirty feet) in depth, but to the east, just a couple of miles from the island, there are sea beds almost 300 meters (one thousand feet) in depth. The underwater features are quite similar on just about the entire northeastern side, which is without a doubt the most interesting side. There is a small coral cliff about 5-6 meters (sixteen or twenty feet) in height, which terminates on the sandy bottom at about 15 meters (fifty feet) in depth. The setting is not particularly spectacular (there are no gorgonians) but there is a

great abundance of fish. In just one dive, one is extremely likely to see a good portion of the fish species found in the Red Sea, including some major encounters, such as those with large schools of barracuda and batfish, manta rays, pelagic fish, and the amiable grunts *(Plectorhynchus* sp.) which may be the most representative of this location, along with the endemic *Pomacanthus asfur* with their handsome blue and yellow colors. There are not many sharks around during the daytime, but it is wisest not to dive at night, since tiger sharks come up from the depths; they are not much fun to encounter, nor very safe.

One should also note there are some handsome bottlenose dolphins living around Difnein, but they are not easy to approach.

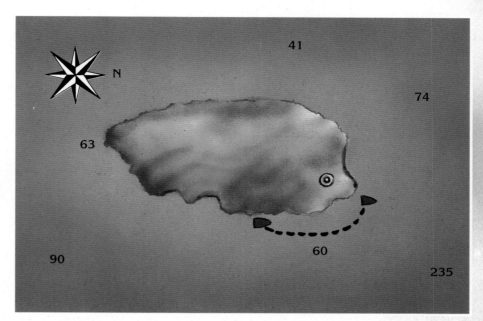

SEIL ISLAND

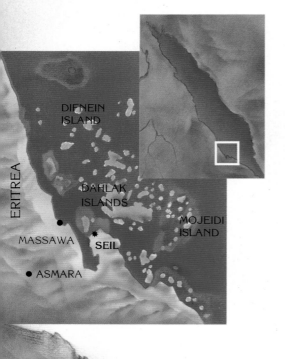

Asmall and rocky islet, indeed, one of the only two rocky islets of the Dahlak Islands, Seil lies quite close to the eastern coast of the island of Dissei, and therefore relatively close to Massaua, from which Dissei is about twenty miles away. This is therefore one of the easiest islands to reach by renting a sambuk or some other vessel at Massaua. Seil is little more than a shoal, but it literally pulsates with birds. There one can see herons, storks, fish hawks, terns, seagulls, pelicans, wild doves, and beautiful spoonbills, which nest on the western shore. Under the water, it is a strange island and in some ways an unsettling one. Indeed, there are none of the classic coral seabeds which are

fairly reminiscent of their Mediterranean counterparts. The best area for diving is the northern side, where the bed drops at first to a depth of 15 meters (fifty feet), with huge boulders piled up to form dens. If one moves toward the northeast, the bottom drops to 30 meters (one hundred feet) or so, and moving toward the north with a sort of promontory, which then plunges down to a depth of 45-50 meters (one hundred and fifty or one hundred and sixty-five feet) in a sheer drop. By following this ridge toward the north, one notices that the seabed begins to take on a very strange appearance, made up of vertical fissures and cracks marked off by rock blades, where the fish crowd

in incredible numbers.
The water is green and not too clear, and the entire underwater environment takes on an intriguing and somewhat gloomy appearance.
It is quite common to run into sharks, which are quite numerous in these waters. There are also plenty of good-sized red snappers, spotted rays, twobar anemonefish, with their attendant anemone and, unfortunately, a few coral-devouring starfish (*Acanthaster planci*). Returning to the coastal area, one finds - all around the island, but especially on the western side - a teeming aquarium of small reef fish, which allow one to finish one's dive with a photo fest.

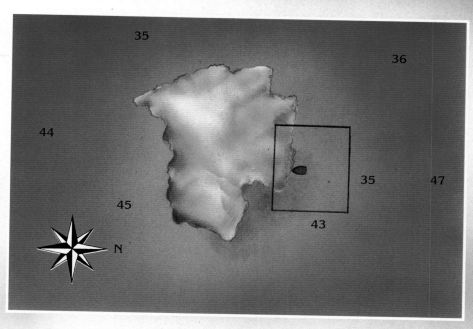

MOJEIDI ISLAND

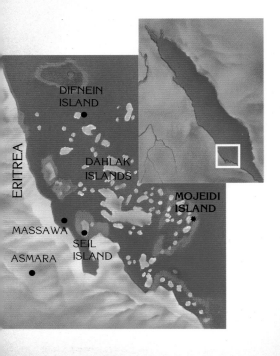

Mojeidi is the easternmost of the Dahlak Islands, extending out into the Red Sea some eighty miles away from Massaua, which is certainly a considerable distance to travel by ship. It is not easy to reach the place, as a great many hours of sambuk are required, while the extremely limited selection of fast vessels at Massaua itself prevents much free travel and exploration of this and the other, more distant islands. Naturally, this is a situation that will not be permanent, and solutions will automatically be found when tourism returns here and when the appropriate facilities are developed. Mojeidi is an unspoiled paradise for a great many species of animals. The beach, which is a marvelous white span of sand, at least a kilometer in length, offers a perfect terrain for the laying of eggs by sea turtles, which land during the night in great numbers. Every morning, it is easy to find the turtle tracks on the sand, and of course it is far from uncommon to run into the turtles themselves at night. Just off the broad beach are a number of coral constructions, which feature considerable smaller varieties of fish, and where we have repeatedly seen manta rays and eagle rays swimming in just two meters of water. In terms of scuba diving, the most interesting side of the island is the southeastern side, where there is a small cut some 4-5 meters (thirteen or sixteen feet) in size about 50 meters (one hundred and sixty feet) off the shore, ending on a sandy bottom at 12-15 meters (forty to fifty feet) in depth, running onward then in a slight slope downward toward the

0 mt

15 mt

open sea, as is the case in most of these islands. The most interesting area to be explored is precisely this small ridge, where coral constructions are the largest and most abundant, forming dens and caves that are always quite well populated with crustaceans and fish of all kinds. The specialty of Mojeidi, aside from the sea turtles and eagle rays, are a numerous school of yellow snappers, which can be found in groups of as many as several hundred.

The macrofauna as well is very interesting, and all those who devote themselves to biology will find them intriguing.

Underwater photography is not highly recommended, at least not waterscape photography, as the water is not very clear because of the wave action in the nearby open sea and because of the sandy sea floor.

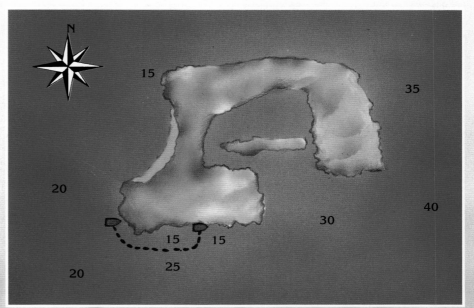

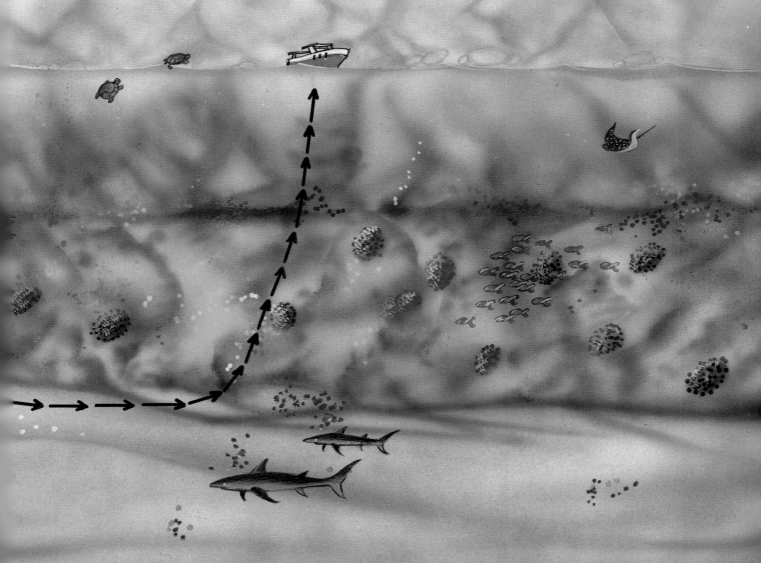

THE FISH
OF THE RED SEA

Because of the long and relatively narrow shape of the Red Sea and its great depth (2,850 meters), the fascinating coral reefs that are its most distinctive feature generally flourish parallel to the coast line, along the brinks of deep abysses, toward which they drop down with their sheer walls.

The seabeds, shallower than fifty meters (one hundred and sixty feet), take up only a fifth of the sea's surface area.

These areas, which enjoy sufficient light to allow vegetation to flourish, especially the microalgae (*Zooxanthellae*) that live in symbiosis with the coral, unfailingly prove to be oases teeming with life.

Competition for space, which is inevitably harsh on hard substrates, has led here to a remarkable development of fauna, creating an incredible "aquarium effect."

In just a few square meters, aside from the remarkable variety of invertebrates (gorgonians, soft corals), it is possible to encounter as many as twenty species of fish at once.

The most recent estimates indicate that there are a thousand species of fish in the Red Sea, and that seventeen percent of those species (though others would put that figure as high as thirty percent) cannot be found anywhere else on the planet.

To describe such an enormous abundance and variety of species is difficult indeed, and a long list of fish is simply not adequate to the challenge.

In the pages that follow, we have attempted to assemble and present a meaningful selection of the most common species or those most representative of the orders and families present in the Red Sea.

Finding one's way through this undersea universe, as alluring as it is complex, is far from simple, and we felt it might be useful to provide some basic information before describing the main groups of fish.

The primary reason for the richness of life on the coral seabeds is a result of the intense productivity of this environment, which is as varied and complex as its inhabitants.

The reefs of the Red Sea, inevitably changeable and undergoing a continuous process of growth - though it may be as little as a few millimeters annually - are jagged and riddled with fissures and crevices, dotted with columnar formations, mushroom-shaped or umbrella-shaped formations.

They border the underwater sands and meadows, and provide limitless habitats to underwater organisms.

Some of these organisms find in the coral an ideal haven to hide from predators; others wait there in ambush, or conceal their spawn, or carry on remarkable interspecies relationships, such as those between anemonefish and sea anemone.

All of them, in any case, find food there: whether they are herbivores, scavengers, omnivores, or specialized carnivores.

The coral reef does not vary only in the forms of life and the landscape that it offers to the eyes of the scuba diver.

There are also gradients of differentiation that are linked to the depth, connected with the dynamics of the water, the lighting, and the temperature, to mention just a few of the many factors.

Only a series of dives can show how many and what sort of relations exist among the various species of fish and the many forms of adaptation, the most distinctive of which must be that connected to the variety of colors seen.

Although these colors are so pronounced and evident to human eyes, they are far less so to other fish, and in fact they often serve as camouflage.

For instance, the common ocellar spots and the dark bands that often cover the fish's eyes - especially in the butterflyfish - serve to deceive attacking predators, who take the spots for real eyes, attacking their intended prey at non-strategic points.

Likewise, the bright colorings with their dots, stripes, and layers of garish colors, which seem like advertising flyers to the human eye, make the outline of the fish incomprehensible, breaking it into many component parts or mingling with the branches of coral or the chiaroscuro of the lacy branches of the gorgonians. And the colors are there more than mere deception. They also serve to trasmit specific messages.

Groupers, for example, can shift their coloring rapidly, when they are threatened, feel fear, or are sleeping and therefore feel relaxed.

It is no accident that marine biologists use the term "pyjama colorings" to describe the patterns that certain fish take on during their evening's rest, so different from the colorings they show during the day that they have been taken for members of two different species.

In other cases, especially among the *Labridae* (genera *Thalassoma, Cheilinus, Gomphosus*) or the parrotfish (*Scarus* sp.), the coloring makes it possible to easily recognize (when one has studied them thoroughly) the sex and age of the individual specimens.

In quite a few fish, the color allows to distinguish the young from the adults, thus preventing pointless intraspecies combat. Color also transmits specific messages, such as: "I am ready for reproduction," "I am dangerous," or "I am inedible."

As attractive as they may be, the reefs of the Red Sea have their dangers, and it is better to be on one's guard.

The old caveat - "Look but don't touch" - is valid here, not only with a view to protecting the environment (it is one of the ironbound rules of guided dives in the Red Sea), but covers a myriad of occasions, and covers not only the organisms that can easily be seen, but especially those that camouflage themselves perfectly as a piece of rock or part of the seabed.

Among the main dangers that the scuba diver might expect to encounter in the Red Sea, there are sharks.

For the most part, these are whitetip reef sharks (*Triaenodon obesus*) and blacktip reef sharks (*Carcharhinus melanopterus*), or shortnosed blackfins (*Carcharhinus wheeleri*), or the silver tip shark (*Carcharhinus albimarginatus*).

These are relatively small species, one and a half to two meters (five to six and a half feet) in length, considered to be relatively innocuous, but it is always well to be careful.

Far more dangerous are the *Synanceja verrucosa*, or stonefish, which are virtually invisible, or the spectacular Scorpionfish (*Pterois* sp.), whose long fin rays are poisonous.

The *Pterois* are slow-swimming fish, easy to approach.

Still, one should keep one's distance, because they can turn swiftly and come on, fins extended, if they feel threatened.

Equally dangerous, though a menace that is usually underestimated, are the surgeonfish and triggerfish.

The former have razor-sharp spines on their caudal peduncle and can cause painful cuts to trusting scuba divers.

It is equally unwise to approach triggerfish when they are protecting their spaw.

The powerful teeth of a large triggerfish, built to crush sea urchins and tough-shelled crustaceans, encounter little resistance when used against the delicate skin of a diver, even if wearing a wetsuit.

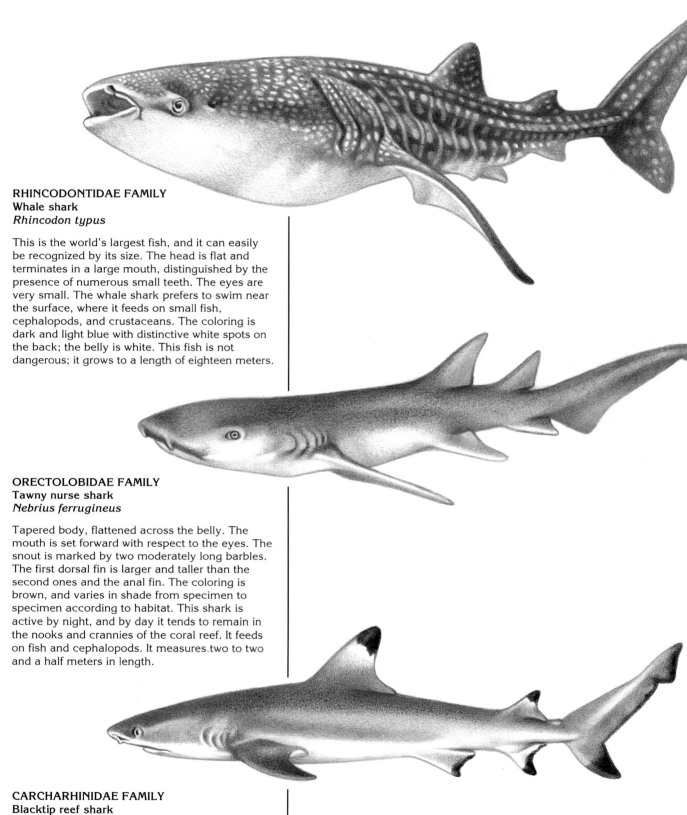

RHINCODONTIDAE FAMILY
Whale shark
Rhincodon typus

This is the world's largest fish, and it can easily be recognized by its size. The head is flat and terminates in a large mouth, distinguished by the presence of numerous small teeth. The eyes are very small. The whale shark prefers to swim near the surface, where it feeds on small fish, cephalopods, and crustaceans. The coloring is dark and light blue with distinctive white spots on the back; the belly is white. This fish is not dangerous; it grows to a length of eighteen meters.

ORECTOLOBIDAE FAMILY
Tawny nurse shark
Nebrius ferrugineus

Tapered body, flattened across the belly. The mouth is set forward with respect to the eyes. The snout is marked by two moderately long barbles. The first dorsal fin is larger and taller than the second ones and the anal fin. The coloring is brown, and varies in shade from specimen to specimen according to habitat. This shark is active by night, and by day it tends to remain in the nooks and crannies of the coral reef. It feeds on fish and cephalopods. It measures two to two and a half meters in length.

CARCHARHINIDAE FAMILY
Blacktip reef shark
Carcharhinus melanopterus

Carcharhinid of moderate size, it is common in shallow coastal waters, especially near open sea reefs. The body is elongated; the snout is short and rounded; the head is flat. The tips of the fins are black. The teeth are triangular. The length is two meters. It seems to have territorial behavior.

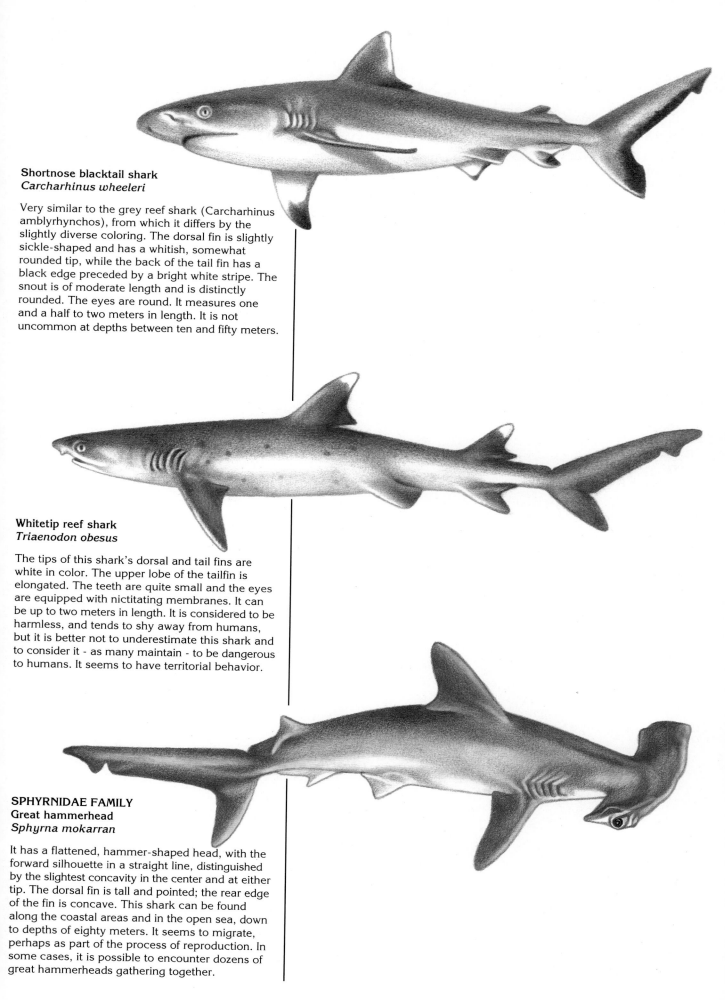

Shortnose blacktail shark
Carcharhinus wheeleri

Very similar to the grey reef shark (Carcharhinus amblyrhynchos), from which it differs by the slightly diverse coloring. The dorsal fin is slightly sickle-shaped and has a whitish, somewhat rounded tip, while the back of the tail fin has a black edge preceded by a bright white stripe. The snout is of moderate length and is distinctly rounded. The eyes are round. It measures one and a half to two meters in length. It is not uncommon at depths between ten and fifty meters.

Whitetip reef shark
Triaenodon obesus

The tips of this shark's dorsal and tail fins are white in color. The upper lobe of the tailfin is elongated. The teeth are quite small and the eyes are equipped with nictitating membranes. It can be up to two meters in length. It is considered to be harmless, and tends to shy away from humans, but it is better not to underestimate this shark and to consider it - as many maintain - to be dangerous to humans. It seems to have territorial behavior.

SPHYRNIDAE FAMILY
Great hammerhead
Sphyrna mokarran

It has a flattened, hammer-shaped head, with the forward silhouette in a straight line, distinguished by the slightest concavity in the center and at either tip. The dorsal fin is tall and pointed; the rear edge of the fin is concave. This shark can be found along the coastal areas and in the open sea, down to depths of eighty meters. It seems to migrate, perhaps as part of the process of reproduction. In some cases, it is possible to encounter dozens of great hammerheads gathering together.

DASYATIDAE FAMILY
Coachwhip ray
Hymanthura uarnak

This ray is shaped like a disk, wider than it is long. The snout is pointed. The tail, which is three to four times longer than the body, is adorned with thirty to thirty-five dark rings, and bears a poisonous spine. The back is marked by a series of tubercules that become particularly distinct between the eyes, and has a brownish-yellow coloring with a number of black spots that in some cases form a sort of network. This ray can be found in relatively shallow waters (one to five meters) on sandy bottoms, between reefs. The disk-shaped body may be as much as two meters in diameter.

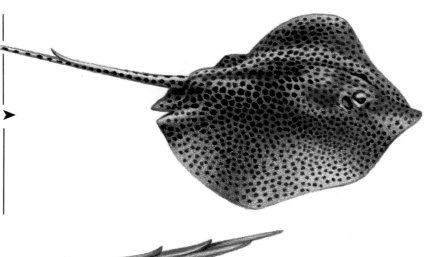

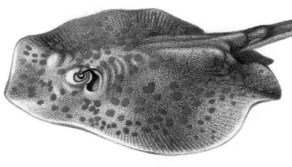

Bluespotted lagoon ray
Taeniura lymma

A more or less elongated disk-shaped body, unadorned in the young rays and marked by a series of denticles at the center of the back in the adults. The coloring is greyish brown or yellowish brown on the back, with bluish spots; the belly is light in color. The tail, with one or two poisonous spines at the tip, has bluish stripes along its sides. The disk-shaped body may grow to about one meter in width. At times, the overall length may be greater than two meters. It lives on sandy bottoms at the base of reefs.

MYLOBATIDAE FAMILY
Spotted eagle ray
Aetobatus narinari

This ray can be recognized easily by the pointed and convex head with large eyes and broad lateral spiracles. The body is diamond-shaped and has broad, pointed pectoral fins. The tail, with one, two, or three denticulated spines, is about three times the length of the body. The ventral fins are broad and fleshy. The back is dark in coloring, with many small white spots. The disk-shaped body measures up to two meters in width. It attains a total length of up to two and a half meters. It can also be found in shallow lagoons (one to five meters in depth) on sandy bottoms.

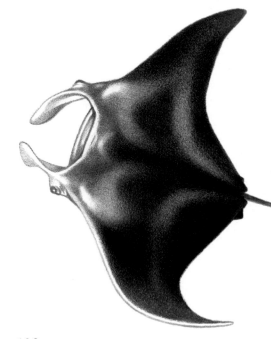

MOBULIDAE FAMILY
Giant manta
Manta birostris

Easily recognized by the well developed pectoral fins, that can attain five to six meters in width. The head is projecting from the body, and is distinguished by a pair of long, flat, flexible cephalic fins, separated by the large arch of the mouth. The upper jaw is devoid of teeth. The spineless tail is long and slim. The dorsal coloring is dark, while the ventral coloring is quite light with dark blotches that can be referred to in order to distinguish one specimen from another.

SYNODONTIDAE FAMILY
Lizardfish
Synodus variegatus

Elongated body, compressed lengthwise. The head is convex toward the rear base. Eyes in an anterior-dorsal position. The snout is pointed, but short. The mouth is wide, and slightly oblique. The jaws are well developed and equipped with numerous needle-shaped teeth. The coloring is variable, but is generally brownish on the back with more or less distinct red spots on the sides. This fish prefers sandy bottoms where it waits in ambush, poised on its sizable ventral fins.

MURAENIDAE FAMILY
Grey moray
Siderea grisa

Small moray with a tapered body and pointed snout, with hard-to-see nares. The mouth is equipped with conical teeth that are more numerous on the upper jaw. The head is brownish, with evident stripes on the back and between the eyes, made up of a series of aligned black points. The rest of the body has a pale brown coloring with violet nuances and brownish marbling. The young are lighter in color. It is not uncommon to see these morays swim in the open on underwater meadowlands. They measure forty to forty-five centimeters in length.

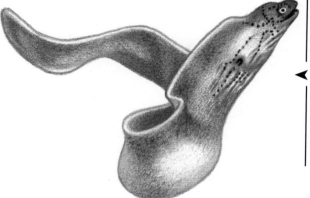

Giant moray
Gymnothorax javanicus

This is the largest of the morays and is fairly common all across the Red Sea. The body is powerful, rather tall on the trunk, and ends in a very well developed head. The snout is short. The mouth is wide. The openings of the opercules are large and black and quite evident. The body is marked by three rows of dark brown spots. The tail is reticulated. It can grow to be as long as two and a half meters.

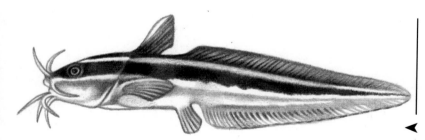

PLOTOSIDAE FAMILY
Striped eel catfish
Plotosus lineatus

This is a social fish found along coastal reefs and near underwater meadowlands. It is easily recognized by the four barbles that surround its mouth. The second dorsal, the caudal, and the anal fin are connected one to the other. The adults are dark on their backs and have two white longitudinal stripes. The young have bright yellow barbles and fins. The dorsal and pectoral fins have serrated spinous rays connected with poison glands, therefore it is not advisable to handle these fish. They measure from thirty to thirty-five centimeters in length.

FISTULARIIDAE FAMILY
Cornetfish
Fistularia commersoni

A cylindrical body that ends in a long and tubular snout. The dorsal and anal fins are symmetrical and set quite far back. The two central rays of the caudal fin are very fine and elongated. The coloring is variable, due to the remarkable capacity for camouflage which this fish possesses and uses to capture - from ambush - the small prey on which it feeds. It is common to see this fish swim along, hidden by the body of a larger, but harmless, fish, so as to steal up unnoticed upon its prey. This fish measures up to a meter and a half in length.

ANTENNARIIDAE FAMILY
Frogfish
Antennarius coccineus

A stout and rounded body, rather tall, so that this fish is a fairly clumsy swimmer. The fish of this species move slowly and at times make use of their pectoral and ventral fins to "walk" on the seabed. Particularly distinctive is the transformation of the first ray on the dorsal fin, which is used as bait to attract prey. Coloring is quite variable, but always well camouflaged. It lives among coral reefs, at times using its pectoral fins to clutch the coral branches.

ANOMALOPIDAE FAMILY
Flashlight fish
Photoblepharon palpebratus

Body with an oval shape, a short snout, a truncated forward profile. The eyes are extremely well developed, and beneath them is a large eliptical light-generating organ, which contains luminescent bacteria. This fish is capable of lighting up or extinguishing this organ by raising or lowering a flap of skin. Dark grey in color, this is a typically nocturnal fish. It measures nine to ten centimeters in length.

HOLOCENTRIDAE FAMILY
Blotcheye soldierfish
Myripristis murdjan

Oval body, moderately compressed and high, covered with stinging scales. The first dorsal fin has some ten well developed spinous rays. The eyes are large. The mouth is wide. The coloring is bright red. This is essentially a nocturnal fish, which remains at the entrance to its grotto during the day, as if it were keeping watch. It attains a length of up to thirty centimeters.

Crown squirrelfish
Adioryx diadema

Oval body, longer and less tall than the preceding species. The eyes are quite large, as this too is a species with nocturnal habits. The coloring is red, with evident white stripes on the sides. A white band runs around the lower portion of the face as far as to the opercules. The forward section of the dorsal fin is black. It measures twenty-five centimeters in length.

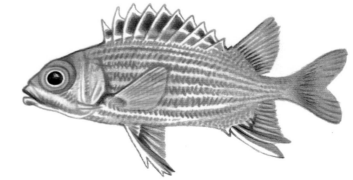

Sabre squirrelfish
Adioryx spinifer

Its body is moderately compressed and tall; the snout is pointed with relatively large eyes. The dorsal fin is well developed with red interradial membranes. Coloring of the body is red with spots of the same color, but darker on the opercula and at the base of the pectoral fins. This is a nocturnal species, and it is aggressive by nature, due to its territorial habits. It measures up to forty-five centimeters in length.

SCORPAENIDAE FAMILY
Clearfin turkeyfish
Pterois radiata

Oblong body with a large head and a large mouth. The rays of the pectoral fins are very long, do not branch out, and the upper ones are joined by a membrane but only at the base. All of the rays are poisonous. The body is a brownish red with white stripes. Above the eyes there are long fleshy papillae. It can attain a size of 25 centimeters.

Turkeyfish
Pterois volitans

Body is similar to the previous species. The coloring presents broad brown vertical stripes; not all the same width. The rays of the fins are not naked, but possess a more or less developed membrane that makes them similar to feathers. The odd-numbered fins bear rows of brownish-black spots. Around the mouth and above the eyes one can clearly see some indented appendages.

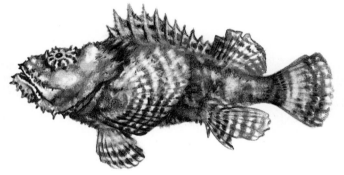

Devil scorpionfish
Scorpaenopsis diabolus

A slightly oval body, massive and high, with numerous fleshy excrescences. The head is large and is covered with spines; the mouth is wide and turns upwards. The pectoral fins extend to the anal fin. The coloring provides excellent camouflage, as this is a species that hunts from ambush. The tailfin has broad dark vertical stripes. The spines of the dorsal fin are poisonous, but not to the same degree as those of the Stonefish. It grows to a length of thirty centimeters.

Stonefish
Synanceia verrucosa

A moderately oblong body, compressed at the sides and free of scales. The head is massive, covered with crests and spines, and the eyes - which are perhaps the most noticeable part - are turned upwards, as is the wide mouth. The pectoral fins are very well developed. The coloring provides excellent camouflage, and the fish is virtually identical to a stone that is, practically invisible. The glands at the base of the spines produce a very powerful poison, which can be fatal.

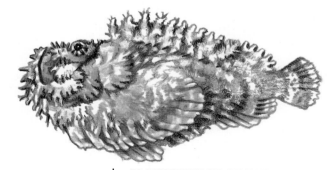

PLATYCEPHALIDAE FAMILY
Crocodile fish
Cociella crocodilus

The body is compressed toward the front and is slightly cylindrical toward the rear; it is covered with rough scales. The mouth is large and is well lined with small, sharp teeth. There are two dorsal fins, the first of which is preceded by an isolated spine. The caudal fin is rounded. The coloring ranges from brownish to olive-grey, with dark spots on the back. Normally, it can be found on the seabed or partly buried in silt, by itself or in pairs. It grows to be sixty to seventy centimeters in length.

SERRANIDAE FAMILY
Scalefin anthias
Anthias squamipinnis

Oval, compressed body, which ends in a sickle-shaped tail with elongated lobes. The snout is short and rounded, and the mouth is terminal. The dorsal fin is well developed, especially in the male, which has several particularly long fore rays. The coloring is reddish, with red spots near the pectoral fins. The females have yellowish shadings. This fish is gregarious, and forms schools dominated by one or two males. They attain a length of fifteen to seventeen centimeters.

Peacock grouper
Cephalopholis argus

The body is massive, tapered, and slightly compressed. The head is powerful, with a slightly prominent lower jaw. The edge of the caudal fin is rounded. The dorsal fin has nine spinous rays and a rounded rear edge that ends in proximity of the caudal peduncle and opposite the anal fin. The coloring is marked by numerous dark blue spots and by ten dark bands on the sides. The fins are dark blue. These fish attain a length of fifty centimeters.

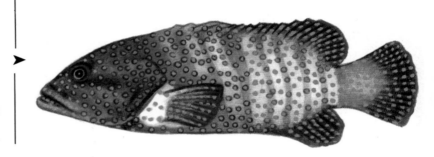

Coral grouper
Cephalopholis miniata

The body is similar to that of *C. argus*. The rear edges of the dorsal and anal fins are less rounded than in the previous species. The coloring is a very bright reddish-orange, with numerous small dark-blue ocellate spots scattered all over the body and fins, and tends to become darker in the adults. A fairly territorial species, it prefers to remain in the general vicinity of grottoes and underwater crannies. According to some observations, this fish tends to become gregarious during the mating season, and to gather to restrict areas. It attains a length of forty to forty-five centimeters.

Lunartail grouper
Variola louti

Tapered body which terminates toward the rear with a tall caudal peduncle supporting an unmistakable tail in the form of a crescent moon or sickle, and with elongated lobes. Dorsal and anal fins have pointed rear edges. The coloring is reddish or brownish, with purple highlights and numerous pale spots. This is a fairly common species and attains lengths of up to eighty or eighty-five centimeters.

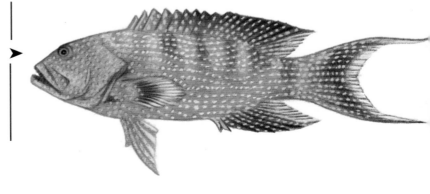

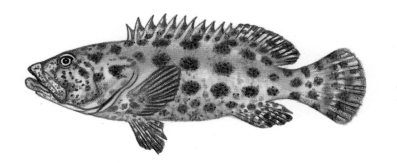

Potato cod
Epinephelus tukula

The body is broad and powerful. The head is tapered, with a convex intraorbital space. The snout is elongated and the mouth is wide. The lower jaw is more developed than the upper. The coloring is greyish-brown, with large, pronounced dark spots arrayed along the sides and on the tail. The fins are marked by smaller but numerous spots. This is one among the largest groupers, and can grow to be as long as two meters.

Giant grouper
Epinephelus tauvina

Tapered body, slightly compressed, but not as tall as other groupers. The snout is pointed, and the mouth is broad and terminal. The caudal fin is rounded. The dorsal fin is not very tall, and has eleven spinous rays. Along the back, at the base of the dorsal fin, it is possible to detect a number of large dark spots. Smaller spots are scattered along the entire body, whose coloring is basically very pale. This species can grow to be longer than two meters.

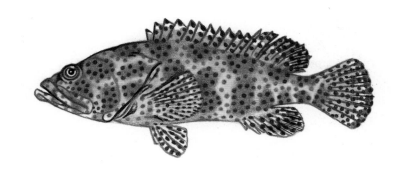

GRAMMISTIDAE FAMILY
Goldstriped goldfish
Grammistes sexlineatus

The body is oval, tall, and compressed, and is covered with many small scales. The mouth is wide, and the lower jaw bears a small fleshy excrescence. This species is easily recognized for its distinctive pattern of whitish-yellow stripes run lengthwise from the head to the caudal peduncle; these stripes are extremely noticeable on the dark brown and blue of the body. If this fish is alarmed, it secretes a mucus that is toxic to other fish. It grows to be thirty centimeters in length.

PRIACANTHIDAE FAMILY
Goggle eye
Priacanthus hamrur

The body is oval, tall, and compressed. The snout is short, and the large eyes stand out, revealing the nocturnal habits of the species. The mouth is turned upward. The caudal fin is shaped like a crescent moon, with elongated lobes, especially in the adults of the species. The coloring is generally a dark reddish hue, but can change rapidly, acquiring more or less pronounced silvery highlights or becoming striped with red on silvery body. The dorsal and anal fins have dark highlights along their edges. This fish attains a length of forty to forty-five centimeters.

CIRRHITIDAE FAMILY
Longnose hawkfish
Oxycirrhites typus

The body is slightly cylindrical, taller at the center, and terminates in an elongated snout. The mouth is small. The spinous part of the dorsal fin bears a series of appendages. Pectoral fins are particularly well developed, and this fish uses them to balance upon gorgonians. Here the fish is perfectly camouflaged, due to a series of red stripes that form a checkerboard on its body. It attains a length of between ten and thirteen centimeters.

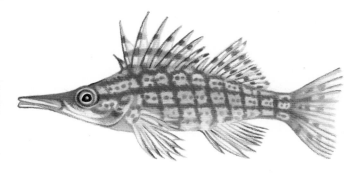

111

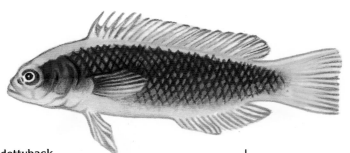

◄

PSEUDOCHROMIDAE FAMILY
Sunrise dottyback
Pseudochromis flavivertex

The body is elongated, compressed, and is distinguished by a very long dorsal fin and a long anal fin. The eyes are in a subdorsal position and protrude slightly. The two-tone coloring is distinctive; it is a bright chrome yellow above, while the rest of the body is light blue. It lives by preference among the branches of coral, near a sandy bottom. This fish grows to be ten centimeters in length.

Olive dottyback
Pseudochromis fridmani

This species is only found in the Red Sea. The body is elongated and tapered toward the front. The snout is short, with large eyes and a terminal mouth. The caudal fin, which is truncated in the young, tends to have a slightly more elongated lower lobe in the adults of the species. This fish has a bright purple coloring, and is almost luminescent. A thin dark band runs from the tip of the snout to the eye. The opercula have a fairly pronounced dark blue spot. The upper lobe of the caudal fin is practically transparent. This species is often found under coral umbrellas that jut from the walls of the reef. They grow to be six to seven centimeters in length.

APOGONIDAE FAMILY
Golden cardinalfish
Apogon aureus

The body is tapered, with a broad mouth, head, and eyes. The two dorsal fins are completely separate and similar in size. Large and pronounced scales. The head is darker in coloring than the rest of the body, which is pale yellow. A broad dark band surrounds the caudal peduncle. In the larger fish, one can see a dark ventral band. These fish tend to be nocturnal, and during the day they gather in groups in dark locations (crevices, grottos, crannies). They attain a length of twelve centimeters.

CARANGIDAE FAMILY
Bluefin Trevally
Caranx melampygus

The body is elongated, and rather tall; forward, it terminates with a convex head and a high forehead. The eyes are small. The caudal peduncle is narrow and reinforced with visible bony plates, the lateral line is complete and arched anteriorly. The coloring is greenish-brown, with numerous small black spots. The long, sickle-shaped pectoral fins with scales on their sides are yellow in the young of the species. This fish grows to be longer than one meter.

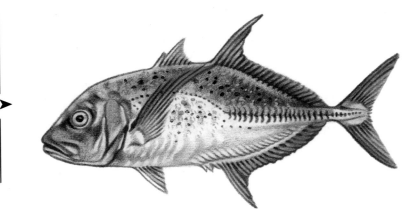

Bigeye Trevally
Caranx sexfasciatus

The body is elongated and compressed; the forward silhouette is rounded. The lower jaw tends to jut. On the caudal stalk, there are evident keels; the caudal fin is sharply forked. The coloring is blue-gray or blue-green on the back. The lobes of the caudal fin show a blackish hue. The sides are greenish-yellow or silvery. The young of the species are golden yellow, with four to seven broad dark vertical bands. This fish grows to be longer than a meter and a half.

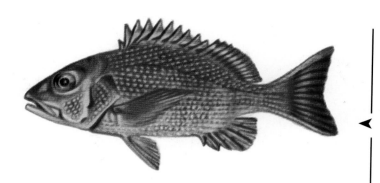

LUTJANIDAE FAMILY
Twinspot snapper
Lutjanus bohar

Elongated, tall, powerful body. The snout is pointed, and the mouth is wide and lined with one row of conical teeth above and below, and there are pronounced front canine teeth. The fins are well developed. There is only one dorsal fin; the sickle-shaped pectoral fins stretch almost all the way to where the anal fin is attached.
The coloring is a reddish-purple, darker on the back, and with yellowish highlights on either side of the head. The fins are dark, and are partly edged with white. The spinous rays of the dorsal fin are white at the tips. This fish attains a length of seventy to seventy-five centimeters.

Bluestripe snapper
Lutjanus kasmira

Tapered body with pointed snout. Large eyes and mouth. The dorsal fin extends to the height of the caudal peduncle. The coloring is golden yellow on the back, becoming gradually paler along the sides and almost silvery on the belly. Typical of the species are the four light stripes running lengthwise; the longest of the stripes runs from the mouth to the caudal peduncle. The edges of the dorsal and the caudal fins are black. This fish measures forty centimeters in length.

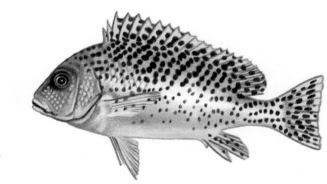

CAESIONIDAE FAMILY
Suez fusilier
Caesio suevicus

The rounded and tapered body is rather elongated. The mouth is small and has thin teeth in front of a row of very small teeth. The upper jaw can be extended forward quite easily while capturing the small prey upon which the species feeds. Particularly distinctive is the forked caudal fin. The coloring is generally silvery, with yellow nuances; the lobes of the tailfin are black. These fish travel in numerous schools. They measure fifteen to twenty centimeters in length.

HAEMULIDAE FAMILY
Blackspotted grunt
Plectorhynchus gaterinus

The body is tapered, tall, and slightly compressed. The head is well developed, the snout is short and convex. The eyes are large. The mouth is not very large and distinguished by a pair of thick lips. The adults are unmistakable, and have a basic coloring of bright yellow, upon which numerous black spots stand out. The young fish, instead, have five black longitudinal bands; the two bands closest to the back extend all the way back to the caudal fin. During daytime, this species tends to form schools close to the reef's slope. It measures up to fifty centimeters in length.

LETHRINIDAE FAMILY
Spangled emperor
Lethrinus nebulosus

The body is fairly tall and compressed. The head is elongated with a sharply oblique forward profile. The snout is pointed. The eyes tend upwards. The mouth is entirely red. The dorsal fin is well developed; the pectoral fins have scales on the inner section. The basic coloring, grey and uniform, is enlivened by light blue stripes and spots, more evident on the sides, on the opercules, and behind the eyes. Present in large numbers on open and shallow seabeds. It may measure seventy-five centimeters or more in length.

113

KYPHOSIDAE
Snubnose chub
Kyphosus cinerascens

The oval body is covered with small scales, rough to the touch, which also extend over the head and fins. The small mouth possesses numerous teeth, which are also present on the tongue. The dorsal fin is rounded and tall toward the rear. The pectoral fins are rather short. The coloring is a bluish silver, and the dorsal fins are darker. A silvery strip runs under the eyes. Along the rows of scales, it is possible to notice a number of yellow or black stripes. During the day, these fish swim in schools in middle layers of water. They measure fifty centimeters in length.

EPHIPPIDAE FAMILY
Batfish
Platax orbicularis

The unmistakably shaped body is tall, compressed, and discoid, with anal and dorsal fins that are symmetrical and well developed. Narrower in the young, these fins tend to broaden and become more rounded in adults. The mouth and the eyes are small. The coloring is distinguished by broad dark vertical bands along the sides, which tend to disappear with age. They live in schools. They measure fifty centimeters in length.

PEMPHERIDAE FAMILY
Vanikoro sweeper
Pempheris vanicolensis

The body is oblong and compressed, taller toward the front and tapered toward the rear. The dorsal silhouette is nearly a straight line, while the ventral profile is concave around the long anal fin. The tail is slightly incised. The mouth is wide, oblique, and terminal. The eyes are large. This species is nocturnal, and forms numerous schools in the shelter of coral reefs. The coloring is light, pink, and translucent. It measures twelve to fifteen centimeters in length.

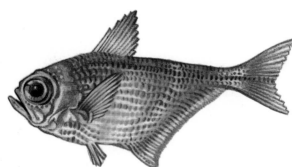

MULLIDAE FAMILY
Yellowsaddle goatfish
Parupeneus cyclostomus

The high, tapered body ends in a jutting snout. The lower jaw is distinguished by the presence of two long barbles that extend back to the ventral fins. The two dorsal fins are sharply separated. The tail is typically two-lobed. The head has bluish stripes that are fairly evident. The second dorsal fin has a dark spot toward the rear. The coloring is brighter in the young. It measures thirty-five centimeters in length.

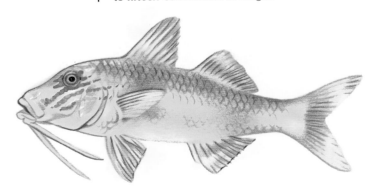

Forsskal's goatfish
Parupeneus forskali

The shape of the body is typical of the genus *Parupeneus*. The barbles, which are still present, are however far smaller than those found in the previous species described. The coloring is a silvery blue with yellow nuances on the back. The caudal peduncle is bright yellow with a pronounced dark spot at the center. Along the sides there is a dark band which covers the eye.

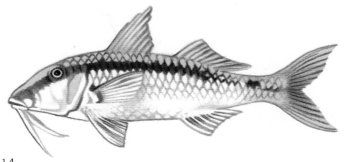

ECHENEIDAE FAMILY
Sharksucker
Echeneis naucrates

Elongated body with a head that is flattened dorsally, where the suction cup is found that is typical of remoras, and which is nothing more than a modified dorsal fin. The mouth features a well developed lower jaw. The dorsal and anal fins are similar and symmetrical. The coloring is dark grey or brownish with a darker band running lengthwise. The edges of the fins are whitish. This species attains a length of about a meter.

SPHYRAENIDAE FAMILY
Great barracuda
Sphyraena barracuda

The body is elongated and slightly cylindrical. The snout is long and pointed, and the lower jaw is prominent. The teeth are numerous and canine-shaped. There are two dorsal fins, clearly separated. The coloring ranges from greyish to greenish-brown on the back, while the sides and the belly are silvery. The adults have irregular dark spots along their sides near the caudal fin. This species attains a length of 1.5 to 1.8 meters.

Blackfin barracuda
Sphyraena qenie

The body is elongated and is typical of the barracuda. The lower jaw, devoid of any fleshy excrescence, is prominent, but the back of the jaw goes no further back than the forward margin of the eye. The first dorsal fin begins after the pectoral fins. The second dorsal fin is symmetrical with the anal fin. The caudal fin is forked, and strangely can have three lobes in the larger specimens. The coloring is silvery, with eighteen to twenty-two dark vertical bands. The dorsal and caudal fins are dark, as is the anal fin, while the last two anal rays are white. This species grows to over a meter in length.

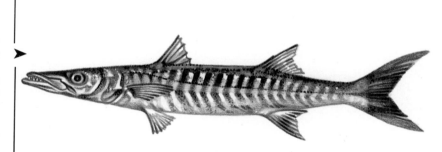

POMACENTRIDAE FAMILY
Sergeant major
Abdudefduf saxatilis

Configuration of the body is similar to the other described species. The greyish silvery coloring shifts toward bright yellow on the back. Along the sides of the fish, there are five dark vertical bands, the first of which intersects the rearmost edge of the operculum. The coloring becomes lighter when the fish lives near sandy seabeds, and darker near coral. Adult males acquire bluish and purplish nuances when they are guarding the spawn. They attain a length of ten to fifteen centimeters.

Sergeant scissortail
Abdudefduf sexfasciatus

Compressed body, ovoid in shape and fairly tall, covered with rough scales which extend to the fins. The head is pointed; the snout is short. The mouth is small, slightly protractile, and is lined with conical teeth. The dorsal fin has mostly spinous rays. The caudal fin is forked. The coloring is whitish-silvery, and there are six black bands, the first of which covers the rearmost edge of the operculum. The lobes of the caudal fin are each marked by a black stripe. This fish is gregarious, and tends to live in schools near the shallower coral formations. It attains a length of seventeen to twenty centimeters.

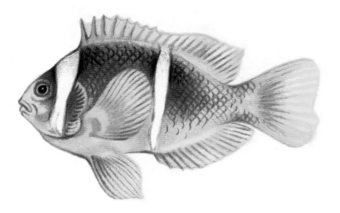

Twobar anemonefish
Amphiprion bicinctus

The body is oval and rounded. The snout is short and stubby, with a small mouth. The dorsal fin extends along much of the dorsum and presents a slight saddle formation which separates the spinous portion from the part with soft rays. The caudal fin has two lobes. The background coloring ranges from orange to brownish orange, with two white vertical strips. The younger specimens may have a third stripe on the stalk of the tailfin. It generally tends to live in symbiosis with anemonefish of the genus *Heteractis*. It attains a length of thirteen to fifteen centimeters.

Bluegreen chromis
Chromis caerulea

The shape of the body is roughly similar to the damselfish of the Mediterranean. The coloring tends to bluish, and is relatively intense, with slight nuances along the edge of the scales. This fish is gregarious, and tends to form large groups, each of which seems to colonize a specific coral formation, favoring those near the sheer walls at the outer edge of the reef. They measure from eight to ten centimeters in length.

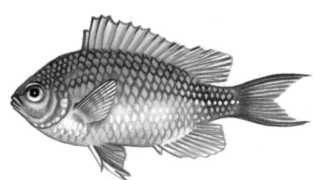

Half-and-half chromis
Chromis dimidiata

The shape of the body is similar to the species described immediately above. The coloring, however, is radically different, and allows one to recognize this species quite easily; half the body is white and half is dark brown or black. This fish is gregarious, and tends to form huge schools near large coral formations, venturing to greater depths than the *C. caerulea*. It measures seven centimeters in length.

Banded dascyllus
Dascyllus aruanus

The body is fairly stubby, squarish, tall, and compressed. The mouth is small with a slightly prominent lower jaw. The background coloring is whitish, with three distinctive diagonal dark bands, the first of which covers the eye and the mouth. This fish forms small groups, each of which is closely associated with a single coral colony. Only larger specimens venture at any distance from the corals, while smaller ones remain in permanent residence among the branches. They measure eight to ten centimeters in length.

Sulphur damselfish
Pomacentrus sulfureus

The body is slightly oval, tall, and compressed. The snout is short. The mouth is small and protractile and lined with small teeth, arranged in a number of rows. Near the eye is a flat spine pointing backwards. The edge of the opercula is serrated. The caudal fin is slightly inset. The coloring is yellow, with a black spot at the base of the pectoral fins. These fish do not move in large, closely packed schools, though a number of individual specimens may be found close together. This fish measures from eight to ten centimeters in length.

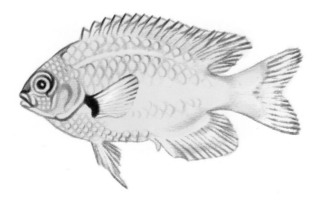

Domino damselfish
Dascyllus trimaculatus

The shape of the body is typical of the genus. The mouth is small, considering that this is a fish feeding on plankton. The coloring is the most distinctive feature, and quite sufficient to make the fish unmistakable. In fact, this species is either completely black or dark brown, with three white spots: one on either side and a third on the forehead. These spots are most pronounced in the young, and tend to fade in adulthood. The species is quite common around anemonefish, amidst long-spined black urchins (Diadema antillarum), and amidst acroporas. It measures up to fourteen centimeters in length.

LABRIDAE FAMILY
Yellowtail wrasse
Anampses meleagrides

Tapered body, with a generally oval silhouette, and with a slight frontal hump, more pronounced in females. The mouth is terminal, and protractile, with large fleshy lips. The coloring of adult males is dark and purplish with more-or-less elongated bluish spots along the edge of the scales. Dorsal and anal fins feature bluish stripes, as does the rearmost edge of the caudal fin, the lobes of which are elongated. Females have a dark coloring, spangled with numerous white spots. The snout and the lower head are reddish. The caudal fin is yellow. This fish measures up to twenty-five centimeters in length.

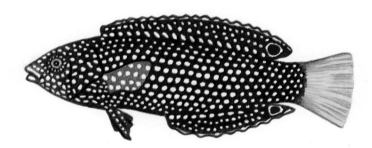

Abudjubbe wrasse
Cheilinus abudjubbe

A member of the Labridae family with a particularly powerful structure, with a tall body covered with large scales. The head is elongated and convex; the mouth is well developed with pronounced canine-shaped teeth. The background coloring is dark, especially along the side, where a number of red spots can be seen. Distinctive red stripes are arrayed around the eyes. The fins are lighter in color and distinguished by yellow-greenish spots, distributed in rows along the rays. This fish often feeds on sea urchins. It measures thirty-five centimeters in length.

Broomtail wrasse
Cheilinus lunulatus

The body is compressed and tall, with large scales. The head is convex and stubby with a short tail. The mouth is large and protractile. Males have a relatively dark background coloring, especially on the head, and feature purple stripes that are sometimes particularly pronounced along the edges of the scales. The pectoral fins are yellow. Bluish nuances distinguish the mouth and fins. The caudal fin is distinguished by a fringed rear edge that is peculiar to the species. This fish measures up to fifty centimeters in length.

Humphead wrasse
Cheilinus undulatus

The humphead wrasse is the largest known member of the *Labridae* family, and has a very distinctive tall and stubby structure. The mouth is large and features thick protractile lips which allow this fish literally to suck up its prey. In the adults, the head is marked by a pronounced bump on the forehead. The greenish-grey coloring has irregular greenish-yellow stripes along the sides, shifting to orange on the head. These fish can be as long as two meters, and can weigh more than 170-180 kilograms.

African coris
Coris gaimard

Tapered, slender body, with a silhouette reminding one of the Mediterranean rainbow wrasse. The first two rays on the dorsal fin are generally elongated, in adult specimens. The reddish coloring features fine greenish stripes at the base of each scale. The head is greenish and has broad greenish bands, the widest of which runs from the rear edge of the mouth to the operculum. Males have a green stripe along the side, just above the point of origin of the anal fin. This fish reaches a length of thirty-five to forty centimeters.

Eightline wrasse
Paracheilinus octotaenia

Tapered body and a rounded forward profile. The silhouette differs from that typical of the *Labridae*, especially because of the remarkable development of the dorsal and anal fins. These fins are quite high, rounded, and toward the rear they almost seem to join the fan-shaped caudal fin. The yellowish body is marked by eight bluish horizontal lines. The fins are bright red in color, with white edges. They measure up to ten or twelve centimeters in length.

Axilspot hogfish
Bodianus axillaris

It has a tapered and compressed body with a pointed snout. The ventral fins are well developed and the longer ventral rays reach almost to the anal aperture. The caudal fin is truncated in adults and rounded in the young. The forward portion of the body is dark and contrasts sharply with the lighter hue of the rest. The base of the pectoral, dorsal and anal fins have a pronounced dark spot. The young specimens have nine white spots on their bodies. They reach twenty centimeters in length.

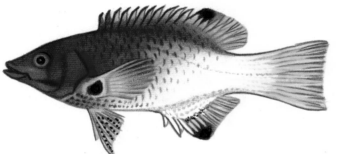

Red Sea bird wrasse
Gomphosus caeruleus

A typically oval body, slightly compressed. The snout is distinctively elongated and tubular in the adults. The mouth is terminal, but sufficiently well developed to prey on small animals. The caudal fin is rounded, but tends to develop elongated lobes with time. The coloring is dark blue in males. Females are green on their backs and yellowish on their bellies, with black spots on their sides. They measure from twenty to twenty-five centimeters in length.

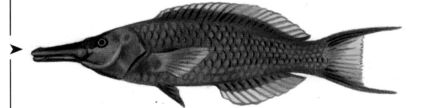

Cleaner wrasse
Labroides dimidiatus

The body is compressed, elongated, and covered with large scales. The head is pointy; the snout is elongated, with a small terminal mouth lined with numerous small and pointed teeth. The upper jaw is longer than the lower. The forward half of the body is brownish, and darker on the back than on the belly. A broad black band runs from the beginning of the snout all the way to the tip of the caudal fin, widening as it goes. The base of the anal fin and the rear part of the body are an intense dark blue. It attains a length of ten centimeters.

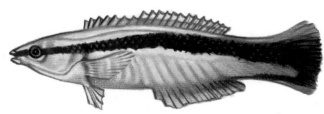

Klunzinger's wrasse
Thalassoma klunzingeri

The body is tapered, powerful, slightly compressed and elongated. The mouth is small and features two clearly visible canine-shaped front teeth. Lips are thin. The body is greenish with fairly dark reddish-brown stripes, along the scales. The head is marked by broad and pronounced reddish-brown stripes, especially between eyes and gullet. The lobes of the caudal fin are also the same color. It attains a length of twenty centimeters.

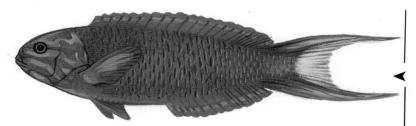

Moon wrasse
Thalassoma lunare

The body is tapered, powerful, and slightly compressed. The head is rounded, the snout is short. The mouth is small and the lips are thin. The caudal fin is truncated in the young; partially moon-shaped in adults, especially larger males, which are also bluish. The coloring is greenish with vertical purplish-red stripes on the sides. The head is greenish-blue with broad pink bands running roughly lengthwise. The caudal fin is yellowish at the center with pink stripes along the lobes. It attains a length of twenty-five to thirty centimeters.

SCARIDAE FAMILY
Rusty parrotfish
Scarus ferrugineus

The body is tapered, slightly compressed at the sides, and covered with large scales. The head is large and the mouth is in a terminal position. The upper jaw is slightly prominent. One distinctive feature is the large teeth of the jaws, which join together so as to form a beak of four plates. The male, which has a greenish snout and fins edged in blue-green, is more colorful than the female. This fish prefers a protected coral seabed. It attains a length of forty centimeters.

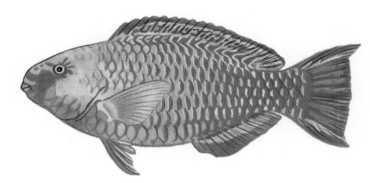

Steephead parrotfish
Scarus gibbus

The body is oval, tall, and powerful. The head has a forward silhouette that is quite convex, and nearly vertical. The dental plates are not particularly pronounced. On the cheeks, are three rows of large scales. The caudal fin is semilunar. The coloring is brownish yellow, while the lower part of the snout is green in the females. On the scales, are fairly intense pink stripes. These remain in males as well; males have on their dorsal area a greenish coloring with touches of violet. The ventral section is blue-green. The rear of the caudal fin has a green edge. It attains a length of seventy centimeters.

Bullethead parrotfish
Scarus sordidus

The general configuration of the body is typical of parrotfish. The dental plates can be clearly seen. The young present a pattern of coloring with horizontal stripes. As they grow, this coloring turns dark brown. The adult males are green in color, and the edges of their scales are salmon pink. The cheeks are bright orange, fading to yellow on the opercula. Strangely, their teeth are green, while the female of the species has a pink mouth.

Bumphead parrotfish
Bolbometopon muricatum

The body is powerful, tall, compressed at the sides, and covered with large scales. At the sides of the snout and near the mouth there are three rows of scales. The coloring is greenish-blue both in males and females. The snout and the gullet are pink, as is the forward portion of the prominence of the males, which can be thus easily recognized. The young of this species are dark brown, with a double row of white spots along the upper half of the body. They grow to be one and a half meter long.

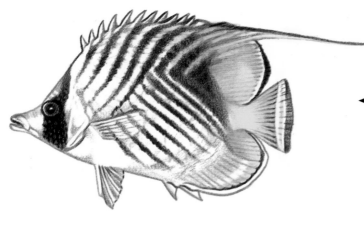

CHAETODONTIDAE FAMILY
Threadfin butterflyfish
Chaetodon auriga

The body is nearly rectangular, very tall and compressed. The head is concave toward the front, and terminates in a pointed, short snout. A broad dark band covers the eye, narrowing on the back. The dorsal fin features a dark ocellate spot along the rearmost edge, topped by a number of elongated and filamentous rays which constitute one of the distinctive features of this species. The *C. auriga* swims alone or in pairs. It measures twenty to twenty-five centimeters in length.

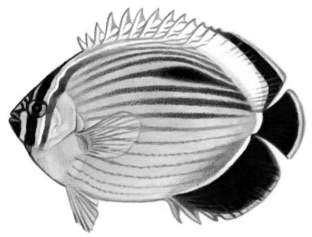

Exquisite butterflyfish
Chaetodon austriacus

The body is typically oval and compressed. The snout is short. The dorsal fin is very long. The anal fin is well developed. The rear edges of the fins just mentioned seem to shade into the caudal fin. The background coloring is yellow. Along the sides, there is a series of slightly diagonal stripes of a blue-black color. The snout is dark and a vertical black stripe entirely covers the eye. The anal fin, the caudal fin, and the rear edge of the dorsal fin are black. This species feeds entirely on polyps. This fish measures twelve centimeters in length.

Striped butterflyfish
Chaetodon fasciatus

The shape of the body is similar to that of *C. austriacus*. The background coloring is yellow. Along the sides, nine or ten slightly diagonal bands of a dark color stand out, and merge into a single band of the same color parallel to the dorsal fin. The dorsal, caudal, and anal fins are trimmed with a brownish-yellow band.
The black eye bands is followed by shorter white band. It measures eighteen centimeters in length.

Blackback butterflyfish
Chaetodon melannotus

The body appears nearly oval, tall and compressed. The head has an oblique and slightly concave forward profile. The snout is short and pointed. The most distinctive feature of this species is the black band that vertically cuts across the snout, covering the eye. The rear portion of the caudal peduncle and forward portion of the anal fin have black spots. All of the fins are yellow. On the sides of this fish there are diagonal rows of points that converge in a dark dorsal band. These fish attain a length of eighteen centimeters.

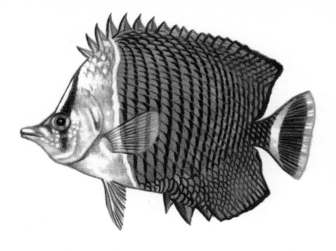

Paleface butterflyfish
Chaetodon mesoleucos

A slightly square body, extremely compressed laterally, and tall. The forward profile is convex. The snout is short. The forward portion is white and the rear portion is brown, with twelve black vertical stripes. The caudal fin is black and is trimmed in white, with a whitish, orange tipped crescent. The upper silhouette of the snout is marked by a black band that covers the eye. It measures fourteen to sixteen centimeters in length.

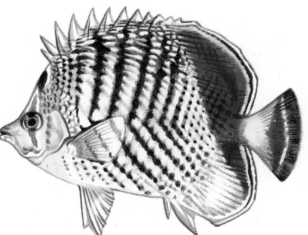

Crown butterflyfish
Chaetodon paucifasciatus

The body is tall and compressed. The snout is pointed. The background color is quite pale. The forward section is whitish with a strip of tawny reddish-yellow covering the eye. On the sides are four or five bands of black diamond shapes. On the rear part of the body there is a distinctive red spot. A band of red distinguishes the caudal fin. In young specimens, at the center of the red spot there is an ocellar dot. This fish generally swims in pairs or in small groups near the underwater meadows. It measures fourteen centimeters in length.

Masked butterflyfish
Chaetodon semilarvatus

This species is peculiar to the Red Sea. The shape is almost discoid, with a small prominent snout. The coloring is almost uniformly orange-yellow with fine dark diagonal stripes. The eye is surrounded by a dark bluish spot that extends as far as to the operculum. A dark narrow line underscores the outline of the dorsal and anal fins. The pectoral fins are transparent; the ventrals fins are yellow. These fish are often found in schools. They grow to be eighteen to twenty centimeters in length.

Pennantfish
Heniochus intermedius

The body is tall, disk-shaped, and extremely compressed. The head is small, the snout is slightly elongated. The forward portion of the body is distinguished by a broad black band that covers the eye and the operculum and extends to the base of the dorsal fin. A second band runs diagonally along the rear portion of the body, starting from the caudal peduncle. The spinous ray of the dorsal fin is prominent as a banner. This fish measures twenty to twenty-five centimeters in length.

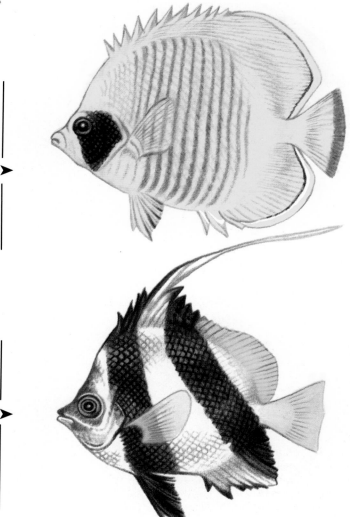

121

Red Sea bannerfish
Heniochus diphreutes

A tall, disk-shaped body, greatly compressed and truncated in the rear. The head has a concave profile. The snout is short and the eyes are large. The coloring is whitish, with two broad dark bands on the sides, which limit the higher and more developed part of the dorsal fin, well extended behind. A dark band partially covers the eyes. The rear sections of the dorsal and caudal fins are yellow. These fish form large schools of many dozens; this is the main feature distinguishing them from *H. intermedius*. Unlike most butterflyfish, they feed on plankton. They grow to be sixteen centimeters in length.

Orangeface butterflyfish
Gonochaetodon larvatus

Tall, oval, and compressed body reminding one of angelfish. The snout, from the root of the dorsal fin to the operculum and all the way to the base of the ventral fins, is orange. The greater part of the body is a glistening light blue, upon which one may note a number of angular white stripes. Another white line ranges from the tip of the dorsal fin to the caudal peduncle. The caudal peduncle and the caudal fin are black. It is common to find these fish near the tops of madrepores. They measure from eight to ten centimeters in length.

POMACANTHIDAE FAMILY
Arabian angelfish
Pomacanthus asfur

The body is tall and compressed. The head has a convex forward profile which ends in a short snout. The lower jaw is slightly prominent. The dorsal and anal fins are very well developed, and their rays extend far backwards, long past the rear margin of the caudal fin. The coloring of the young, with vertical whitish-yellow stripes, becomes a uniform dark blue in adults, which can be distinguished by the large yellow spot on the sides, which extends to part of the back and the tail in the same color. This fish grows to a length of thirty or thirty-five centimeters.

Emperor angelfish
Pomacanthus imperator

The shape of the body is nearly oval, with a practically rectilinear forward profile of the head. The snout is very short. The dorsal and anal fins have a rounded forward edge that just exceeds the caudal stalk. The young of this species are dark blue with lighter concentric bands, the last of which forms a closed circle on the caudal stalk. Adults feature many diagonal yellow bands. The eyes are masked by a black stripe edged in light blue, followed by a similar stripe on the operculum. This fish grows to a length of thirty-five centimeters.

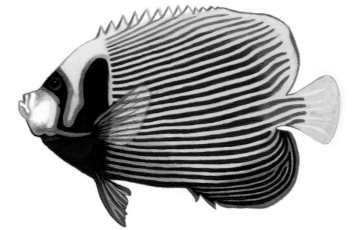

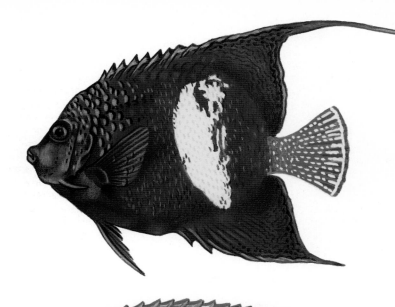

Yellowbar angelfish
Pomacanthus maculosus

The shape of the body is quite similar to that of *P. asfur*. The young of the species have light vertical stripes on the sides, and can be distinguished from the young of *P. asfur* because their caudal fin is light in color and translucent. The adults feature a large yellow spot on their side, which however does not extend to the dorsal area or the base of the dorsal fin. These fish tend to be solitary, and grow to a length of thirty centimeters.

Royal angelfish
Pygoplites diacanthus

The body is less tall than usual in angelfish. The rear edges of the dorsal and anal fins are well developed, but do not exceed the caudal fin. The body has a background coloring of orange yellow, with eight or nine dark blue bands. The eyes are surrounded by two sharply defined dark blue stripes. The dorsal fin has a fairly dark vermiculation, while the anal fin has parallel yellow stripes along the edge of the fin. The young of this species are fairly similar, and have a posterior ocellar spot. This fish grows to a length of twenty-five or thirty centimeters.

ACANTHURIDAE FAMILY
Black surgeonfish
Acanthurus nigricans

The body is oval, tall, and slightly compressed. The forward profile is rounded. The dorsal and anal fins are well developed. The caudal fin, distinguished by a white band at its base, is sickle-shaped, with the upper and lower lobes elongated. A short black band can be seen behind the eyes alongside the spines of the caudal peduncle. The pectoral fins have a dark yellow border. This fish grows to a length of forty centimeters.

Brown surgeonfish
Acanthurus nigrofuscus

The body is oval, tall, and compressed. The forward profile is extremely convex. The snout is short. The caudal fin is concave. The coloring is dark brown or purplish-brown, with or without thin bluish-grey lines running lengthwise along the side. The lips are black. The rear edges of the anal and dorsal fins are distinguished by a black spot. The head and chin have numerous orange spots. The spine on the peduncle is bordered in black. This fish grows to a length of twenty centimeters.

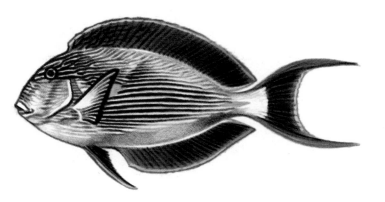

Sohal surgeonfish
Acanthurus sohal

The body is oval, tall, and compressed. The head is powerful and rounded. The mouth is distinguished by thick lips and spatulate teeth suited to grazing on algae, on which this fish feeds. The coloring is bluish-grey, with numerous dark stripes along the side and the upper part of the head. The cheeks are white. The fins are dark and edged with a light-blue band. The fearsome spines on the caudal peduncle are distinguished by their bright orange color. This fish behaves in a territorial manner, and attains a length of forty centimeters.

Spotted unicornfish
Naso brevirostris

This is the most distinctive of the surgeonfish, easily recognized for its powerful oval body that terminates in a long beak, which in turn extends well beyond the snout. On the sides of the peduncle there are two bony plates which each bear a sharp spine. The caudal fin is rounded. The coloring ranges from greyish-blue to olive brown. The lips are sometimes bluish. The tail features a pale band along the lower edge. This fish has gregarious habits, and attains a length of fifty centimeters.

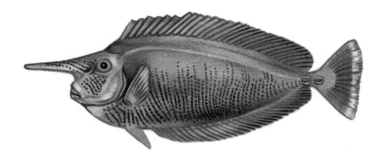

Orangespine unicornfish
Naso literatus

The body is oval, compressed, and tall toward the front. The head is powerful with a dorsal profile that forms a forty-five degree angle. The snout is pointed; the mouth is small and is lined with sharp teeth with rounded tips. On the sides of the peduncle are two bony plates, each bearing a sharp spine which curves forward. The caudal fin is semilunar, with pointed lobes and long filamentous rays. The coloring is yellowish-brown. The caudal peduncle is orange. Between the eyes is a light yellow spot. The dorsal fin is yellowish-orange, black at the base, with a white edge. This fish attains a length of forty-five centimeters.

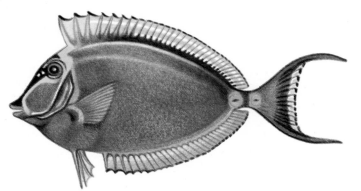

Bluespine unicornfish
Naso unicornis

The body is oval and elongated, tall and compressed. The forward profile is marked by a beak that is not long enough to exceed the mouth. The snout is pointed; the mouth is terminal, with powerful compressed teeth. On the sides of the caudal peduncle are two bluish spines shaped like chisels, which are not movable, but attached to bony plates. The coloring is light grey, and olive. In some cases the lips are blue and the dorsal and anal fins have orange stripes. The caudal fin is crescent-shaped with elongated, filamentous lobes. This fish attains a length of fifty to sixty centimeters.

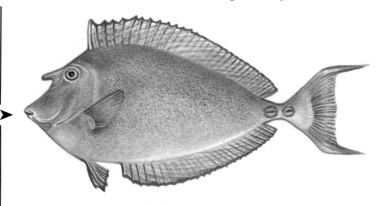

Yellowtail surgeonfish
Zebrasoma xanthurum

The body is compressed laterally and covered with small scales. The forward portion of the silhouette of the snout is typically concave. The mouth is small, terminal, and protractile. The single dorsal fin is well developed, rounded to the rear, and almost symmetrical to the anal fin. The spines on the caudal peduncle can vary in size. The coloring is dark blue, with small reddish spots on the head, which tend to follow a straight-line array behind the eyes, ending at the pectoral fin. The caudal fin and the edge of the pectoral fins are bright yellow. This fish grows to a length of forty centimeters.

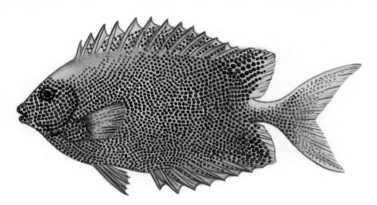

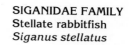
SIGANIDAE FAMILY
Stellate rabbitfish
Siganus stellatus

Oval, compressed body, covered with very small scales. The snout is slightly pointed; the mouth is terminal and is lined with numerous small teeth. The cheeks are covered with large scales. The coloring is generally a greyish-green spangled with small brown spots that tend to become smaller toward the back of the head, where they form a green oval shade at the base of the spines of the dorsal fin. Large black spots are present along the lateral line. This fish grows to a length of forty centimeters.

BLENNIIDAE FAMILY
Mimic blenny
Aspidontus taeniatus

The body is elongated and tapered. Its shape and coloring perfectly mimic the *Labroides dimidiatus*, or cleaner wrasse. Distinguishing between the two species is not a simple matter, even for other fish, which are often thereby deceived by the mimic blenny. The most evidently distinguishing feature is the shape of the snout and of the mouth, which turn downward due to the greater development of the upper jaw. The black band running lengthwise is less developed. This fish grows to a length of twelve to thirteen centimeters.

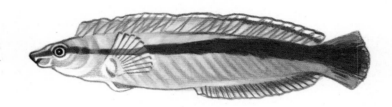

GOBIIDAE FAMILY
Sixspot goby
Valenciennea sexguttata

The tapered body is covered with small rough scales; the snout is pointed and the mouth is turned slightly upward, lined with a great many teeth some of which are quite large. There are two dorsal fins; the first dorsal fin is marked by small round or oblong dark blue spots. Along this fish's sides are one or two barely visible stripes, which do not reach the caudal fin. It lives part of the time buried in sandy seabeds. This fish grows to a length of thirteen centimeters.

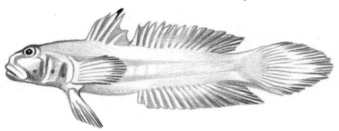

BALISTIDAE FAMILY
Orangestriped triggerfish
Balistapus undulatus

A slightly oval body, tall and compressed, covered with small bony plates. The head is very well developed and measures roughly a third of the length of the body. The eyes are quite far along the side of the fish. The mouth is terminal, and is distinguished by powerful jaws lined with massive teeth. The background coloring is dark, and orange-yellow stripes stand out on it. Bands of the same color surround the mouth. The dorsal and anal fins are light blue. The caudal fin is yellow. This fish grows to a length of seventy centimeters.

Titan triggerfish
Balistoides viridiscens

The shape of the body is typical of the family. The mouth is terminal. There is a deep depression between the eyes. On the stalk of the caudal fin are two to four rows, running lengthwise, of large tubercles. The coloring is greenish; the edges of the fins are black. A black band runs around the upper jaw. The stalk of the caudal fin is fairly light in color. This species is aggressive, especially during the mating season. This fish grows to a length of seventy to seventy-five centimeters.

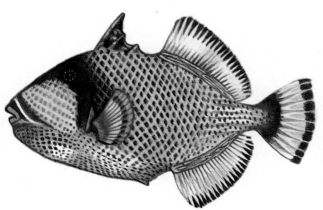

Redtooth triggerfish
Odonus niger

The body is slightly oval. The head is pointed. The mouth is terminal, and the lower jaw is more developed than the upper. The coloring of the body is blue-black while the head is greenish with blueish stripes leading from the mouth. The caudal fin is semilunar, and the lobes are well developed and quite long. This fish tends to gather in small groups, and grows to a length of fifty centimeters.

Blue triggerfish
Pseudobalistes fuscus

The shape of the body is typical of the family. The head is rounded. There are large scales under the opercula. Along the lower portion of the snout there are horizontal channels. The coloring is dark brown with yellow or orange spots on the scales. The edge of the fins is yellowish. The caudal fin is rounded in the young and has elongated lobes in adults. This fish grows to a length of fifty to fifty-five centimeters.

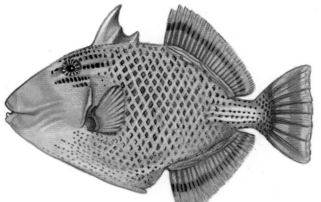

Yellowmargin triggerfish
Pseudobalistes flavimarginatus

This fish has a shape similar to that of *P. fuscus*, but it is more oval. The teeth are white and arranged in two rows on the upper jaw and only one row on the lower. The background coloring is fairly pale. The forward part of the body, between the snout and the base of the pectoral fins, is pale yellow. The sides are distinguished by numerous small black spots. The edges of the dorsal, anal, and caudal fins are yellowish. This fish grows to a length of sixty centimeters.

Picasso triggerfish
Rhinecanthus assasi

The body is oval and the head triangular, the snout is pointed and the mouth is terminal. On the stalk of the caudal fin, there are three rows of small spines. The lips are yellowish and a stripe of the same color extends from the mouth to the operculum. A black vertical band covers the eyes. On the sides are diagonal stripes.
The caudal fin is slightly rounded. This fish grows to a length of twenty-five to thirty centimeters.

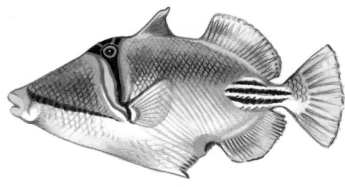

MONACANTHIDAE FAMILY
Harlequin filefish
Oxymonacanthus halli

The body is oval and compressed, and is covered with a rough epidermis, due to the presence of minuscule denticles. The snout is typically elongated and tubular, with a lower jaw that is more developed than the upper. The background coloring is green, with a regular pattern of large bright yellow or orange spots. It forms small groups near branches of acropora, on the polyps of which it feeds. This fish grows to a length of ten or twelve centimeters.

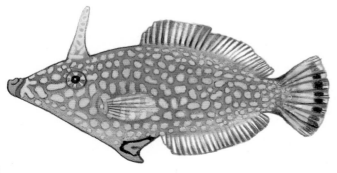

OSTRACIIDAE FAMILY
Cube boxfish
Ostracion cubicus

The body is shaped like a box, rectangular with rounded off angles and corners, and has no spines. The dorsal and anal fins are small, but are driven by powerful muscles which the fish uses for locomotion. The ventral and caudal fins are more developed; the caudal serves as a rudder. Males have a uniform violet coloring. The young of the species are yellow with black spots. This fish grows to a length of forty-five centimeters.

TETRADONTIDAE FAMILY
Blackspotted pufferfish
Arothron stellatus

The body is elongated and globular, with an oval silhouette, and is covered with small spines. The young of the species have a rubbery texture, while adults are more flaccid. The mouth is powerful and equipped with two large adjacent dental plates on each jaw. The coloring is typically mottled. In the young, the belly is marked by pronounced black stripes. The base of the pectoral fins is black. This fish propels itself along with its dorsal and anal fins. It is common to encounter this species on the sandy bottoms of lagoons. It grows to a length of ninety centimeters.

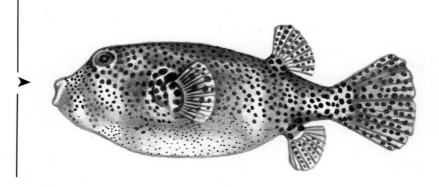

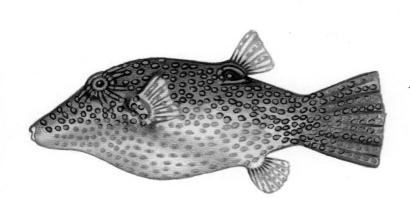

Pearl toby pufferfish
Canthigaster margaritata

This is a blowfish with slightly compressed head and body, dotted with small spines which become pronounced when the fish swells up. The snout is elongated and the mouth is protractile. The caudal fin is truncated. At the center of the back and the belly there is a fold of skin which can erect. The coloring is dark yellow on the back, and shades off on the belly. The body is dotted with dark blue spots edged in black. Around the eyes there are radial stripes, of the same color as the ocellar spots. At the base of the dorsal fin, are two dark blue stripes. This fish grows to a length of twelve or thirteen centimeters.

DIODONTIDAE FAMILY
Burrfish
Diodon hystrix

Tapered body, rounded toward the front, with large sharp spines which generally have split bases. These spines stand erect when the animal puffs up. The mouth has a single dental plate for each jaw. The snout and tail are elongated. The brownish-yellow coloring is fairly dark, with numerous black spots on the sides and the back. Nocturnal by habit, it seeks out sheltered places during the day. It is common, and in certain areas a diver may encounter dozens in a single dive. This fish grows to a length of ninety centimeters.

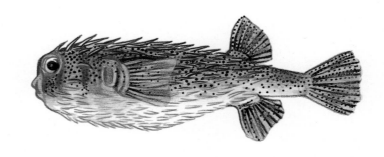

Andrea Ghisotti was born in Milan in 1951. He is considered a specialist in underwater photography. He published more than 400 reports in some of the most prestigious Italian and foreign magazines dealing with nature, travel, the sea, diving and photography. He wrote a number of manuals on diving techniques, an adventure story for children *Fiabasub*, a book about wrecks *Relitti* and has collaborated in the production of many photographic volumes.In 1993 he wrote, together with David Doubilet, the book *The Red Sea* for White Star Publishing House.

Alessandro Carletti was born in Milan in 1963, he is a Pharmacy graduate and a skin-diving instructor. He has worked for a number of years in the Egyptian area of the Red Sea as a skin-diving guide on cruise ships and also at diving centres at Hurghada and Sharm el-Sheikh. He has published his book *Red Sea* on all the Egyptian skin-diving itineraries and is currently contributing to various Italian journals in this sector.

Hanan Golombek was born in Israel in 1963, and lives and works in the coastal city of Eilat. He is a scuba instructor as well as skipper and captain, and currently mans the helm of the *Jacqueline*, the yellow submarine of the Undersea Observatory of Eilat.

Cover
A school of glass fish (Pempheris vanicolensis) splits after the transit of a diver.
Photograph by Norbert Wu.

Back cover, top
The silent arrival of sharks inevitably constitutes a time of tension and excitement.
Photograph by Andrea Ghisotti.

Back cover, bottom
A group of masked butterflyfish (Chaetodon semilarvatus), with their unmistakable yellow colorings, accompany the scuba diver underwater.
Photograph by Vincenzo Paolillo.

128 - A coral grouper (Cephalopolis miniata)swim near the reef.
Photograph by Vincenzo Paolillo.